http://www.lindarasmussenphotography.com



ISBN-13: 978-0-9861661-0-5

Printed in China by Global PSD, www.GlobalPSD.com

Global Printing, Sourcing & Development (Global PSD), in association with American Forests and the Global ReLeaf programs, will plant two trees for each tree used in the manufacturing of a printed book. Global ReLeaf is an international campaign by American Forests, the nation's oldest nonprofit conservation organization and a world leader in planting trees for environmental restoration.

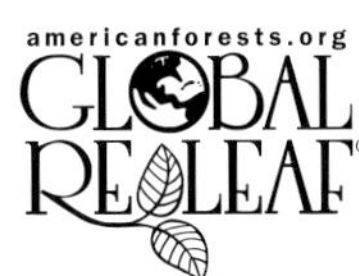


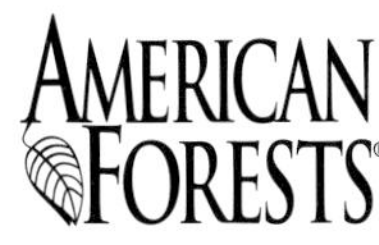


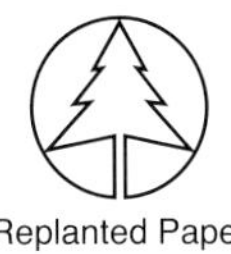

Growing up on a dairy farm at the base of majestic Mount Rainier, Linda's days were spent working with the animals or in the fields, so there was plenty of time to reflect on the surrounding beauty. Once Linda had a camera, that beauty became a passion. Sharing the light and colors from a different perspective was inspirational for her. People are often intrigued with where a photo was taken only to find out that they drive past that spot nearly every day.

After graduation from Saint Martin's University, Linda went on to medical school at the University of Washington. Her caring and compassion for people as well as her mechanical skills are an asset in her orthopedic surgery career. Being able to help people walk without pain following hip and knee replacement became her focus while in her surgical training in San Francisco. Linda moved to beautiful Hawaii over 20 years ago and has been with the Windward Orthopedic Group in Kailua and Kaneohe. Her 3 children share her artistic talents that were passed down from her mother and sister.

In the early morning hours, Linda can be found on the beach with her camera hoping to capture the perfect sunrise. An occasional rainbow can result in a detour from her path to the office or hospital.

"Photography provides a snapshot of inspirational scenery that speaks to each person in their own unique way. Putting these photos together has required a great deal of time and patience, but I am excited to share my work with others. This is what I love. The lens of the camera reflects the eyes of the surgeon and finds the soul of nature's glorious beauty."

Linda Rasmussen, MD

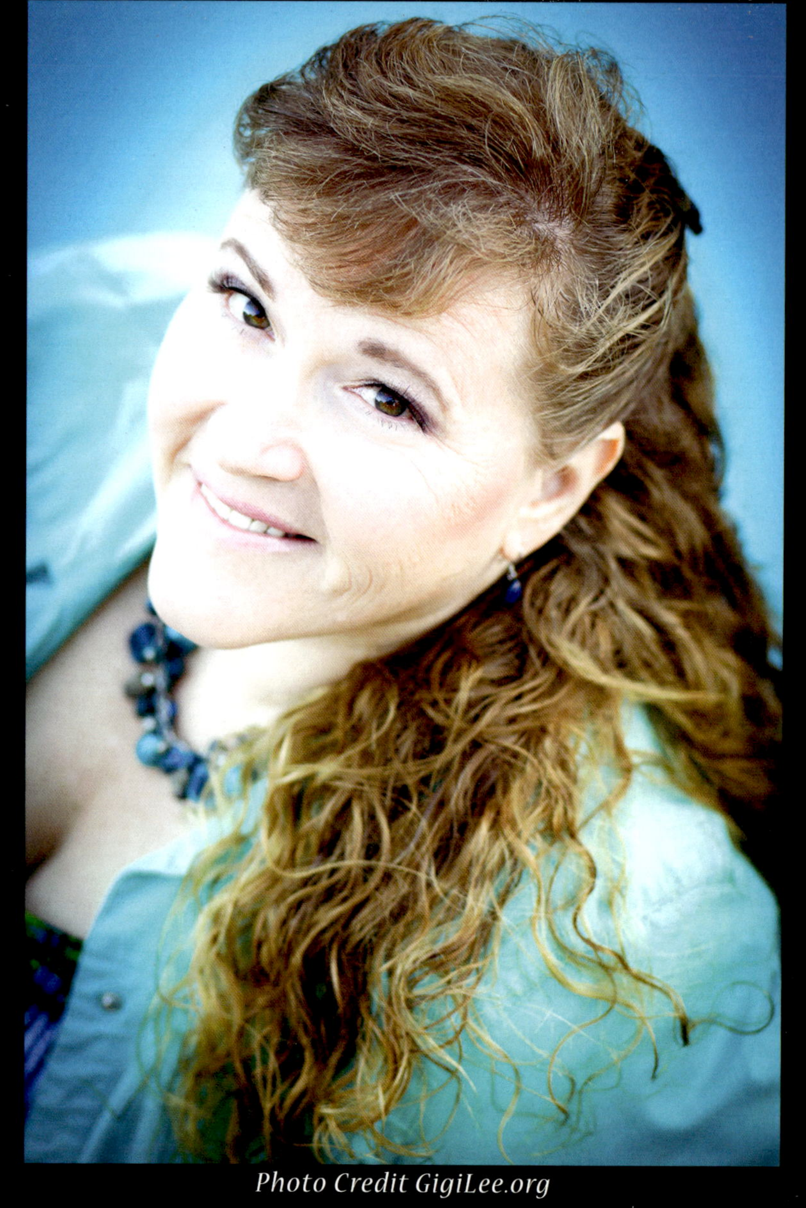

*Photo Credit GigiLee.org*

**All photos available for purchase at:**

**LindaRasmussenPhotography.com**

**Contact Linda at:**

**info@lindarasmussenphotography.com**

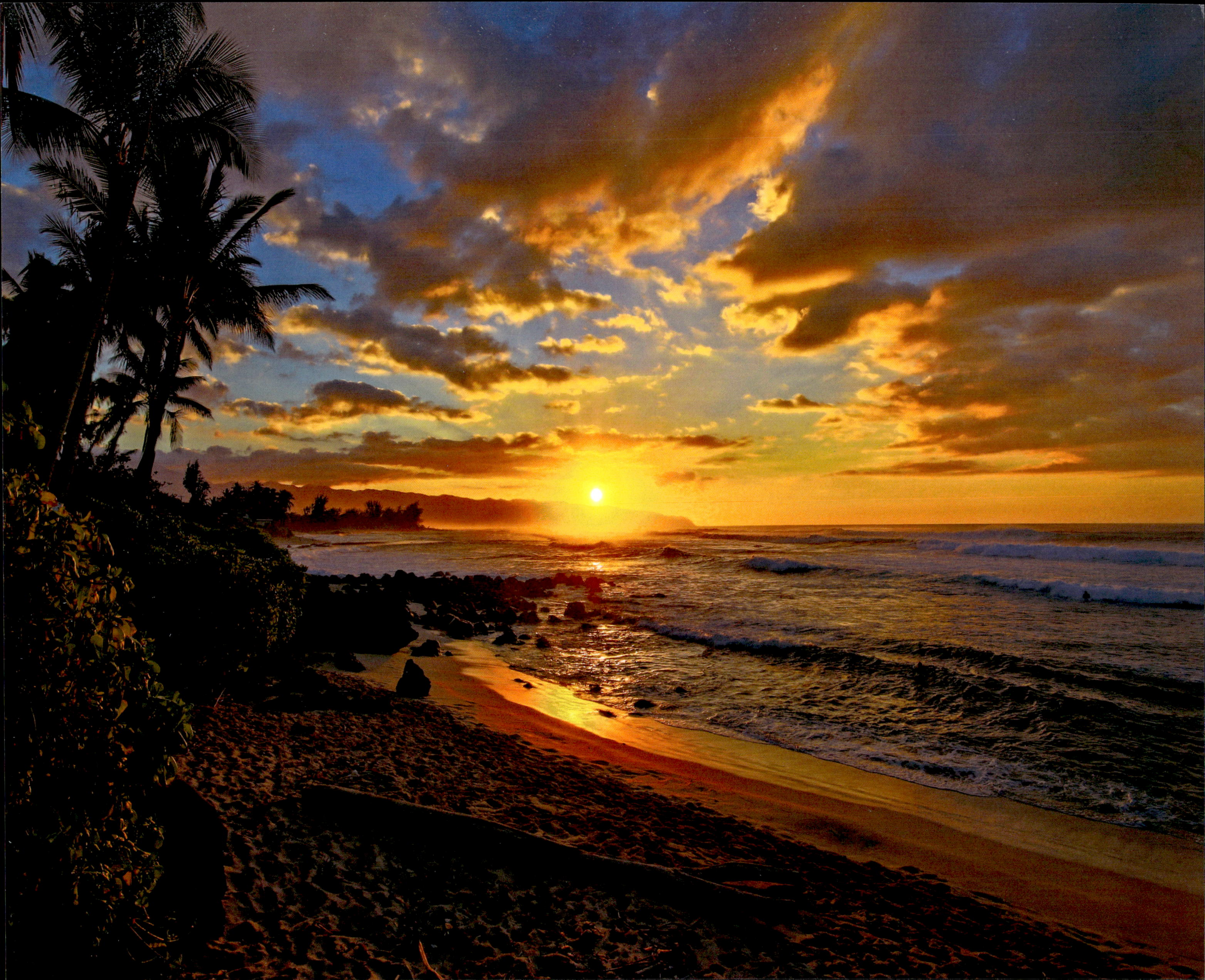

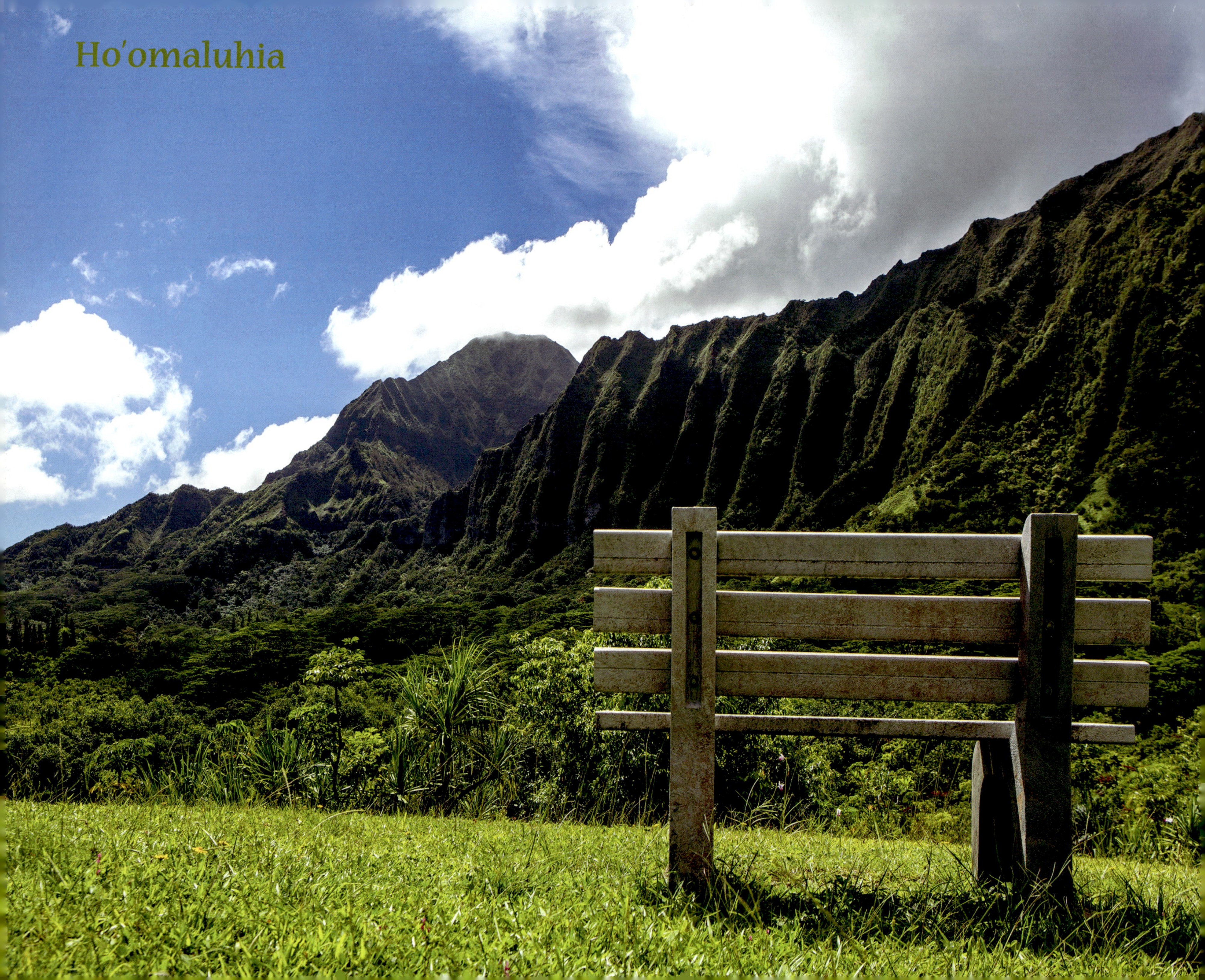

Ho'omaluhia

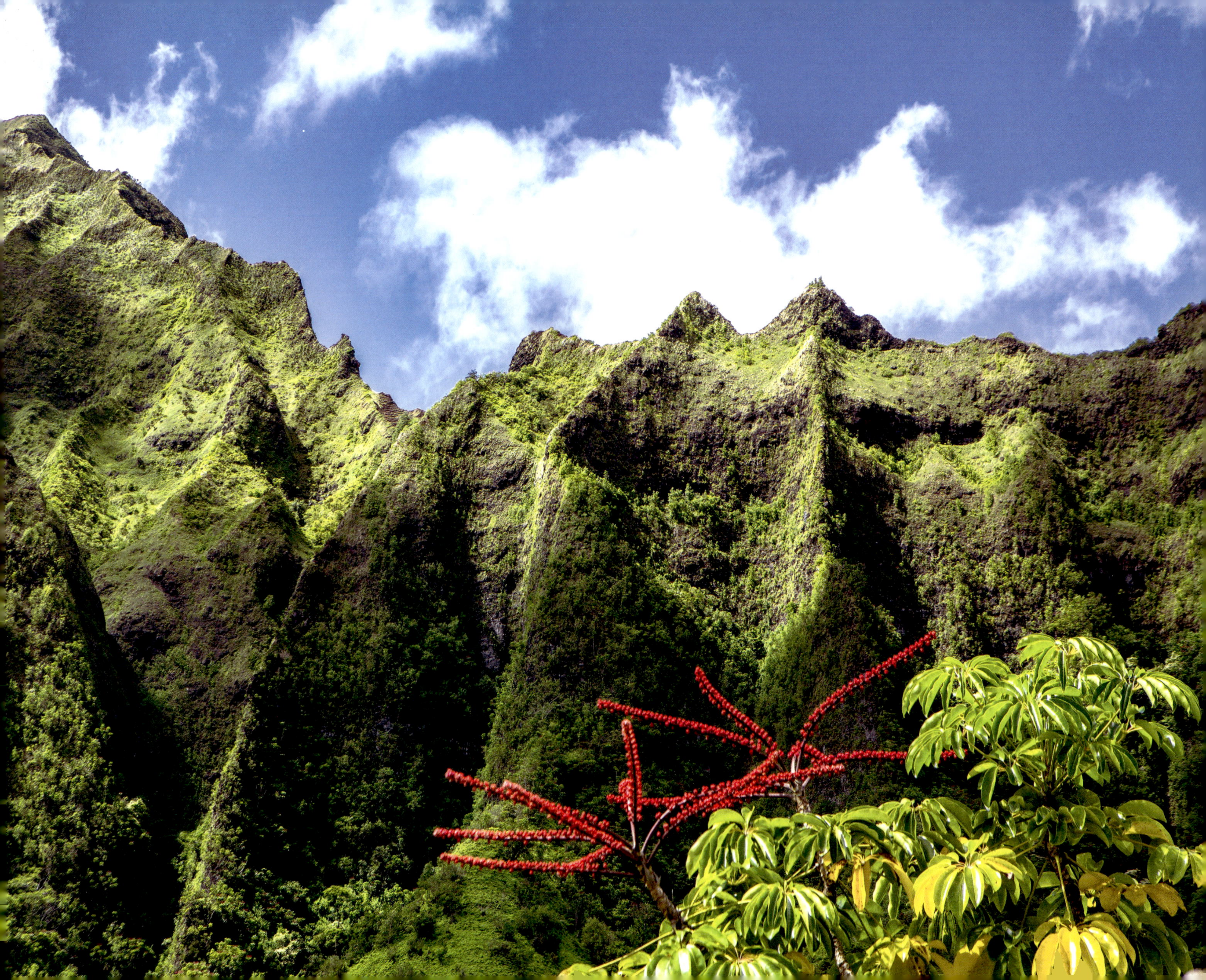

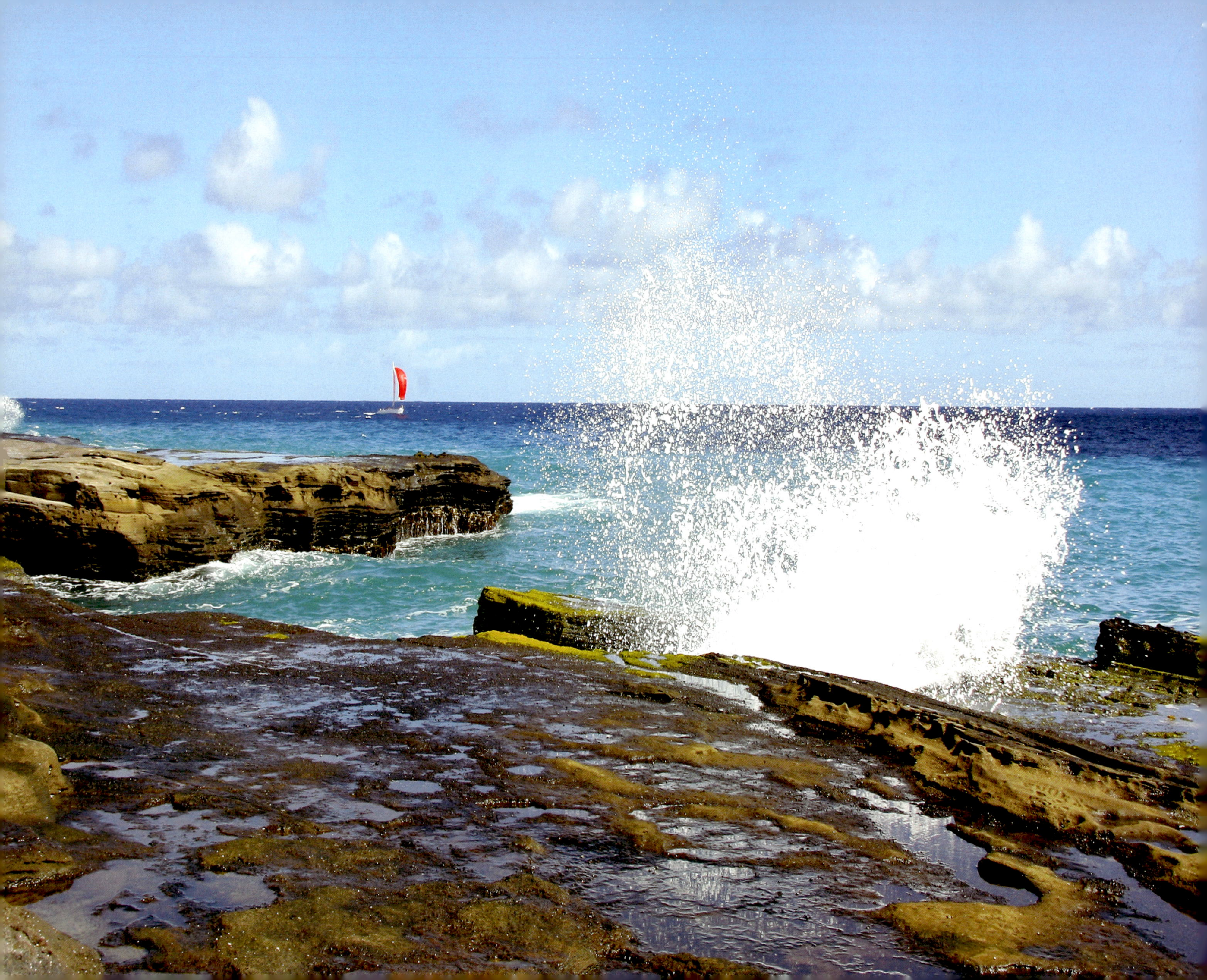

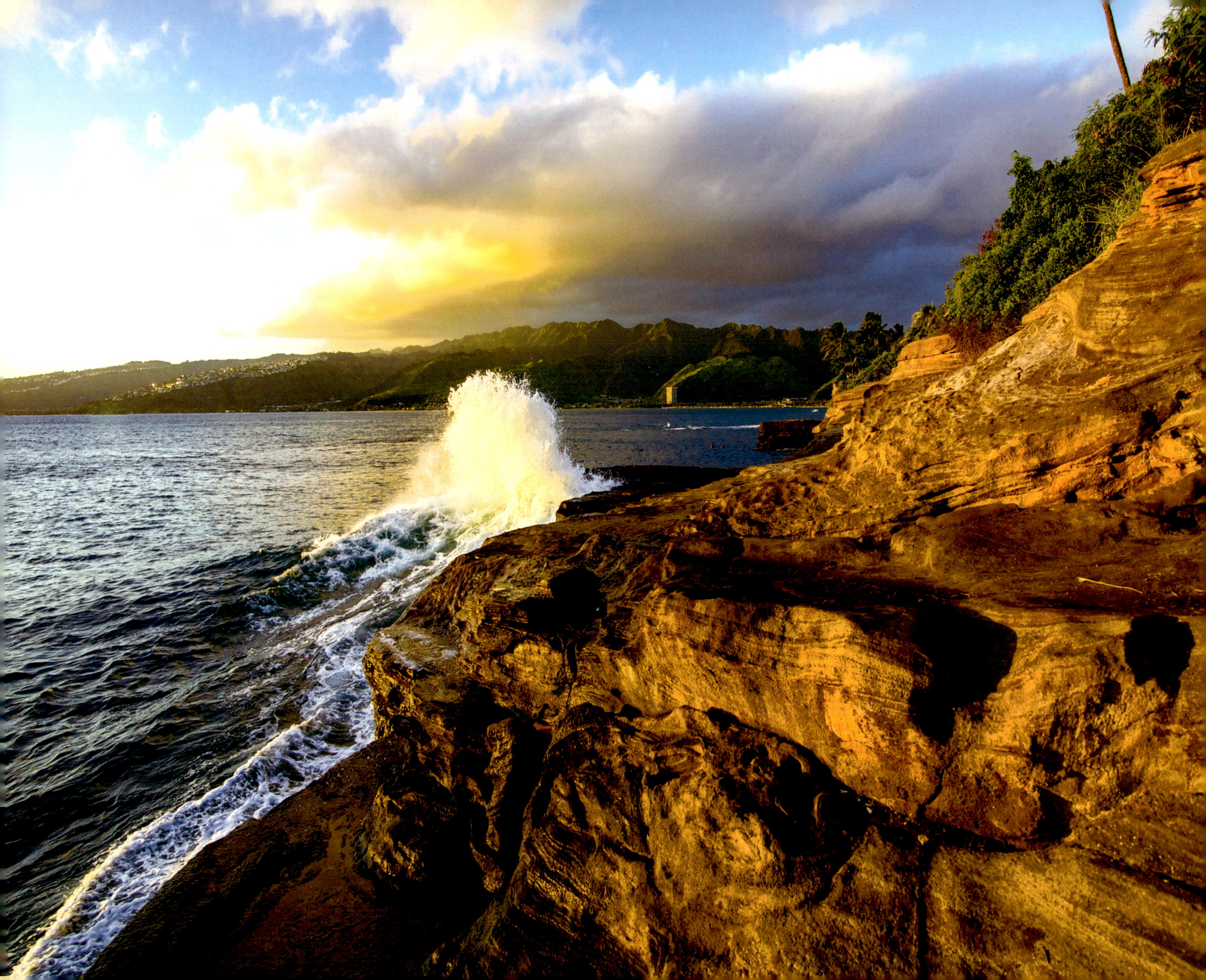

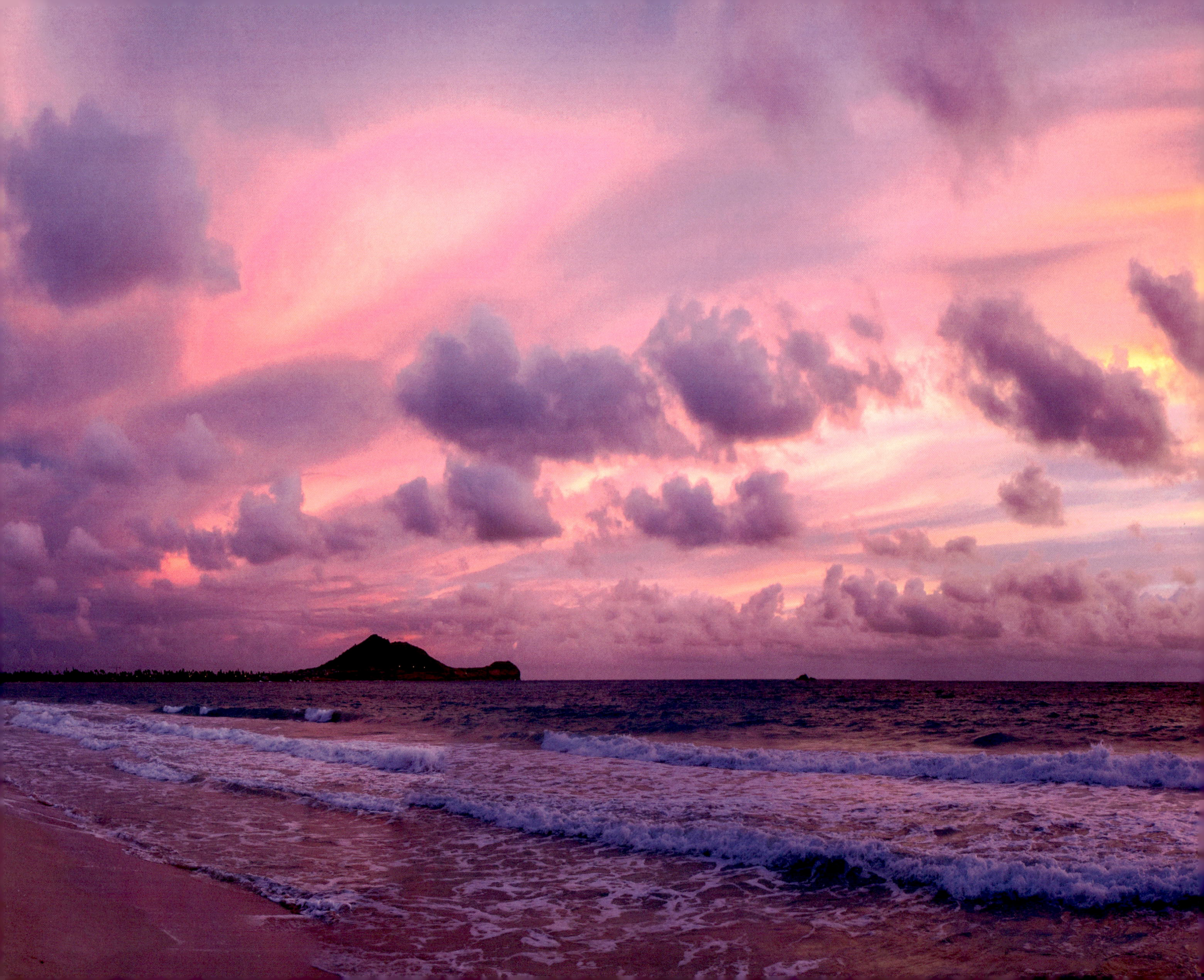

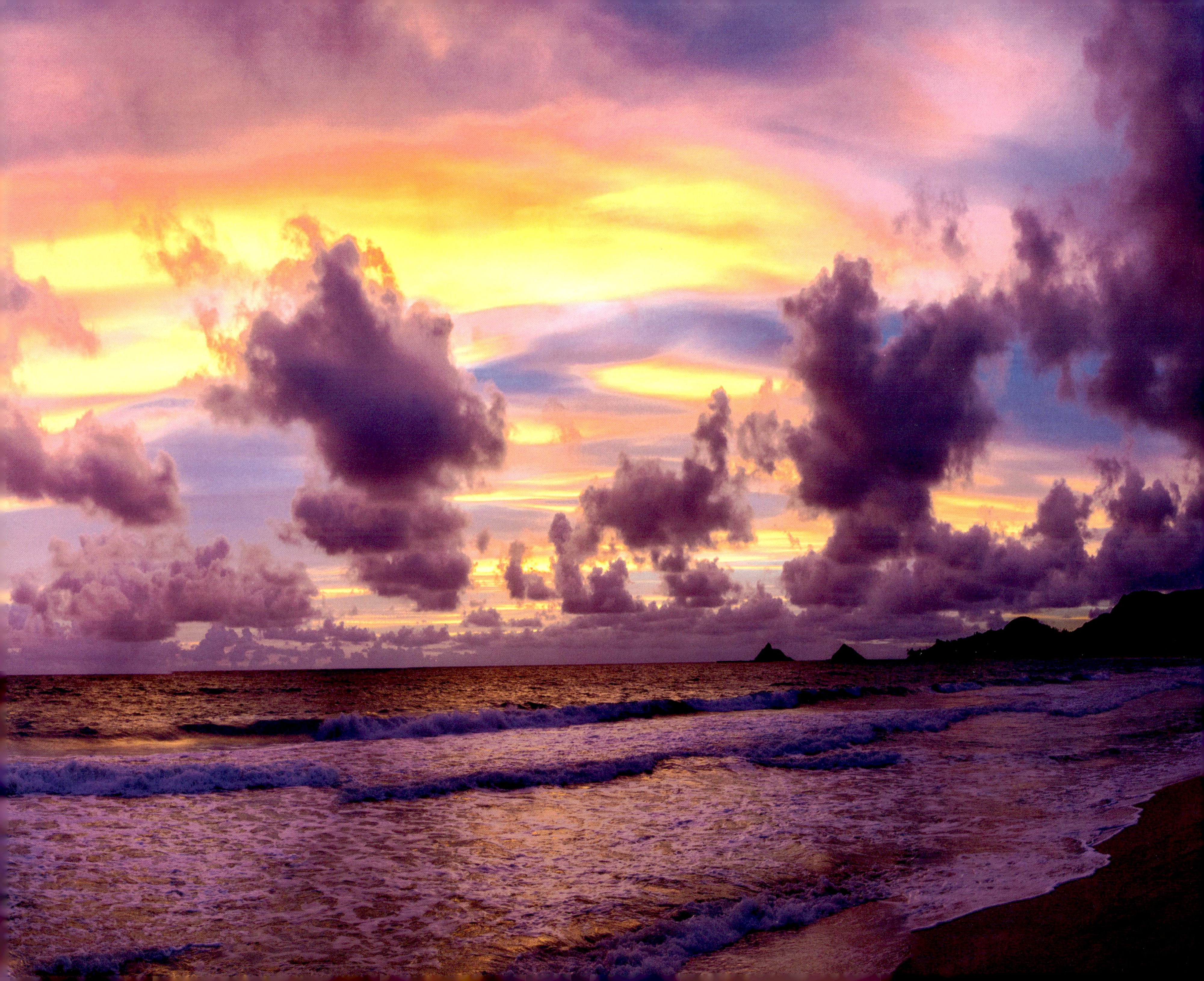

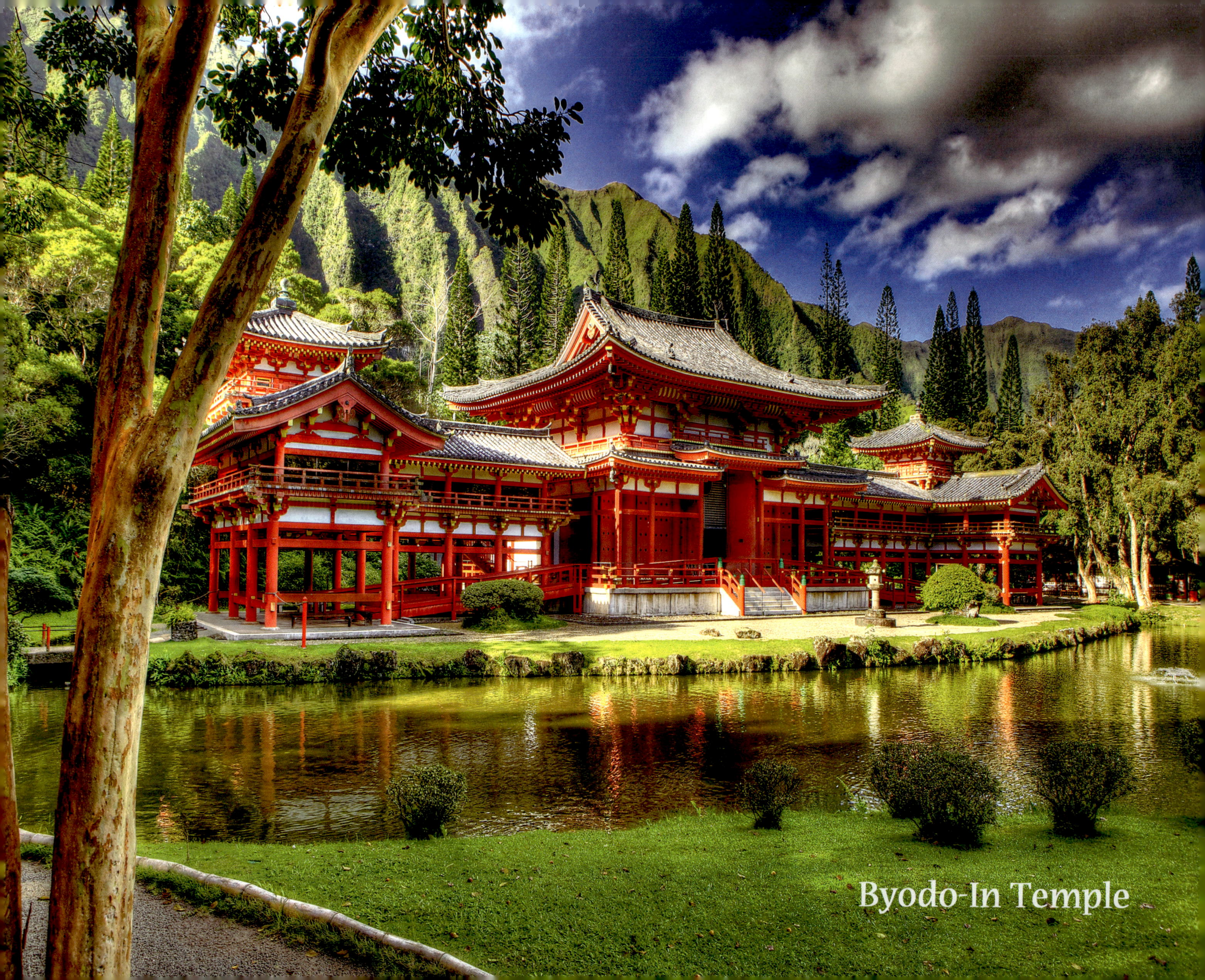

Byodo-In Temple

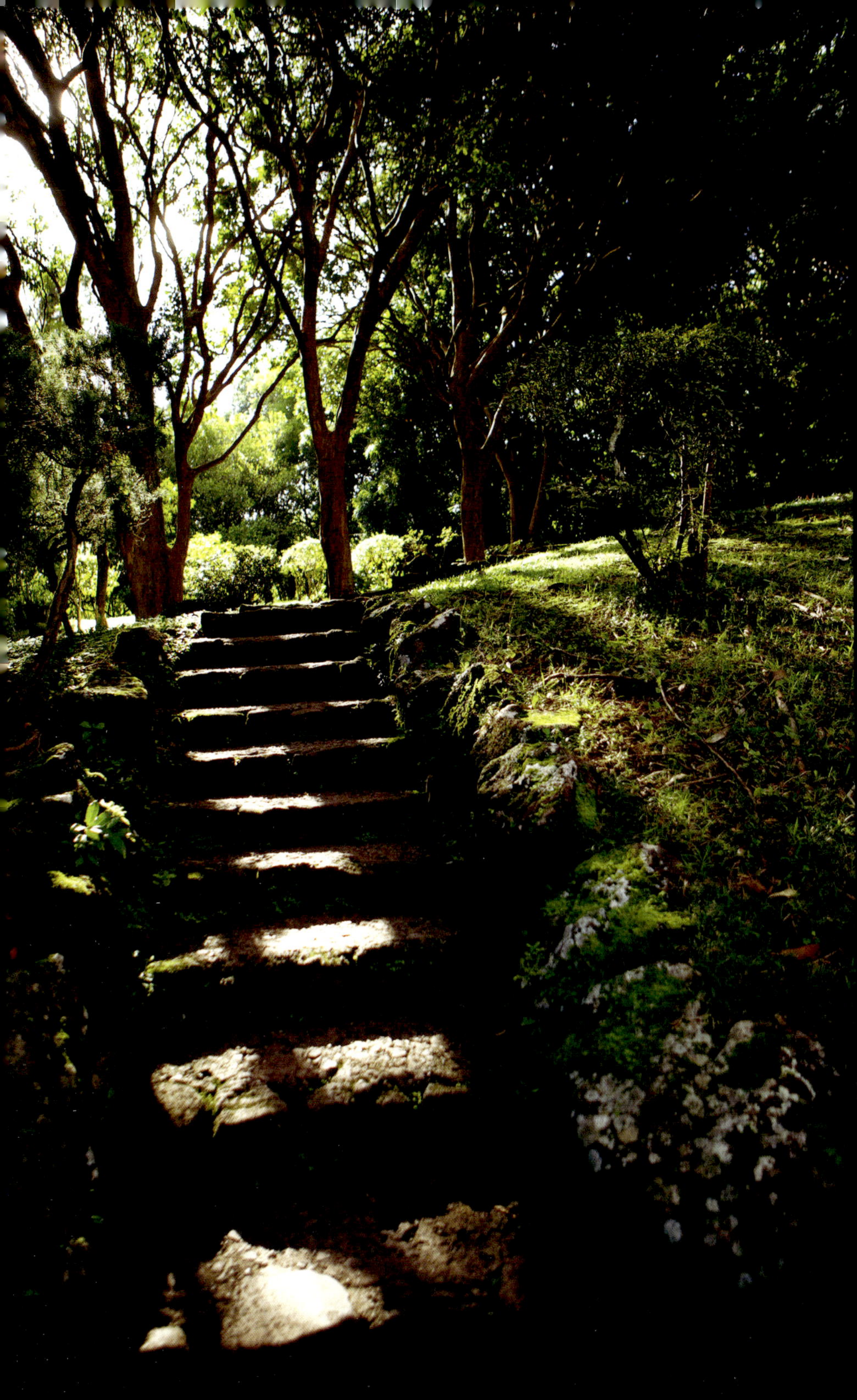

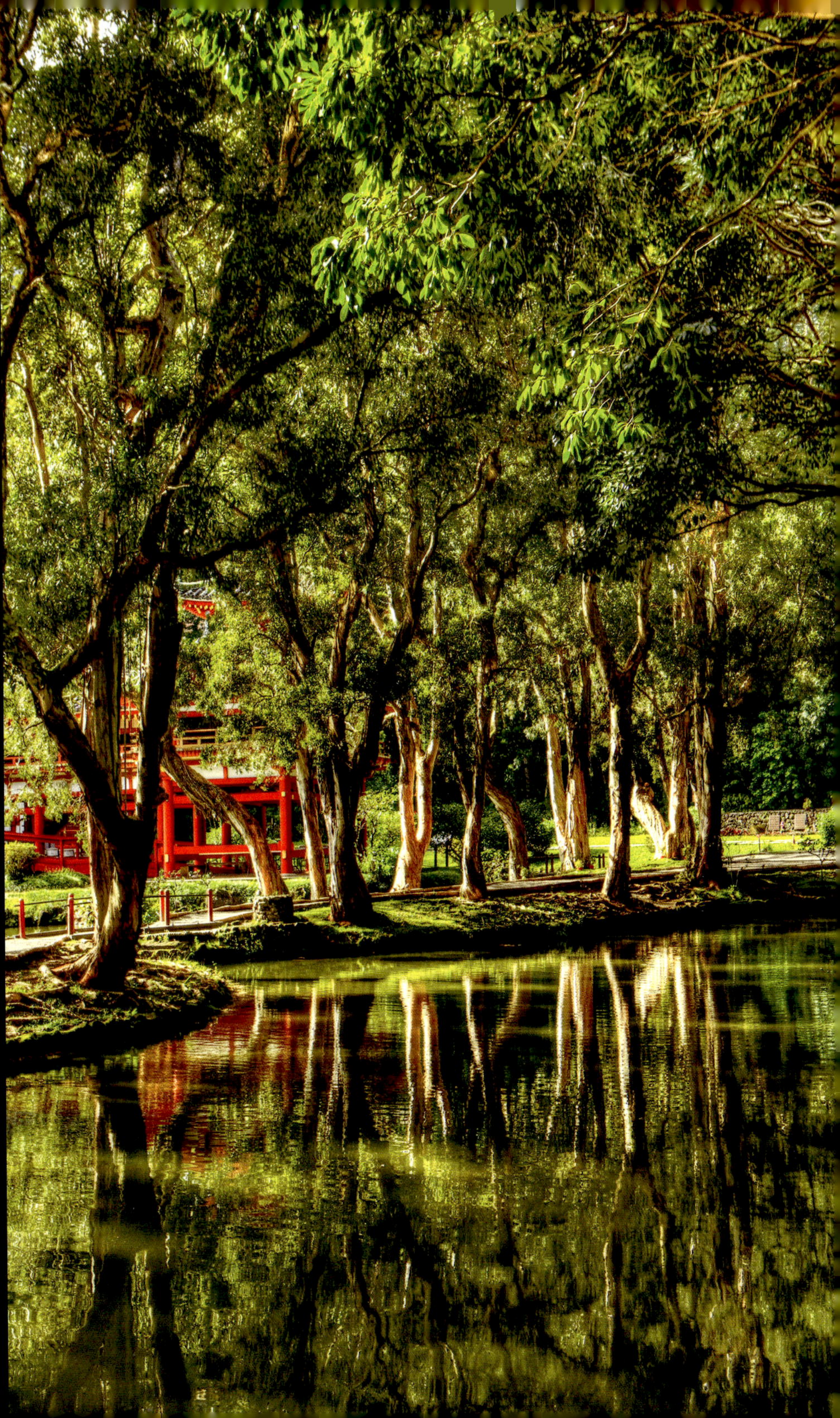

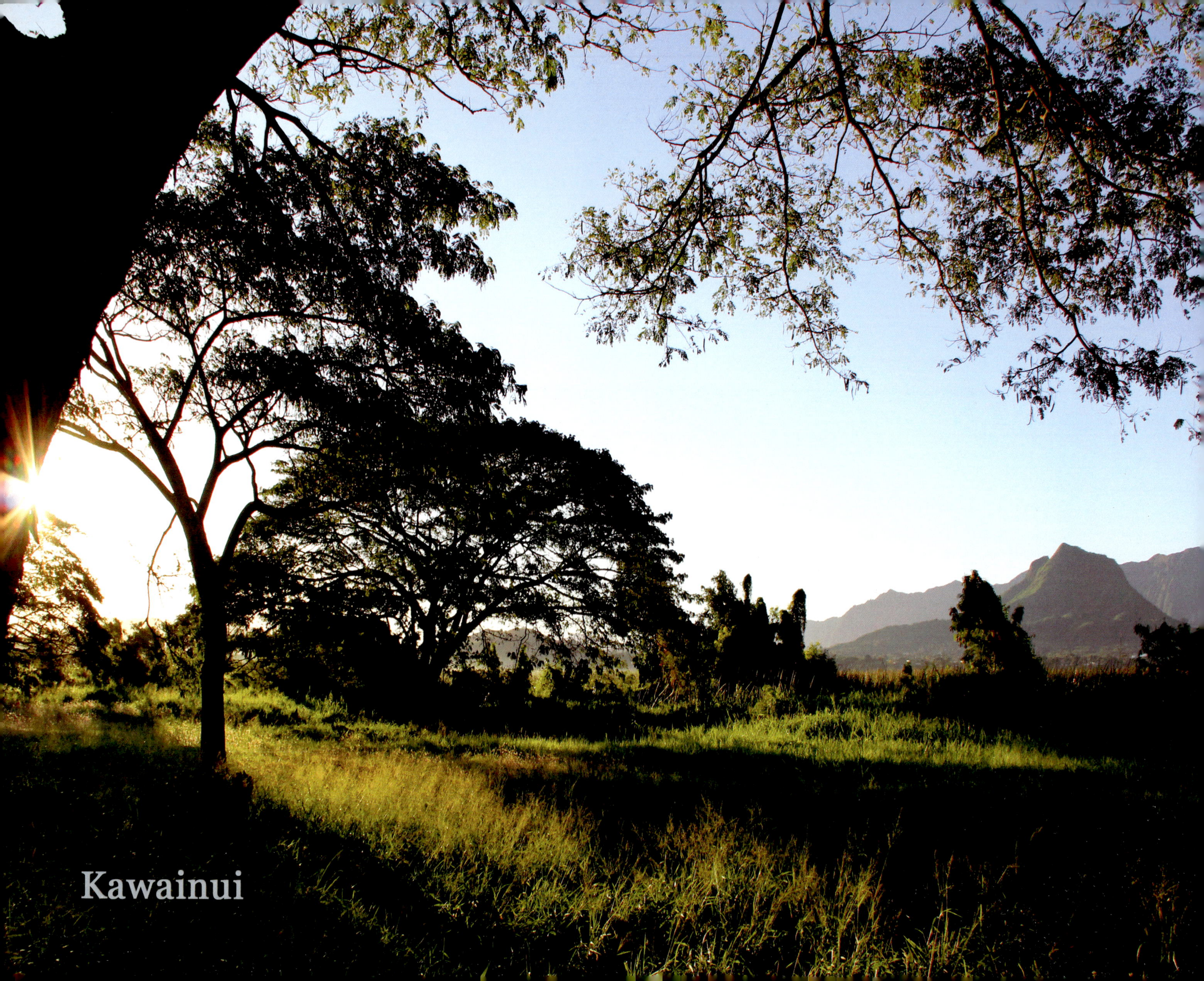

Kawainui

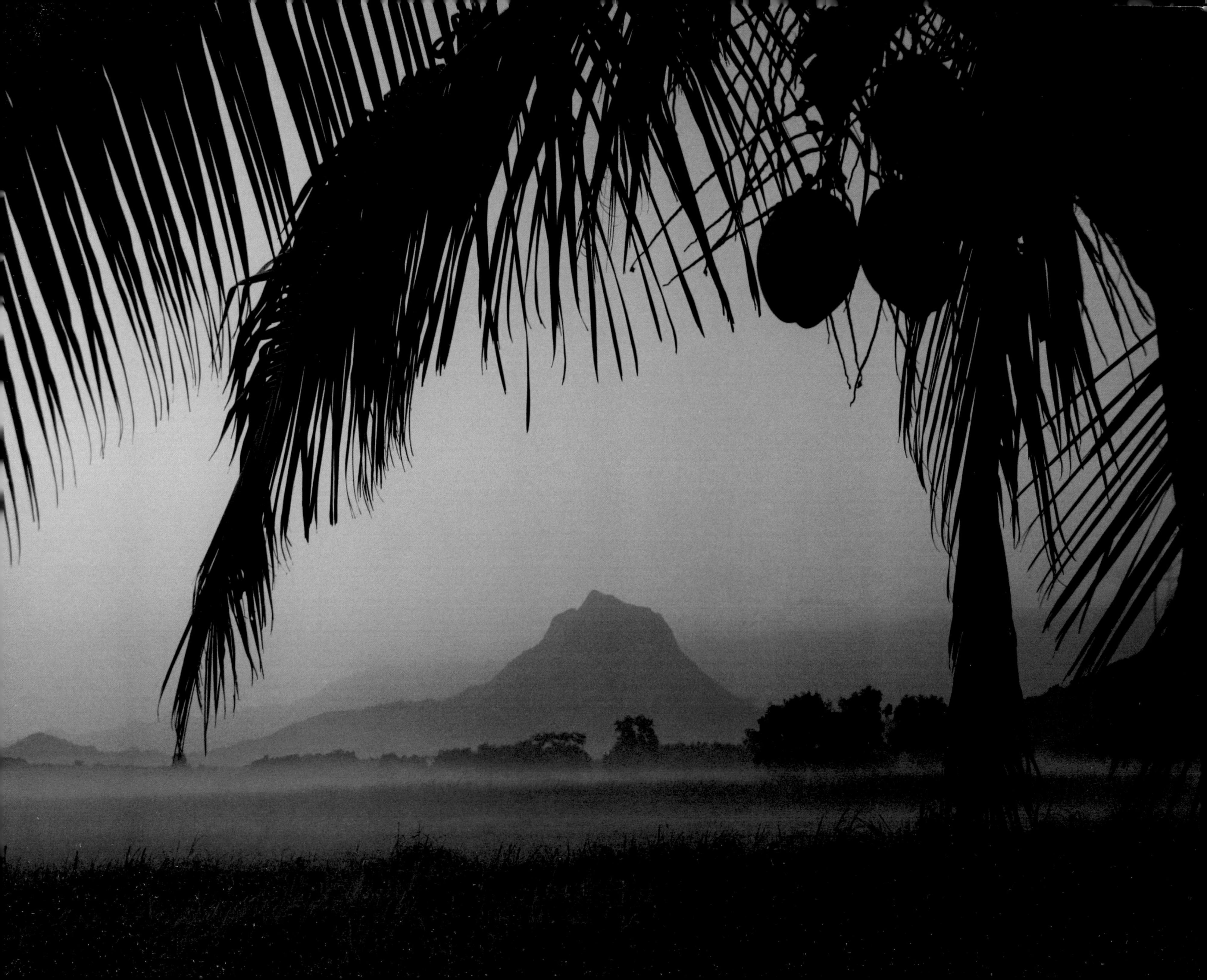

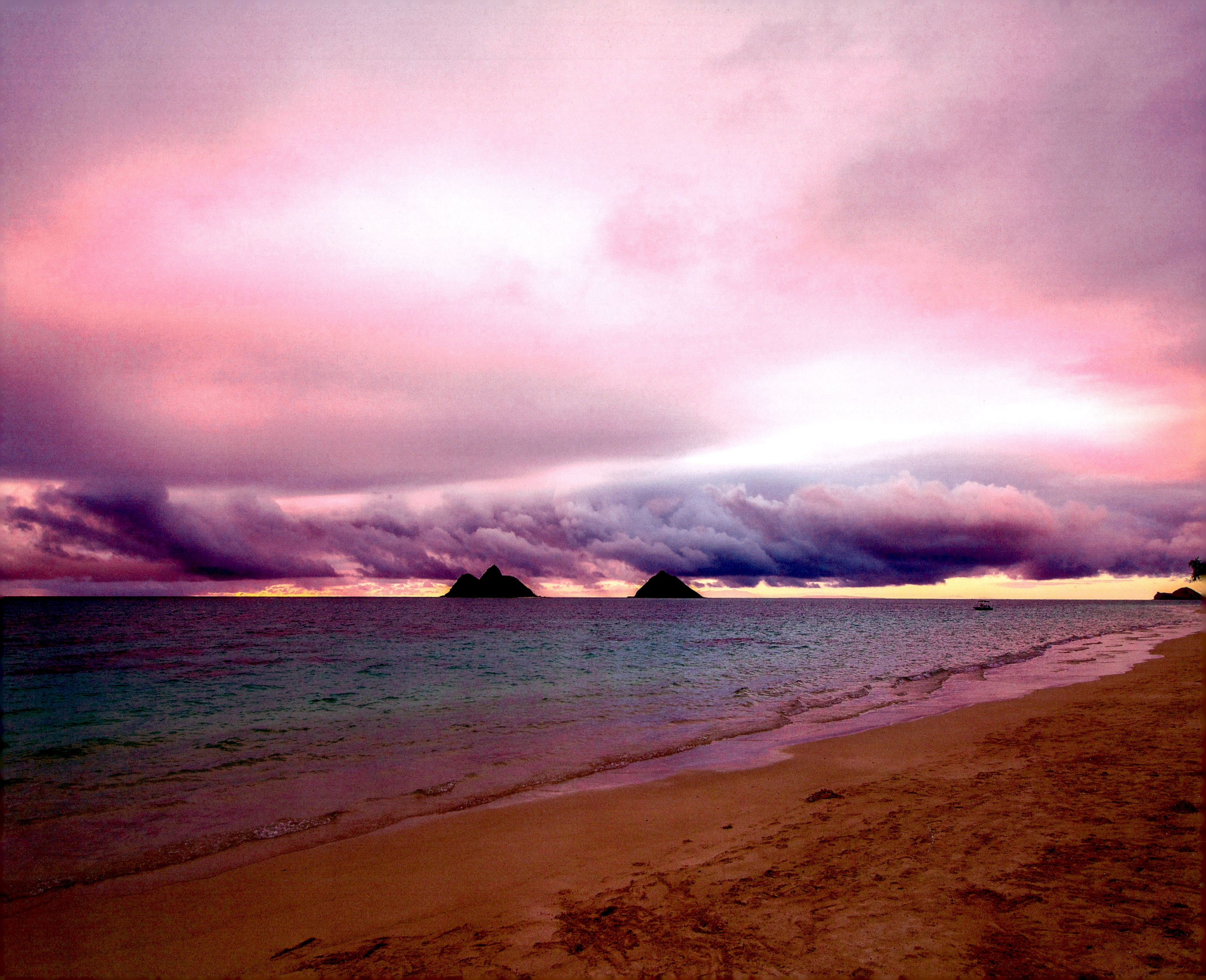

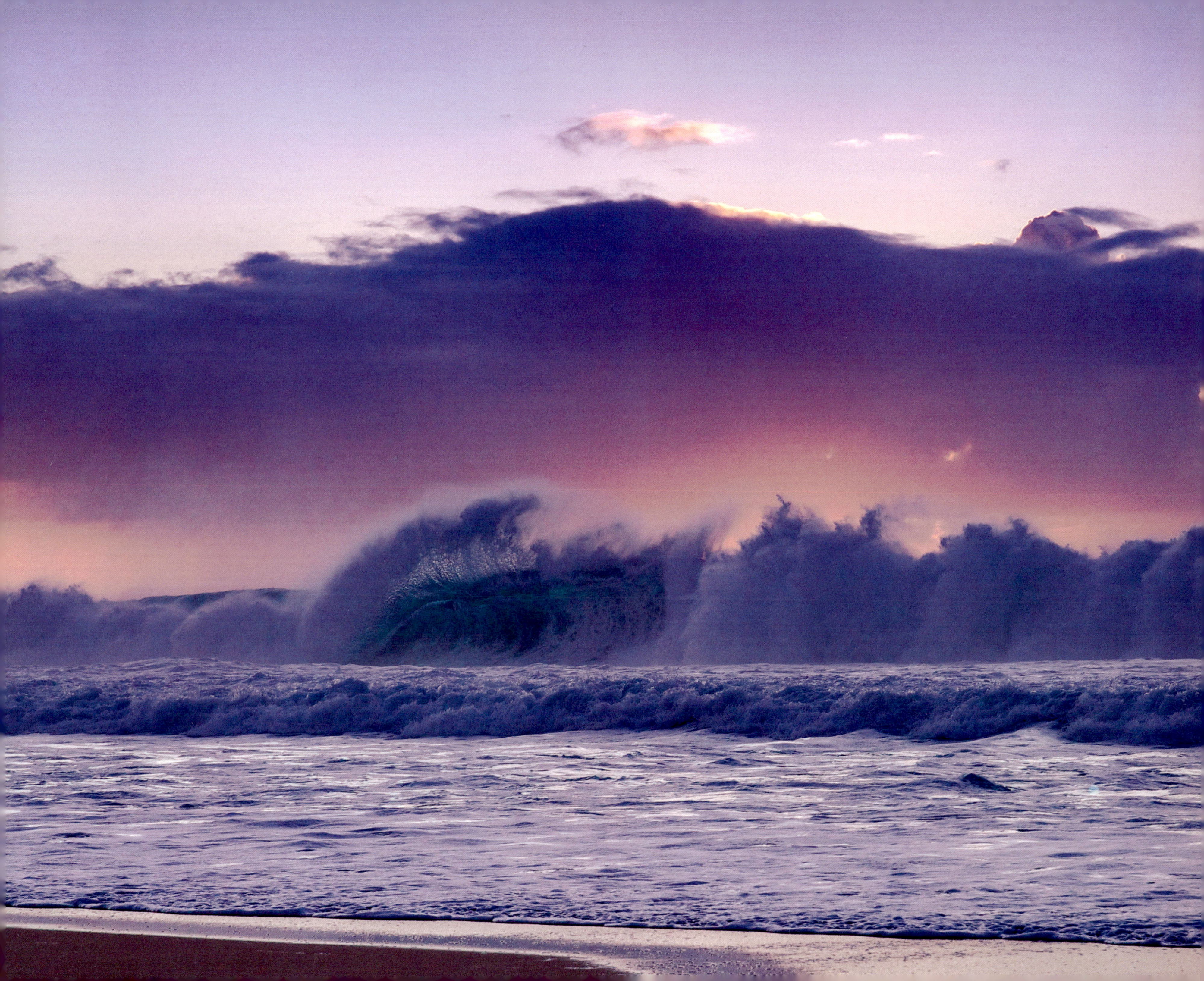

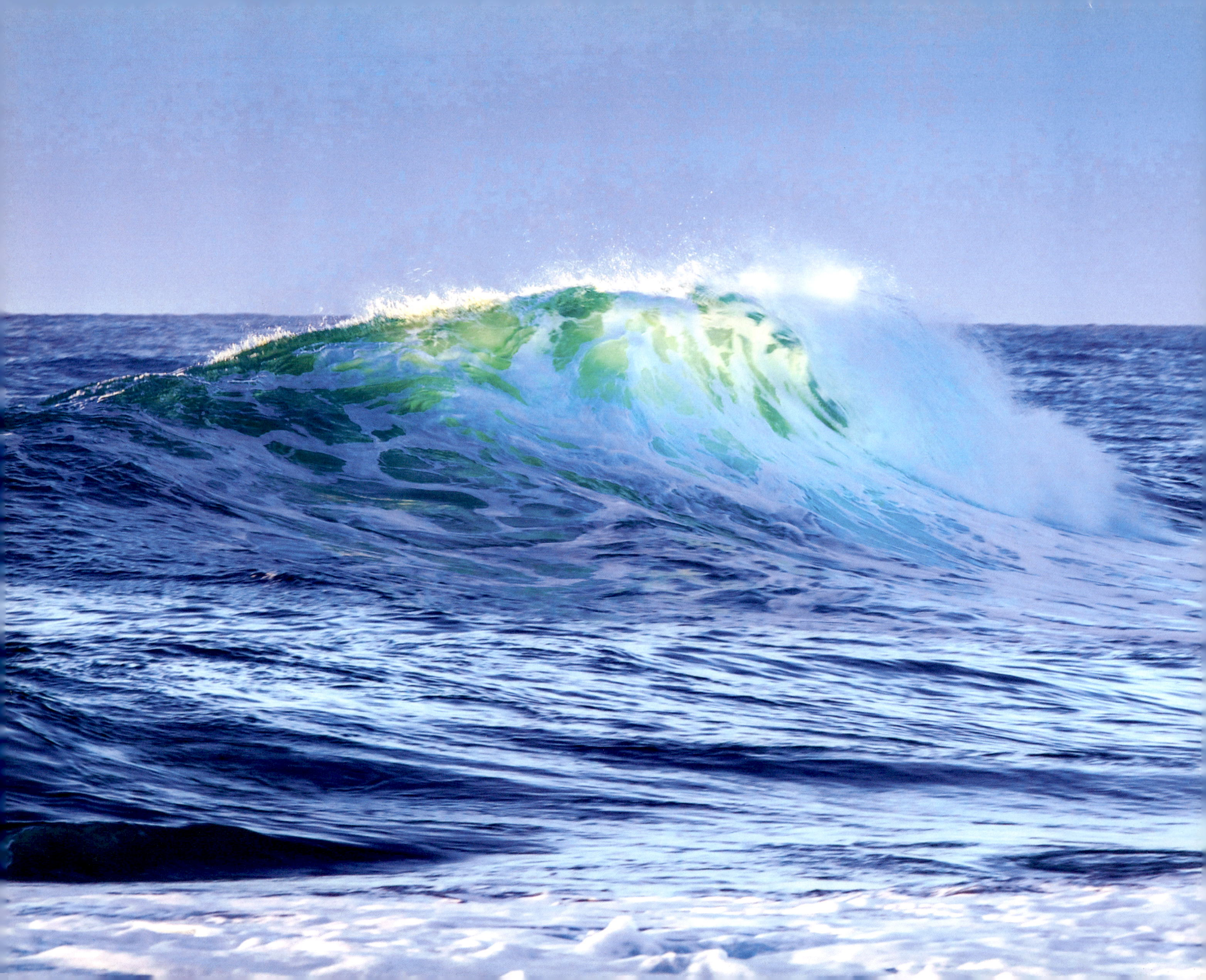

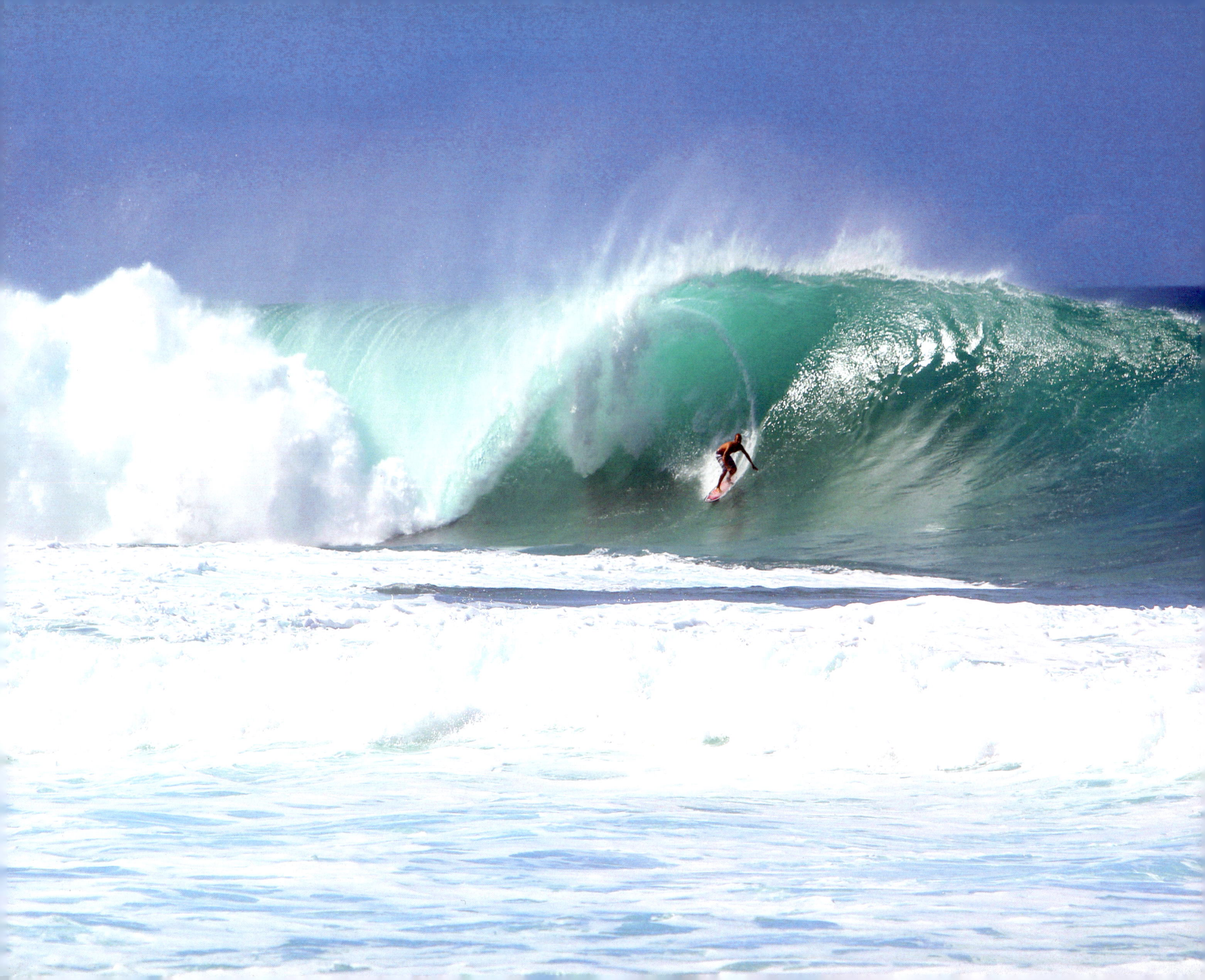

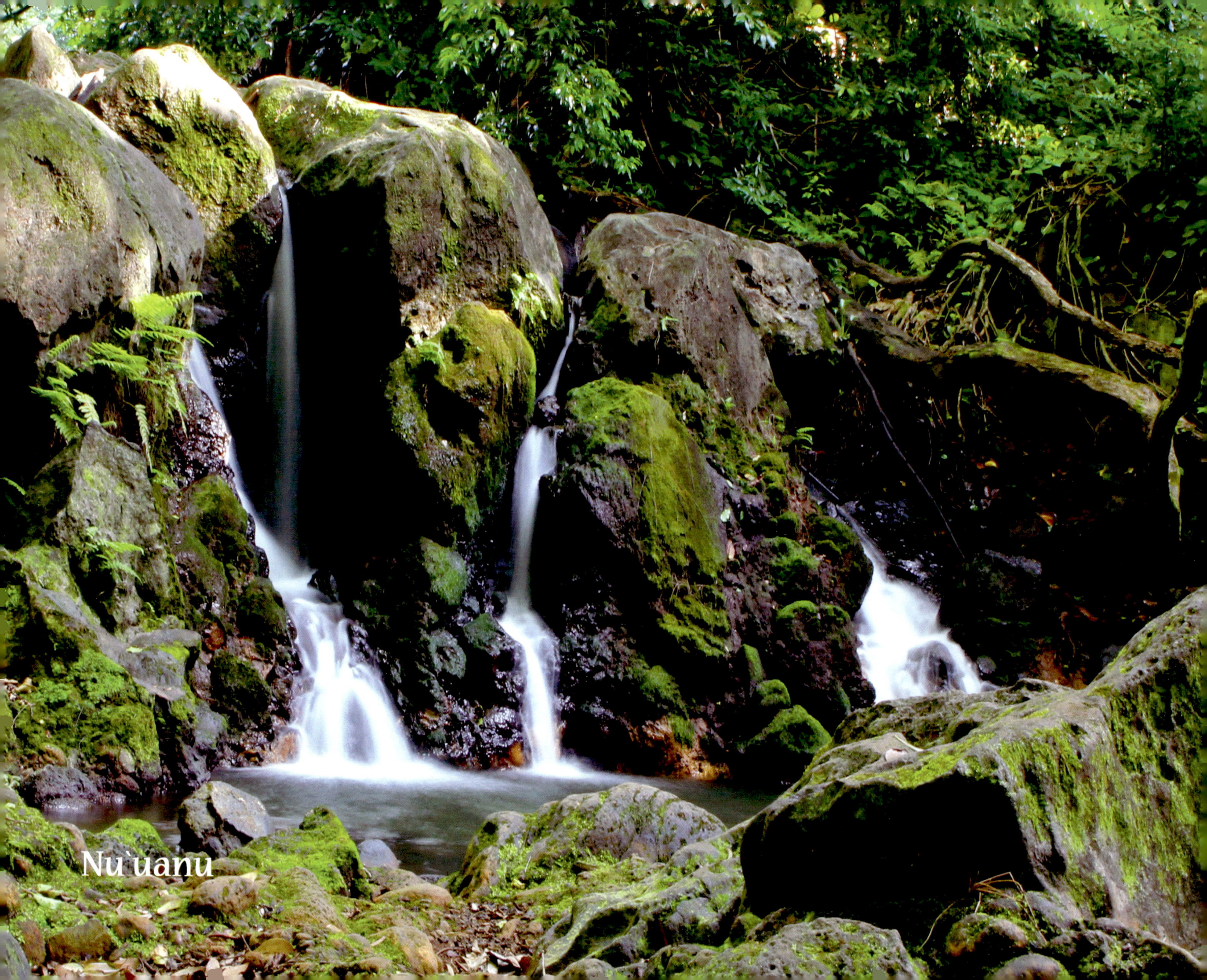

Nu`uanu

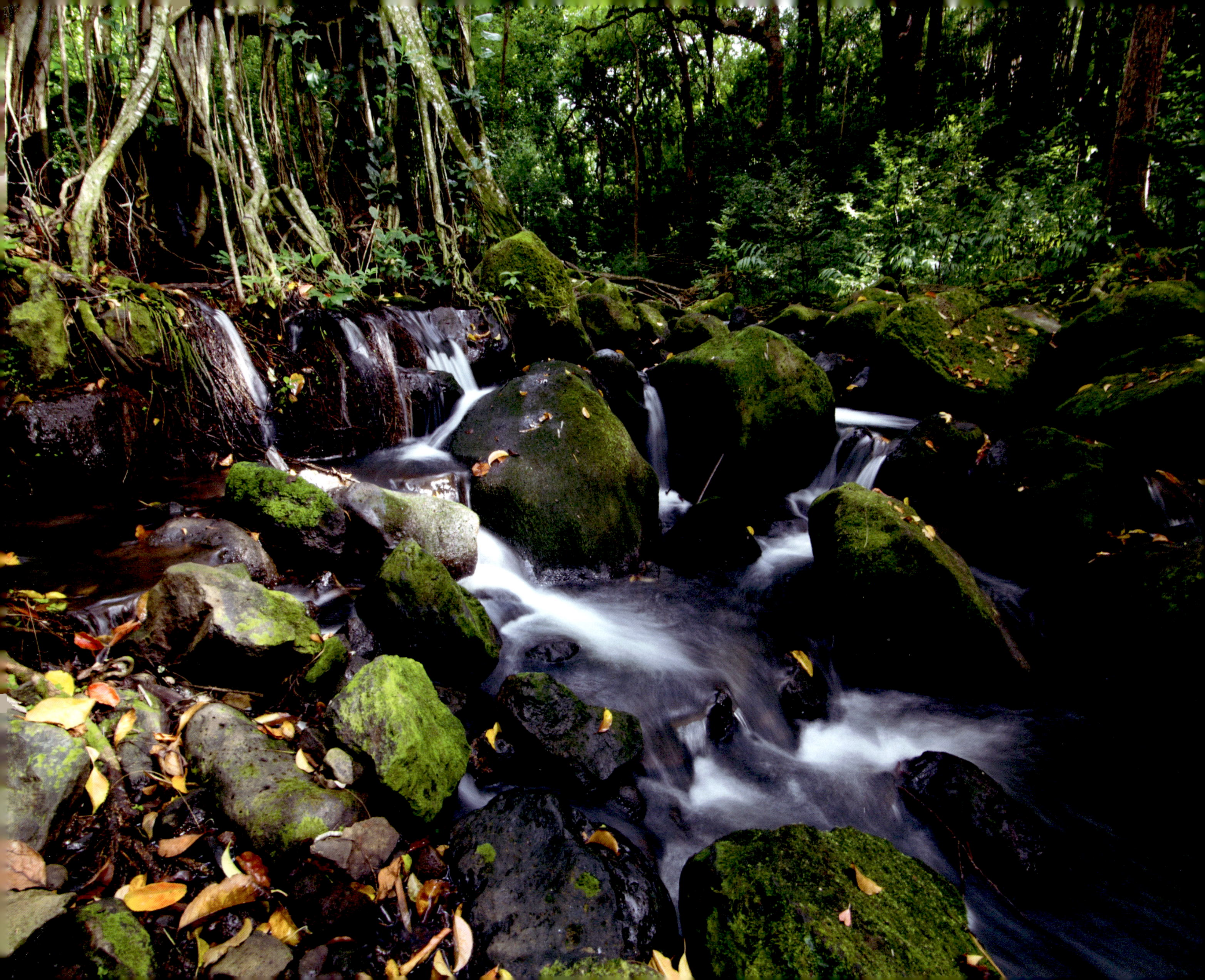

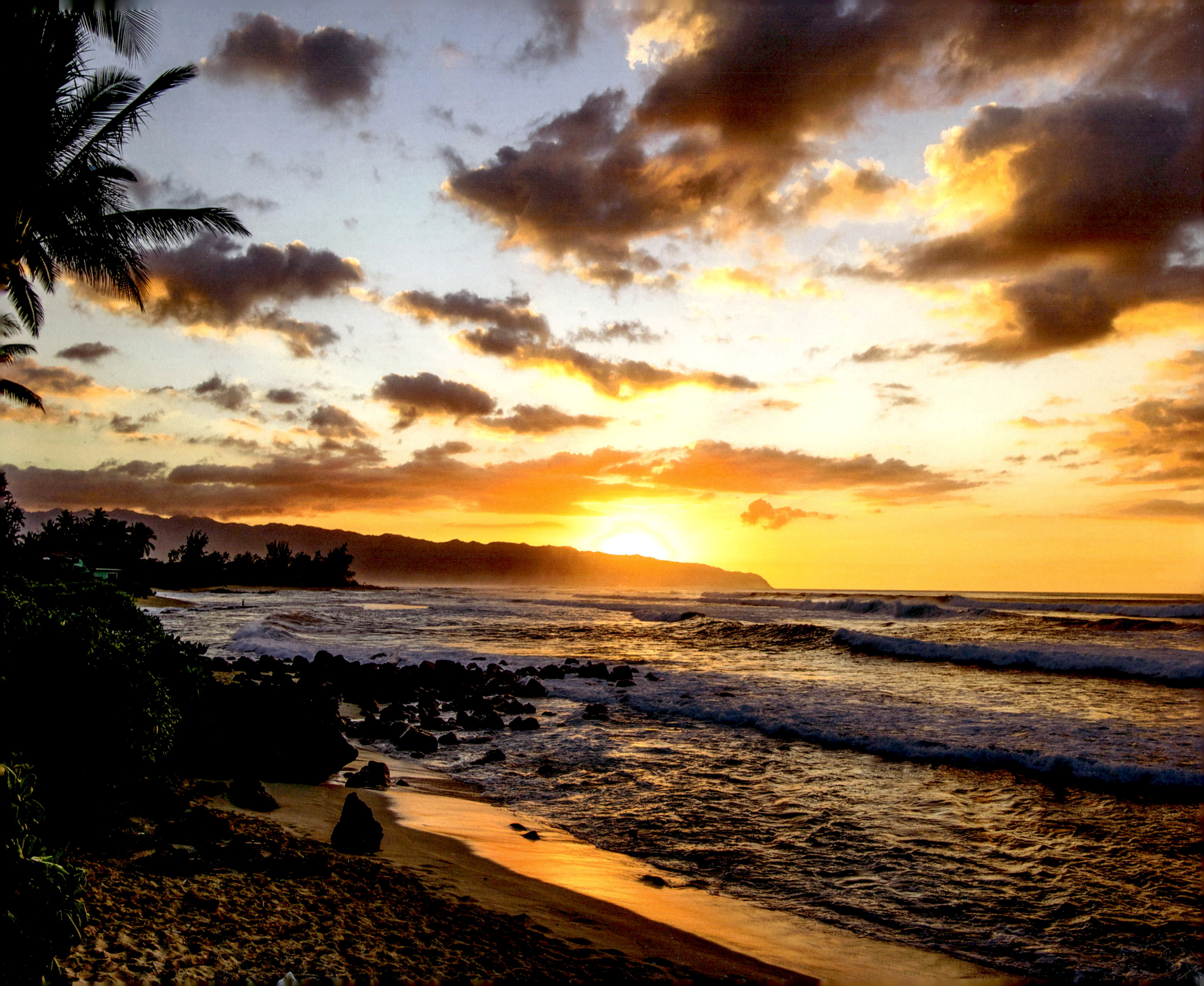

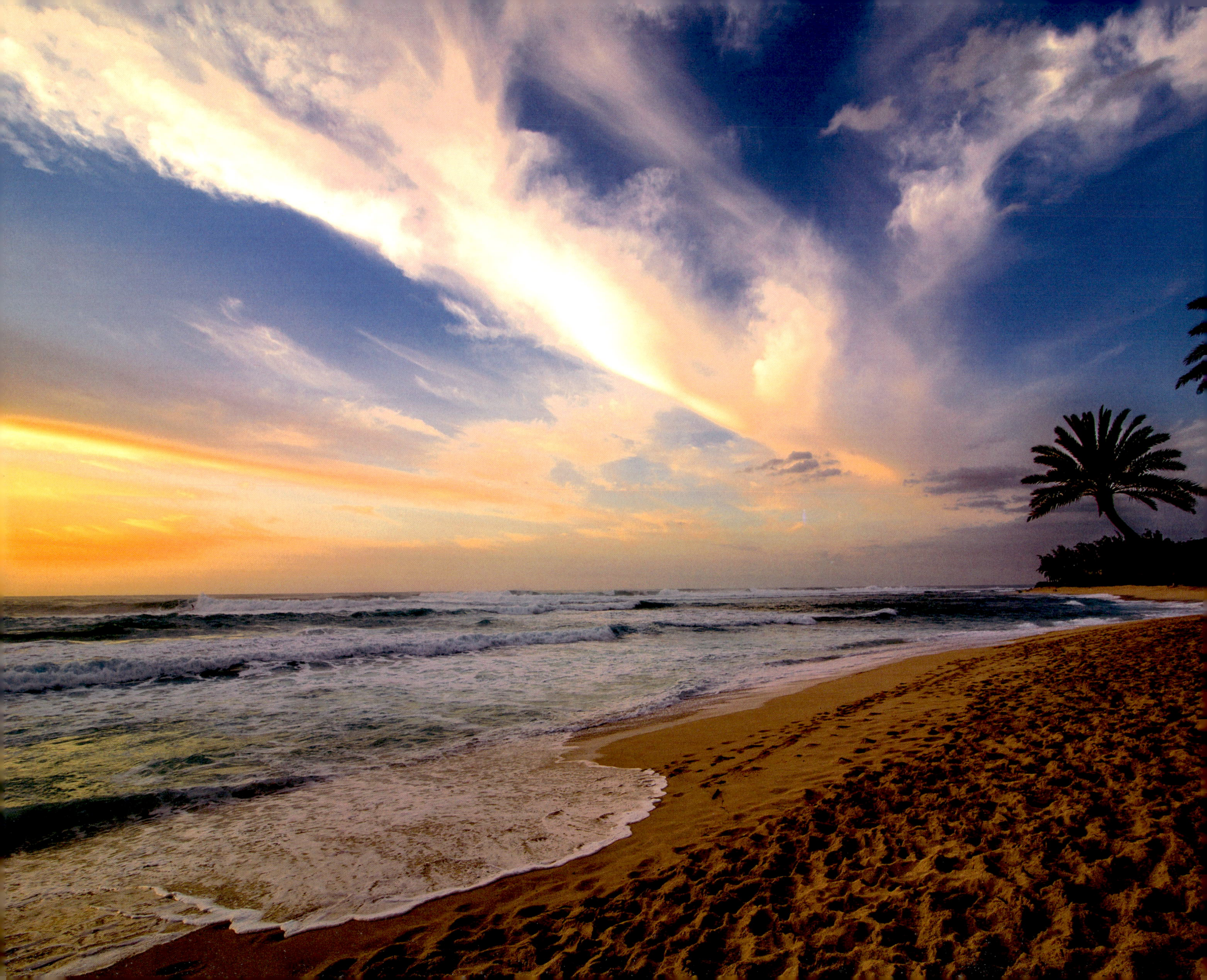

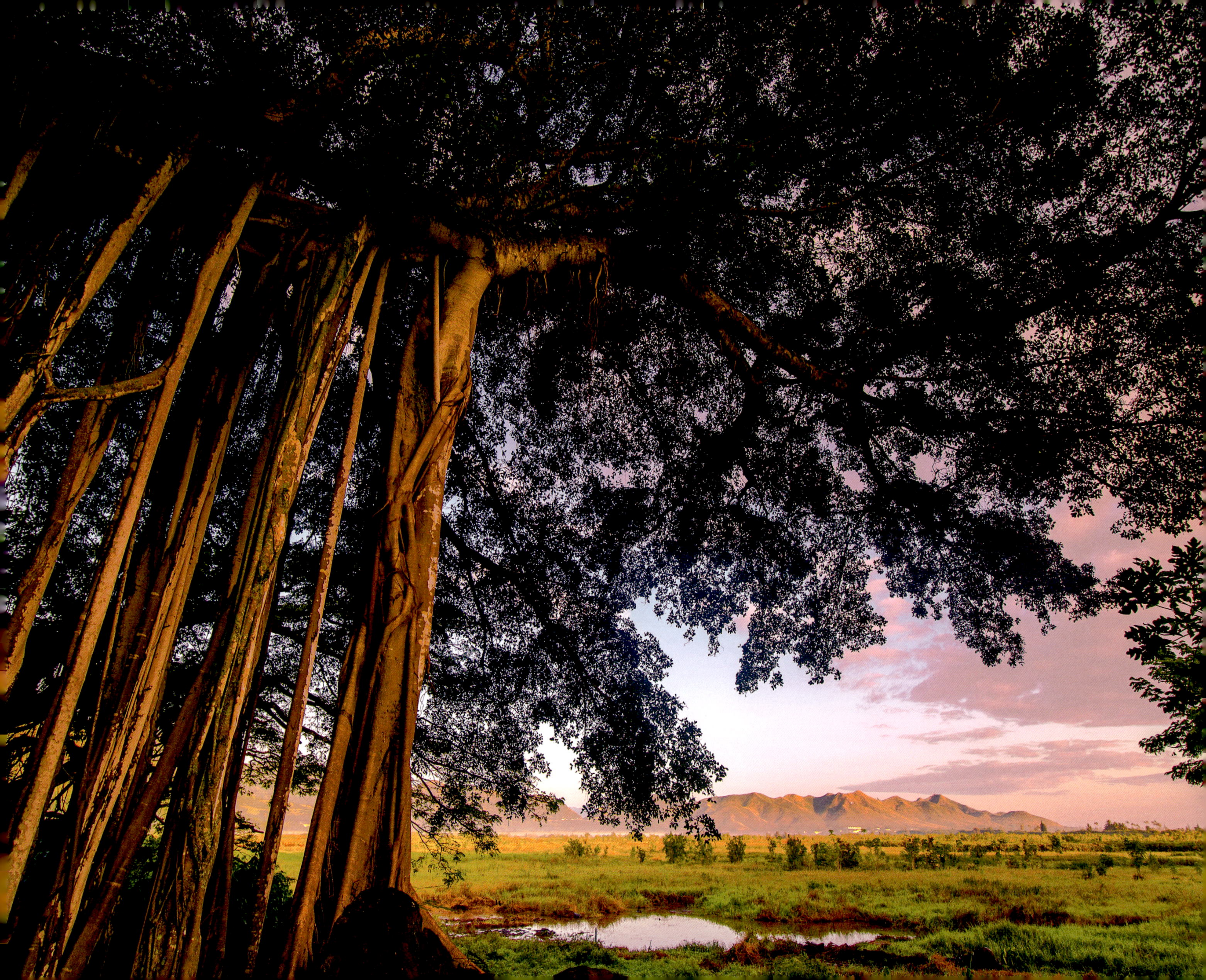

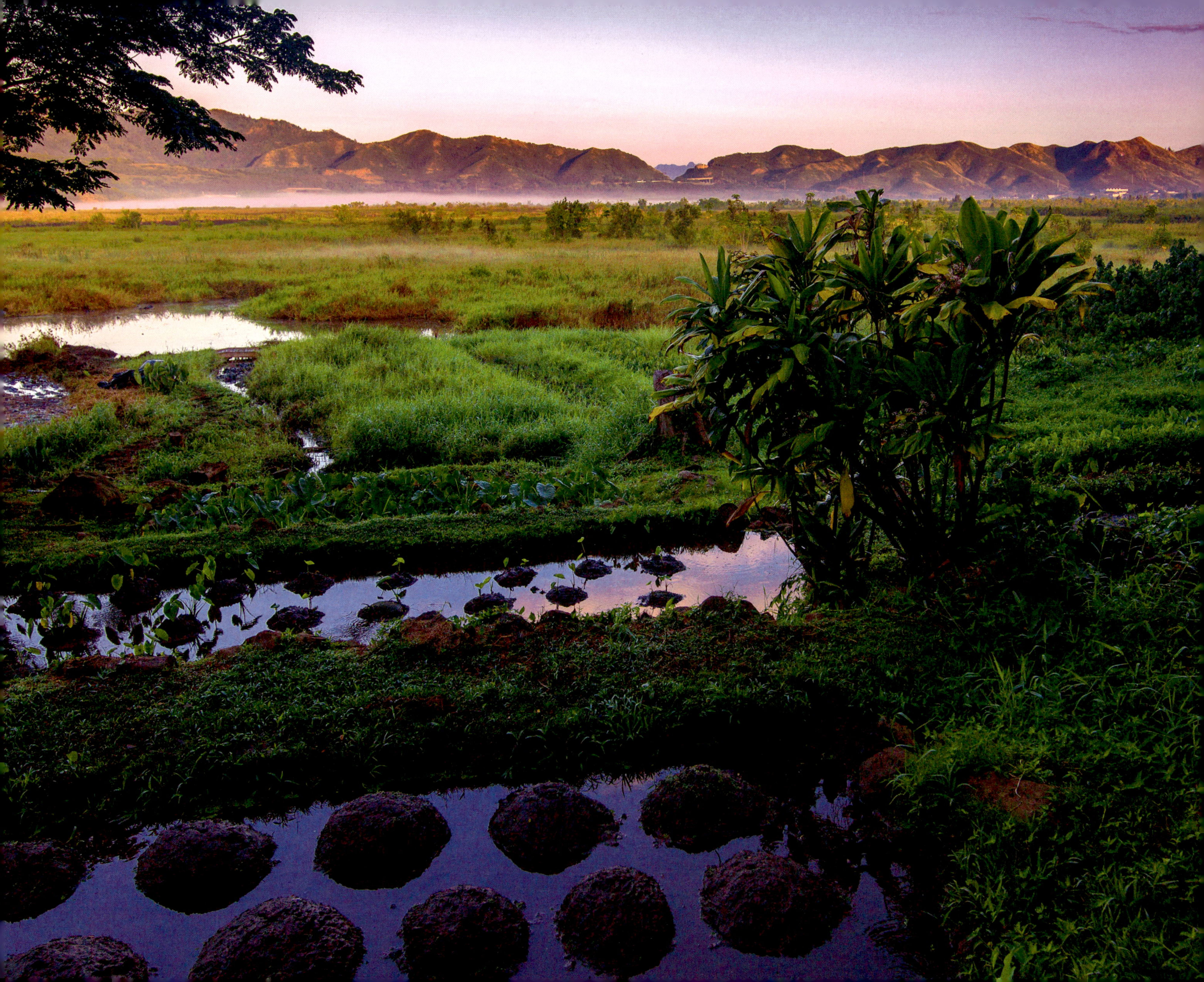

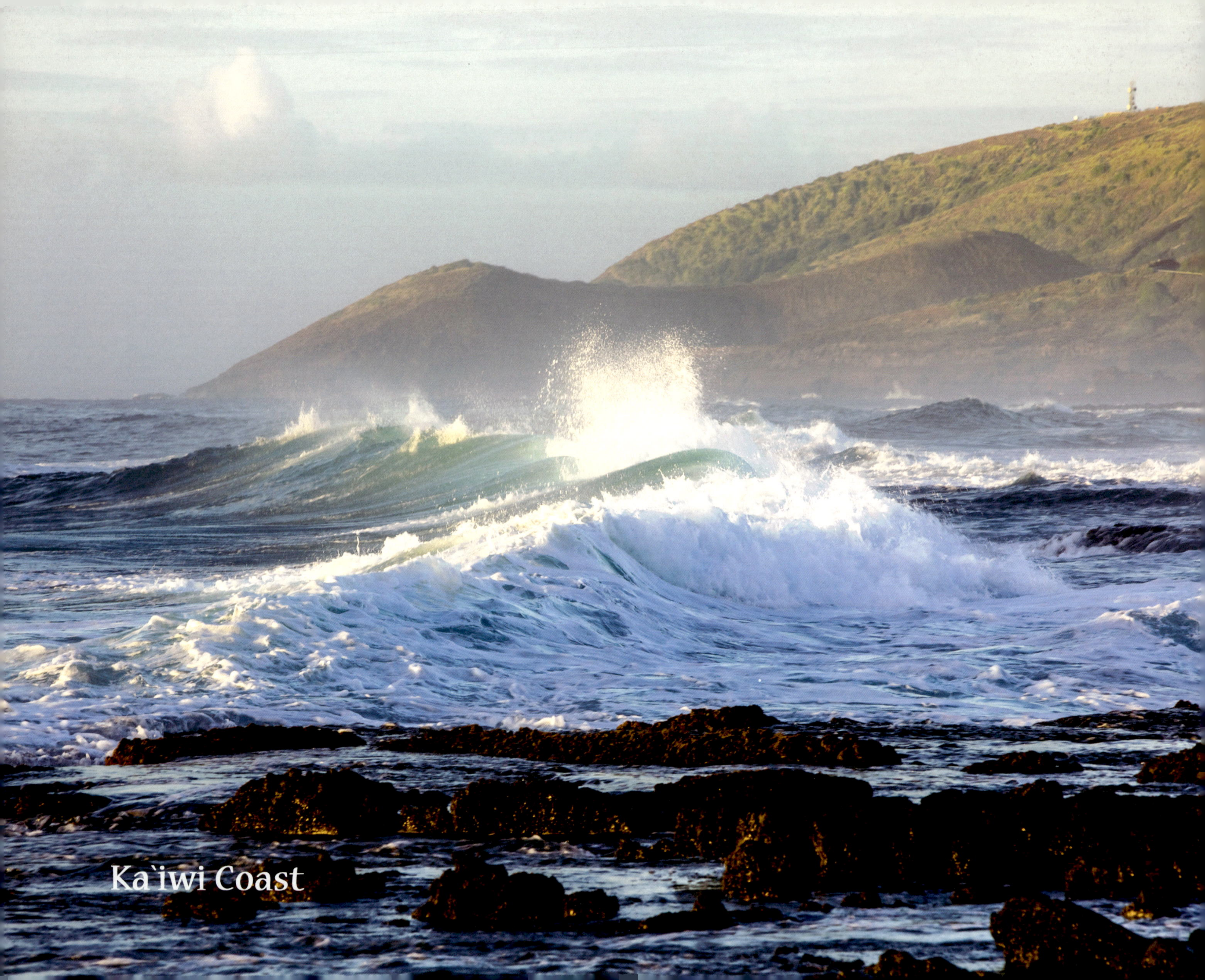
Ka`iwi Coast

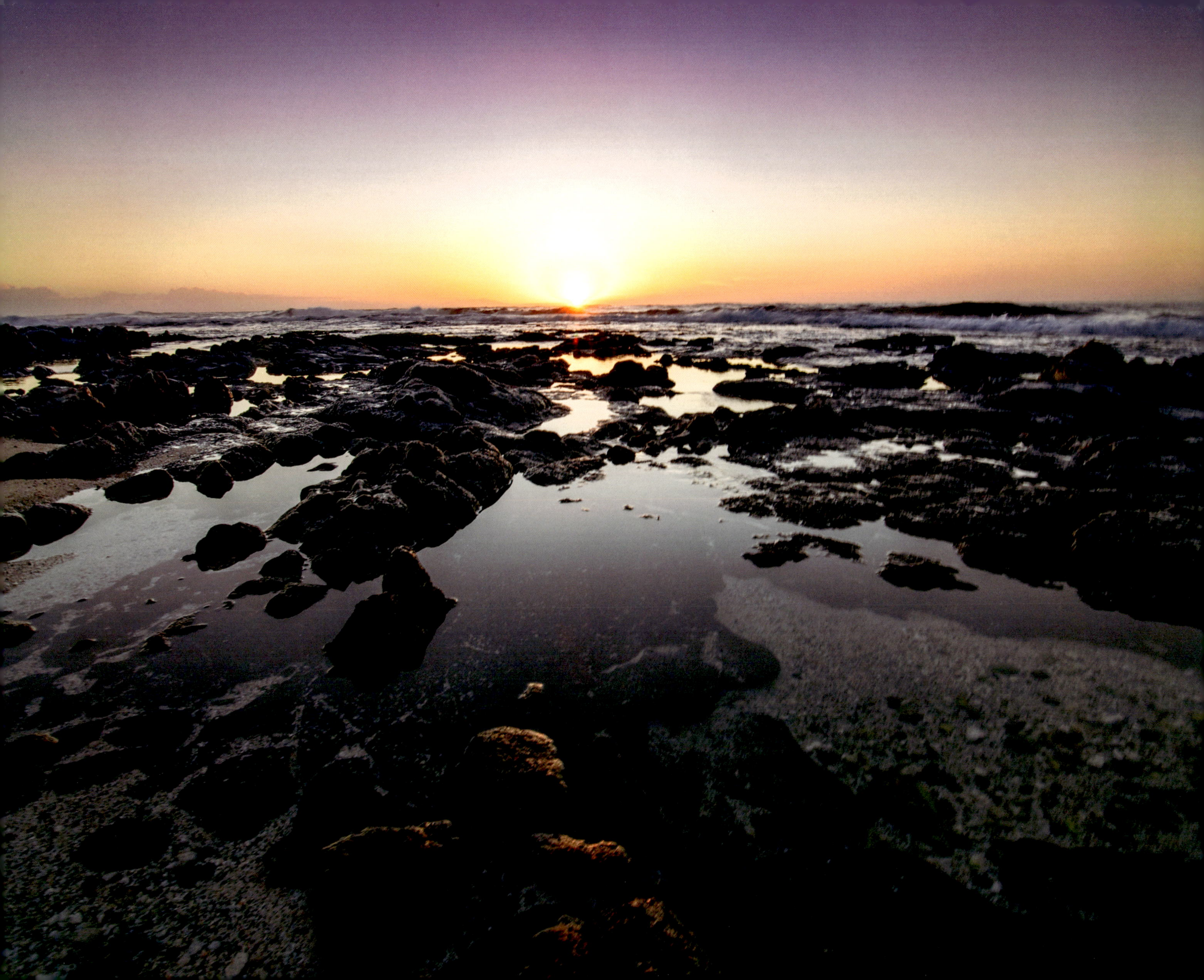

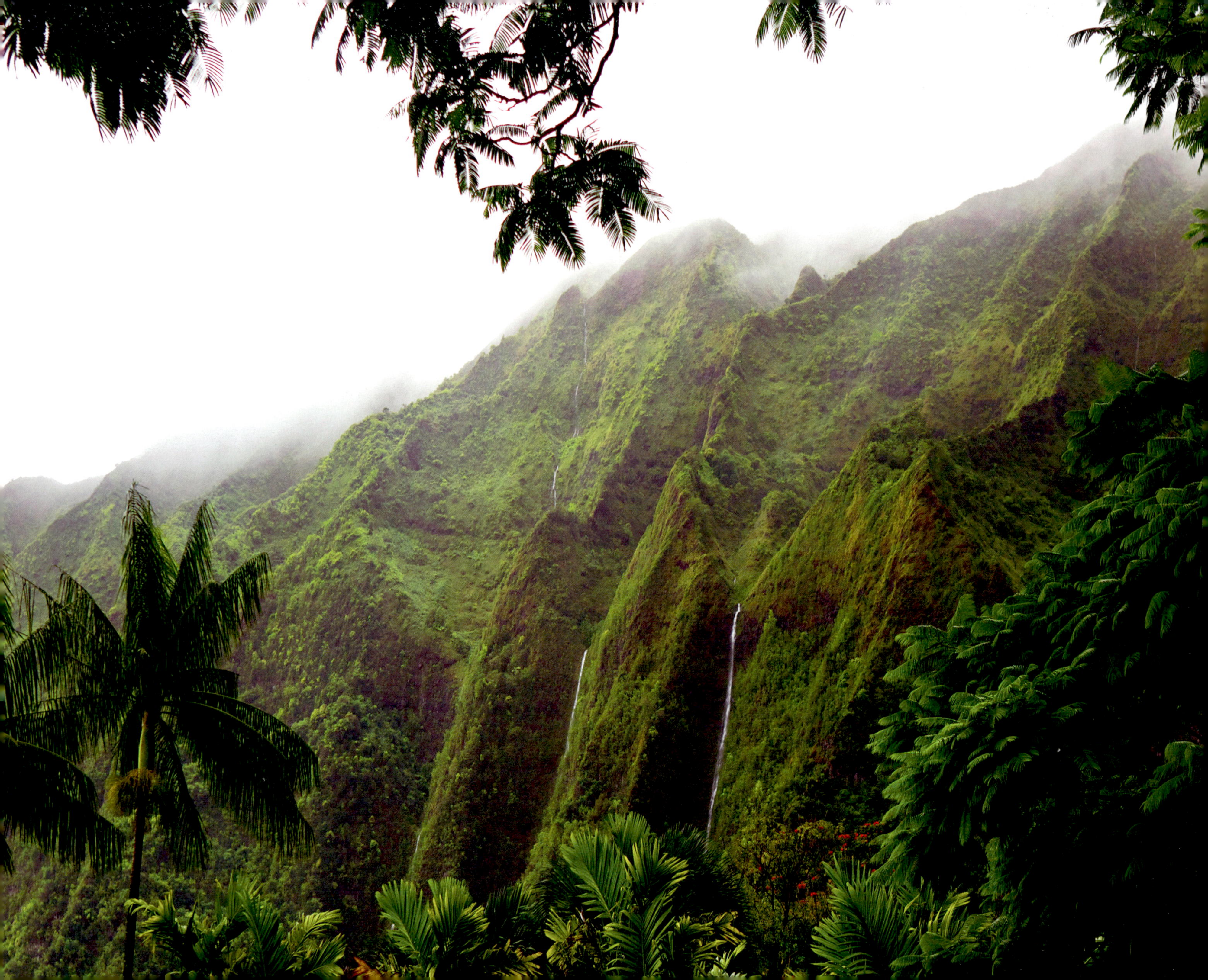

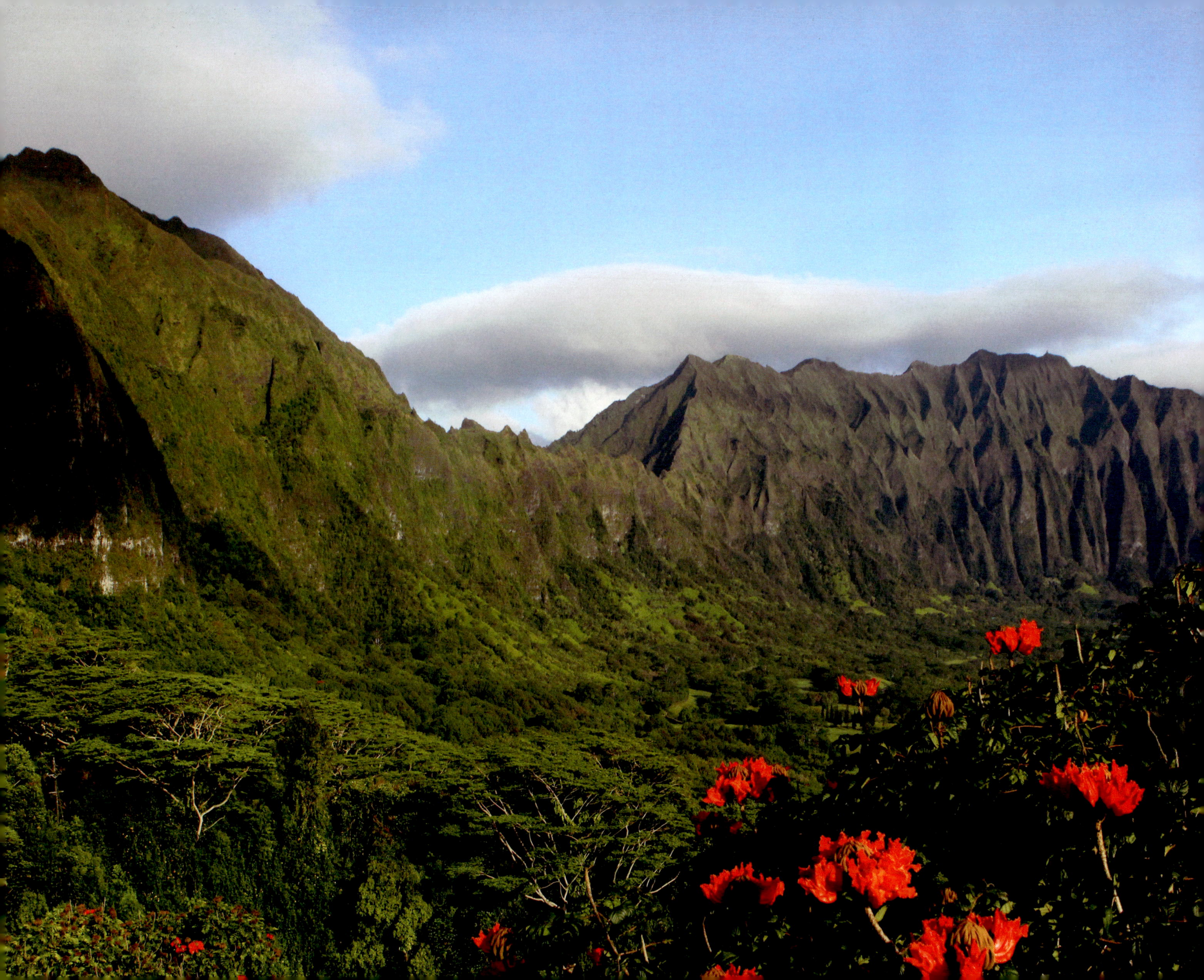

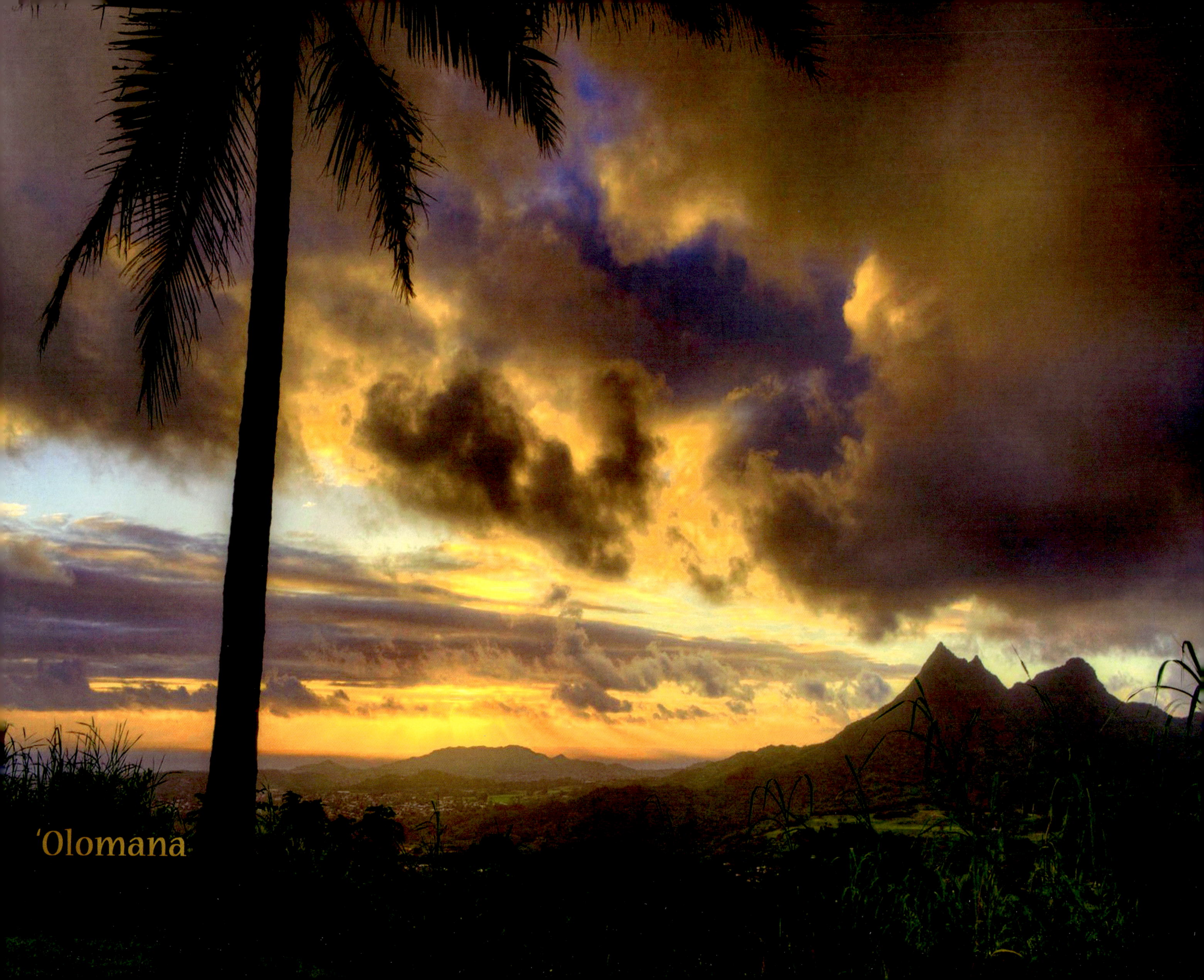

ʻOlomana

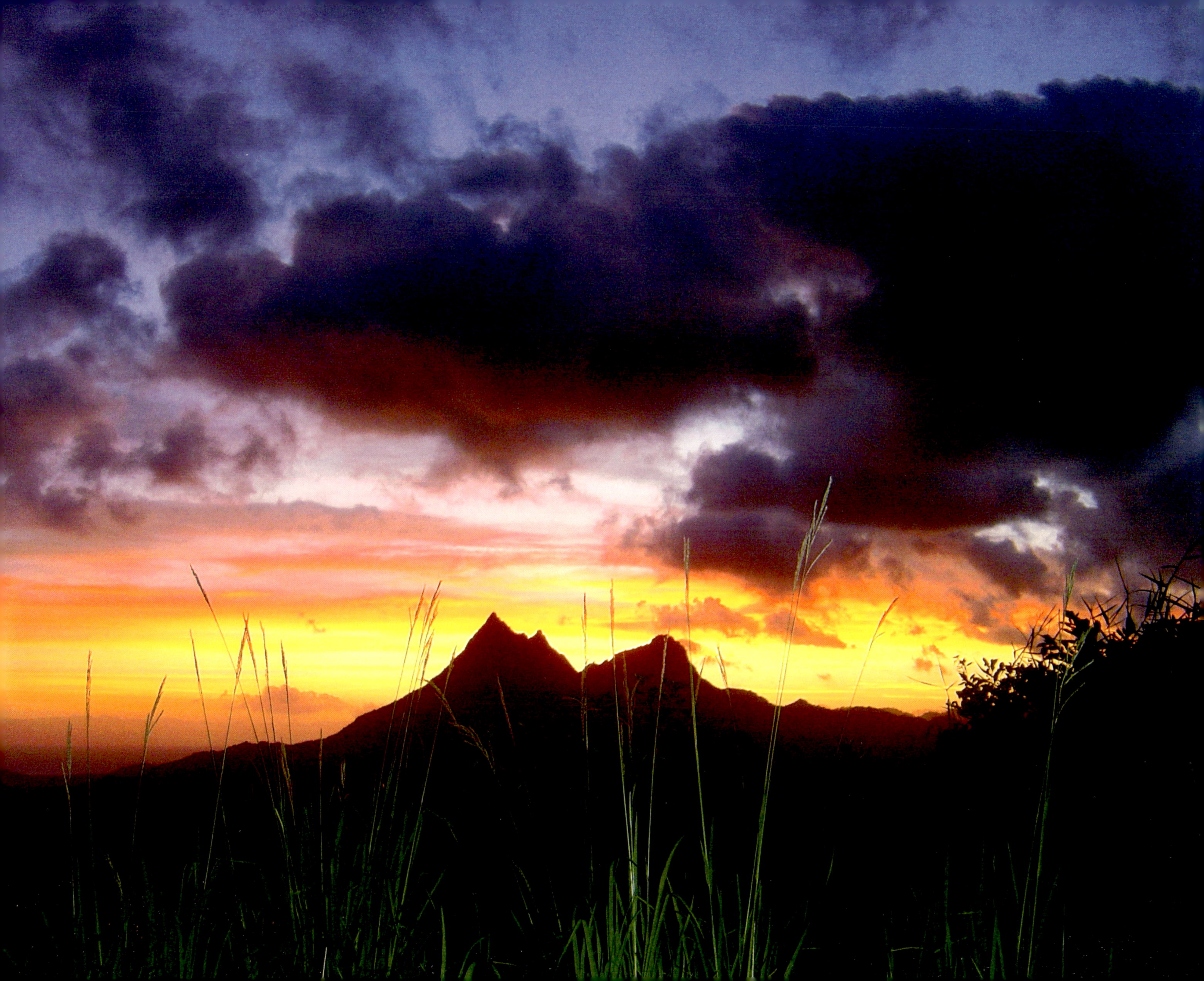

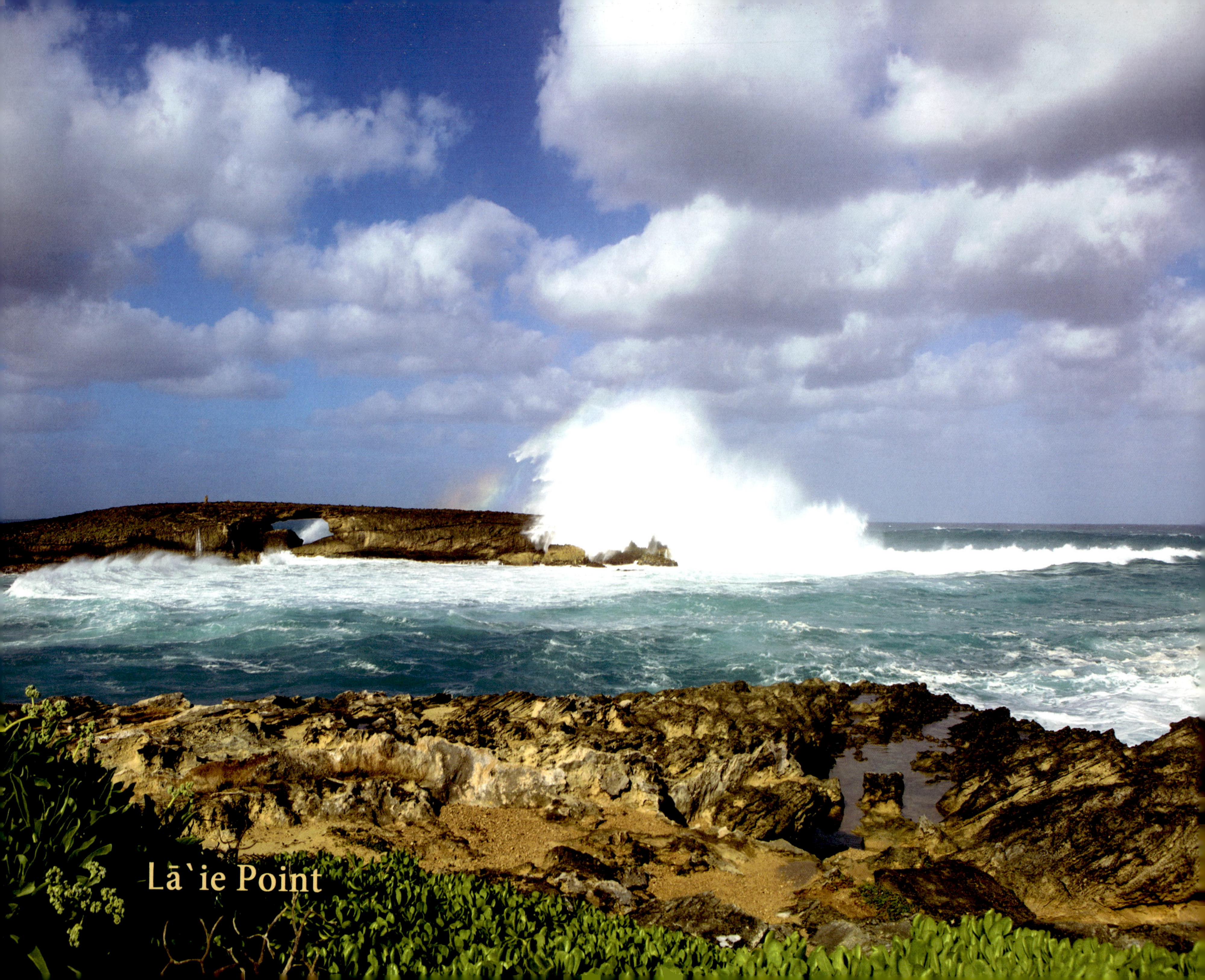
Lā`ie Point

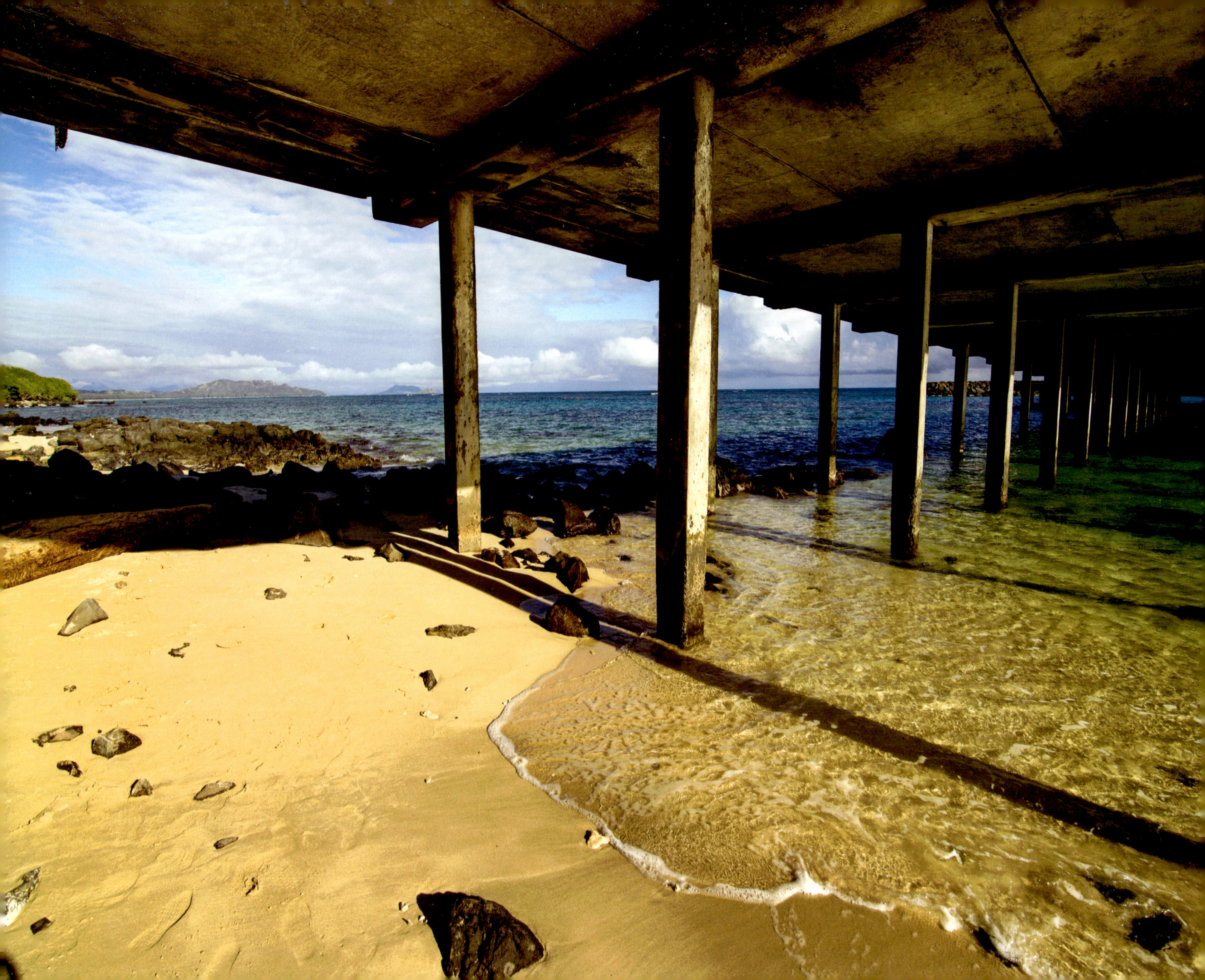

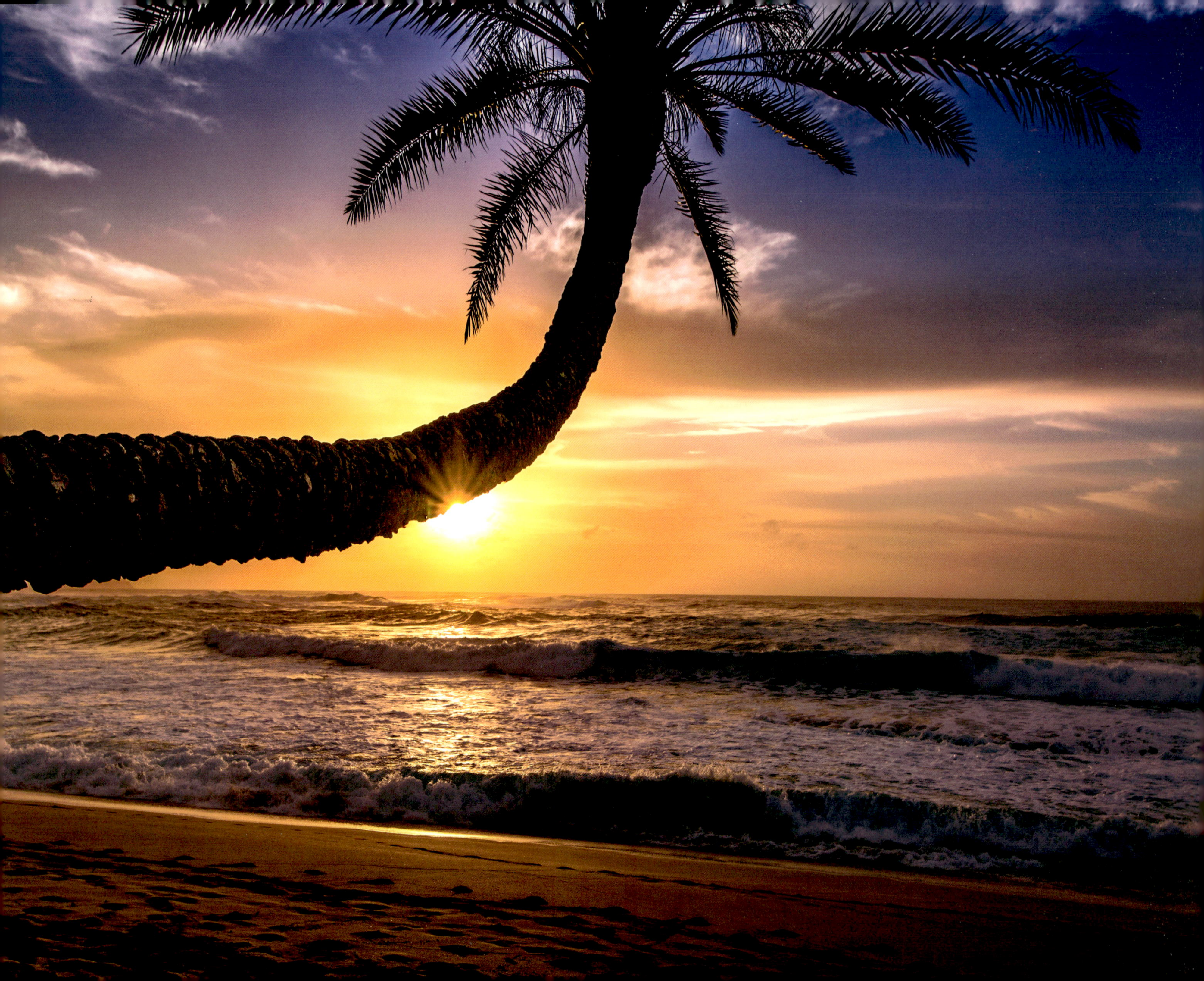

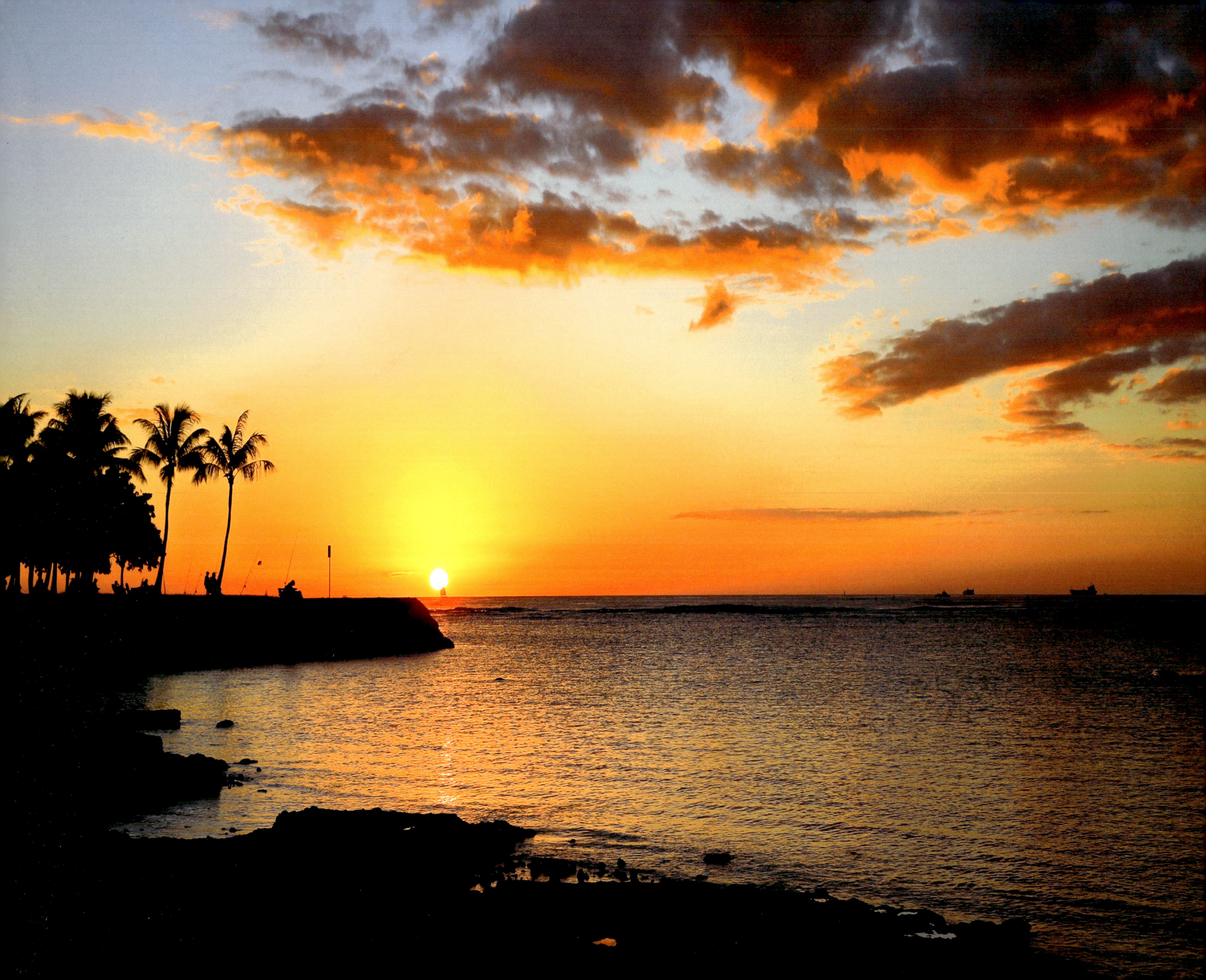

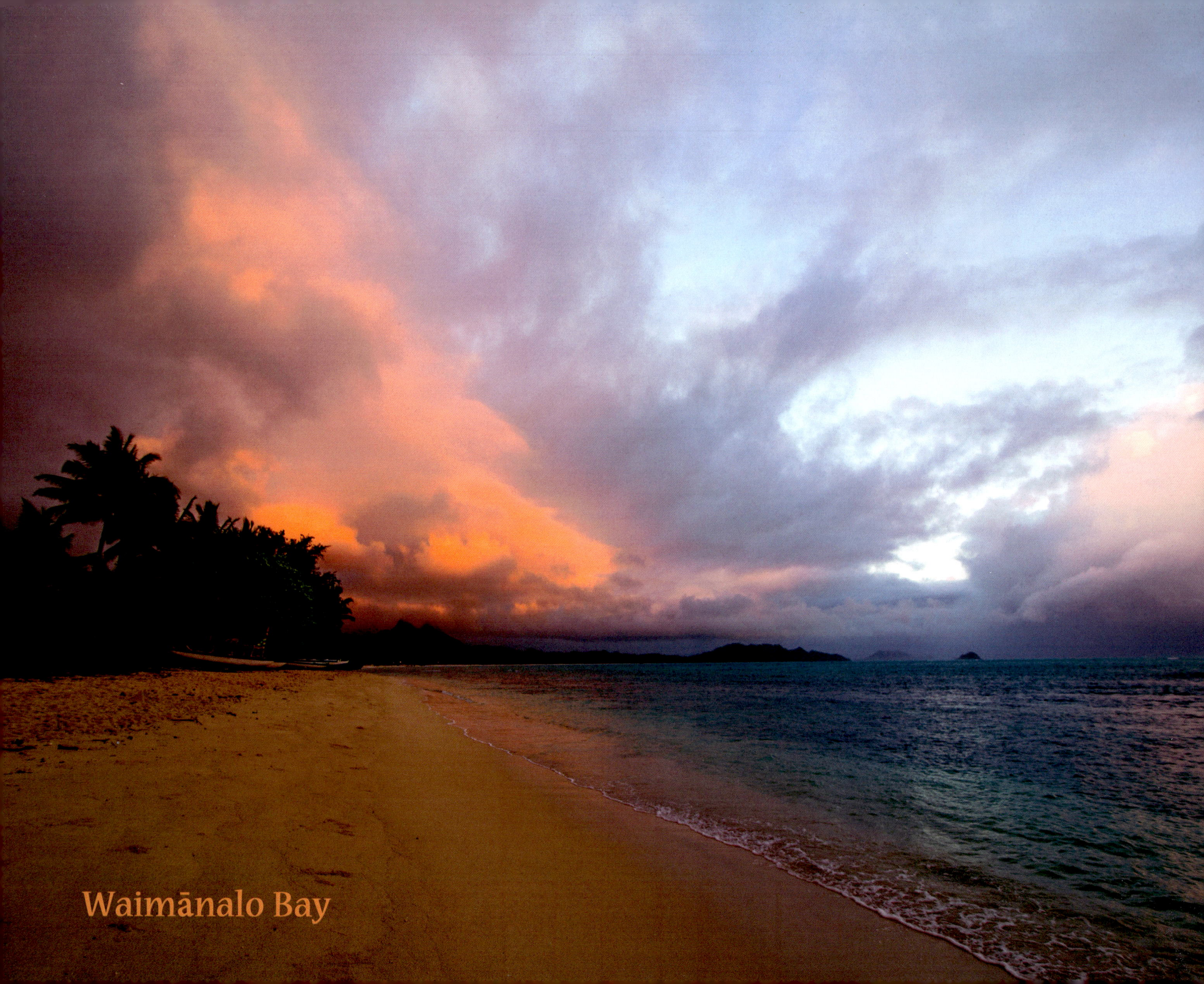

Waimānalo Bay

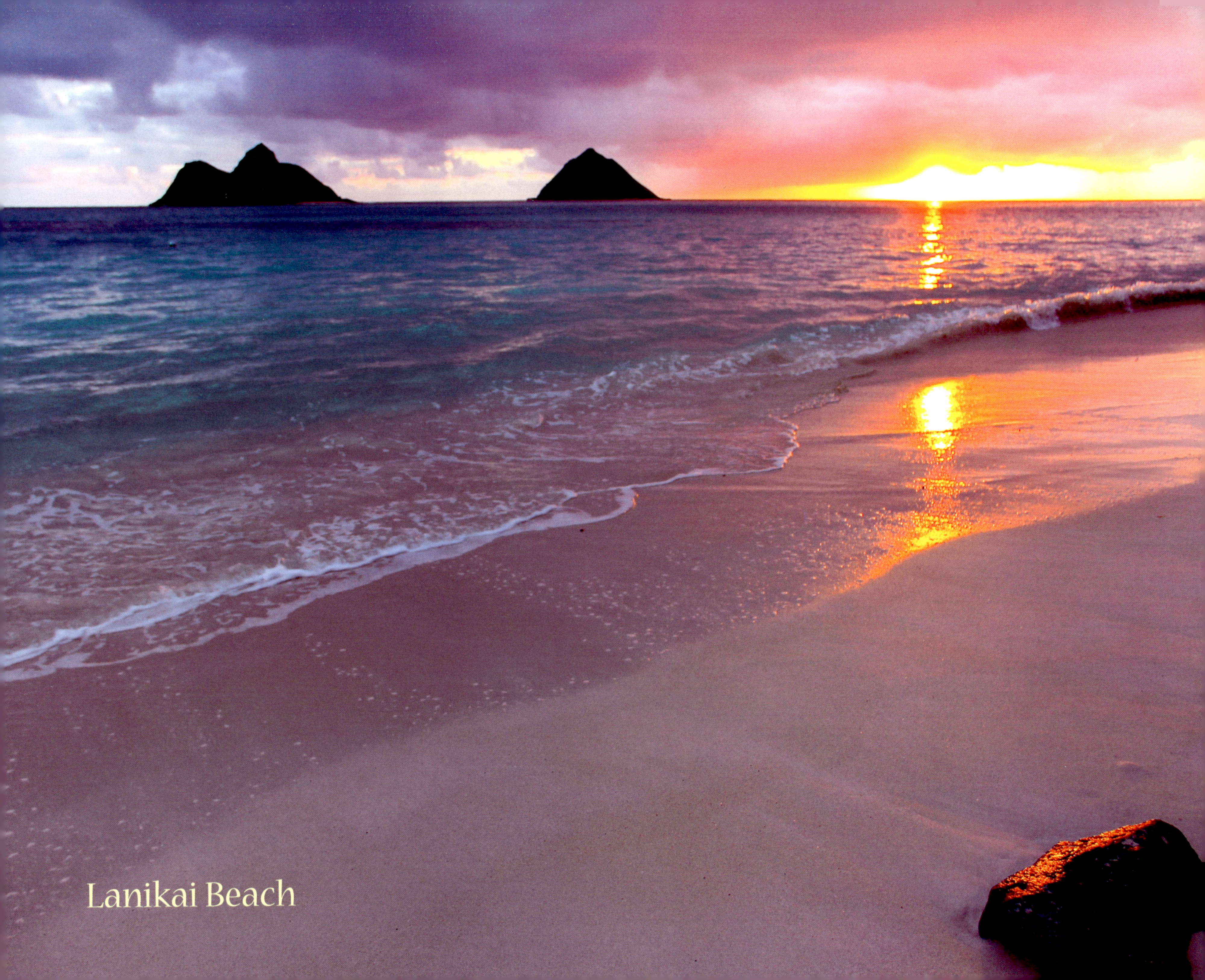

Lanikai Beach

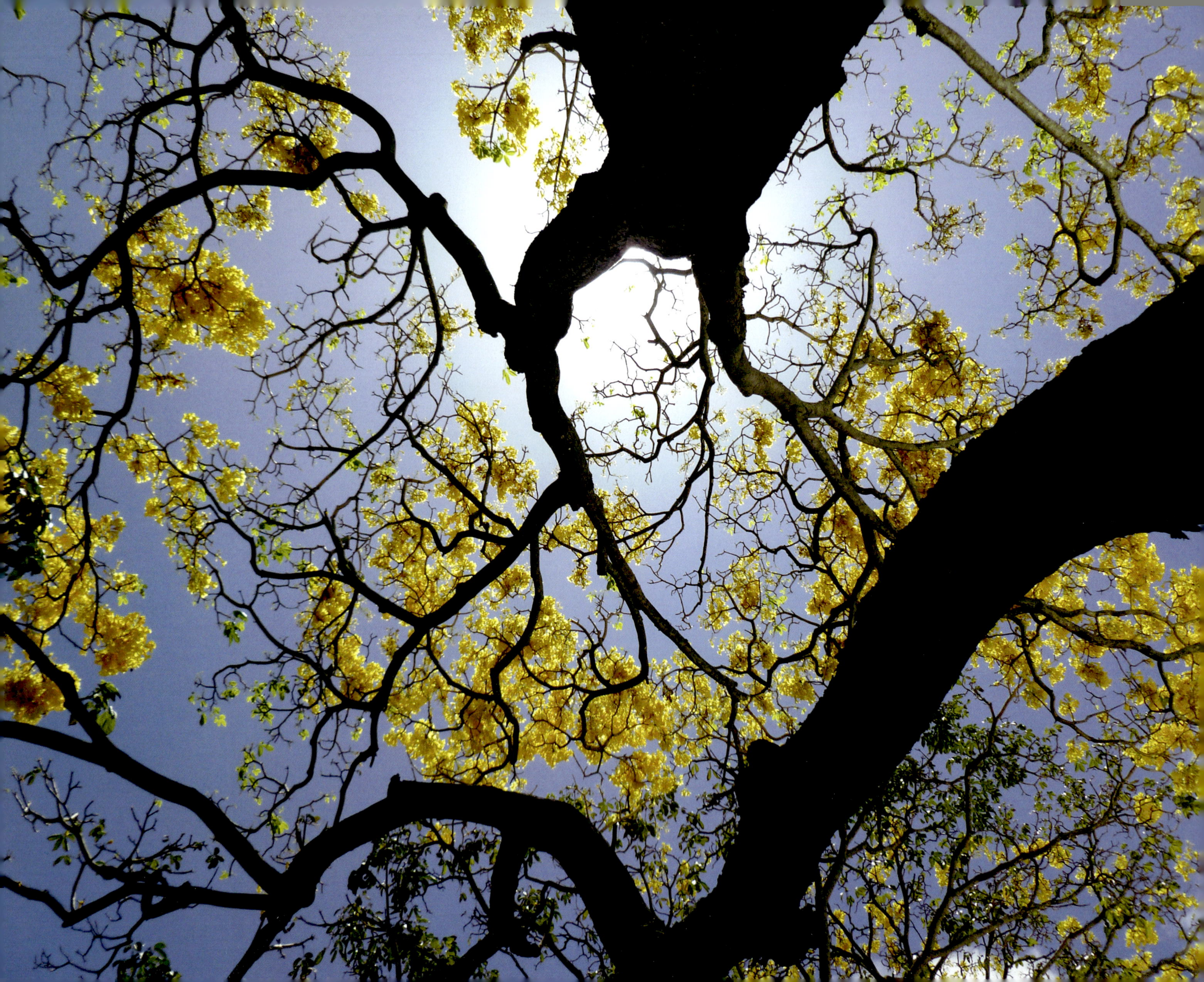

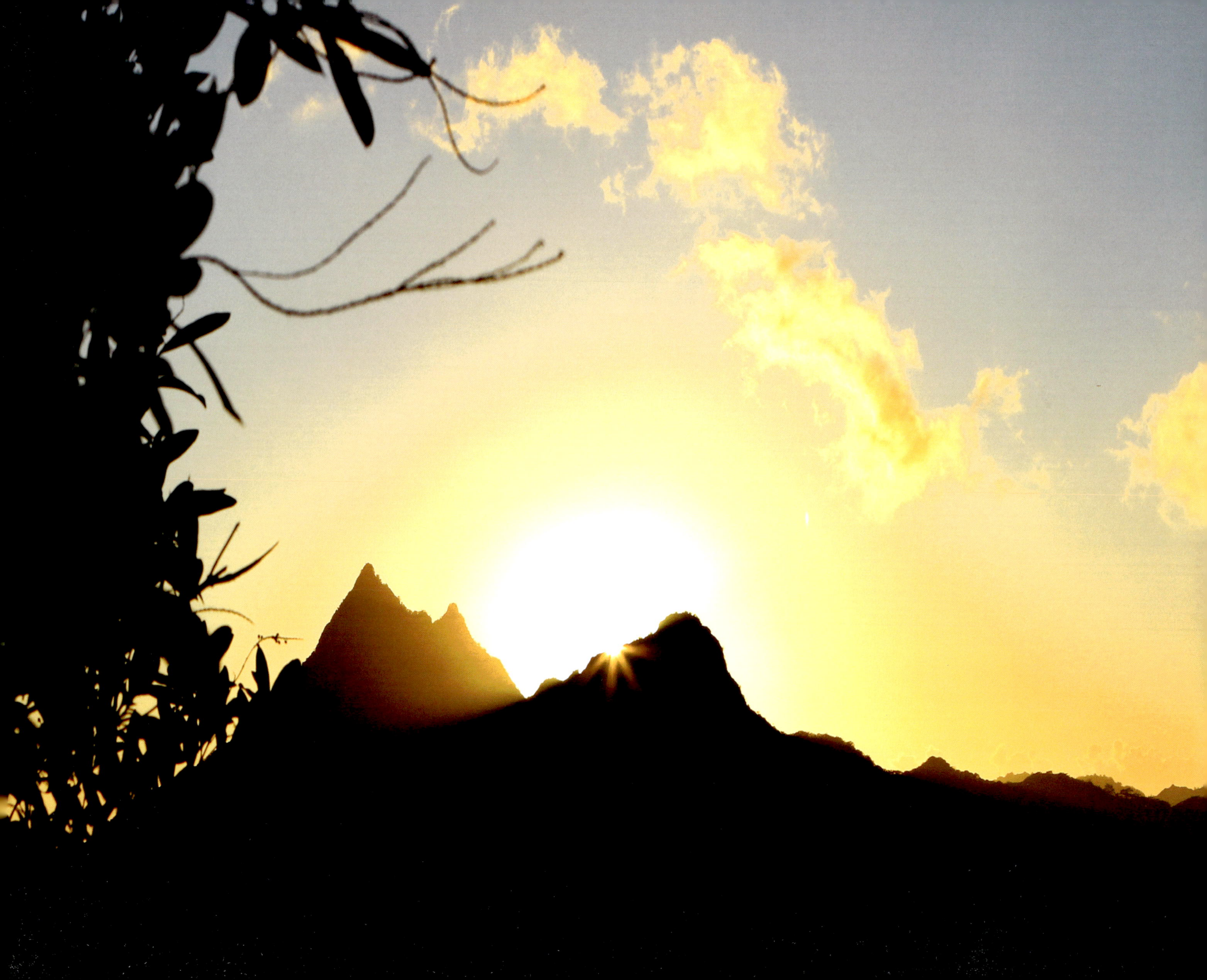

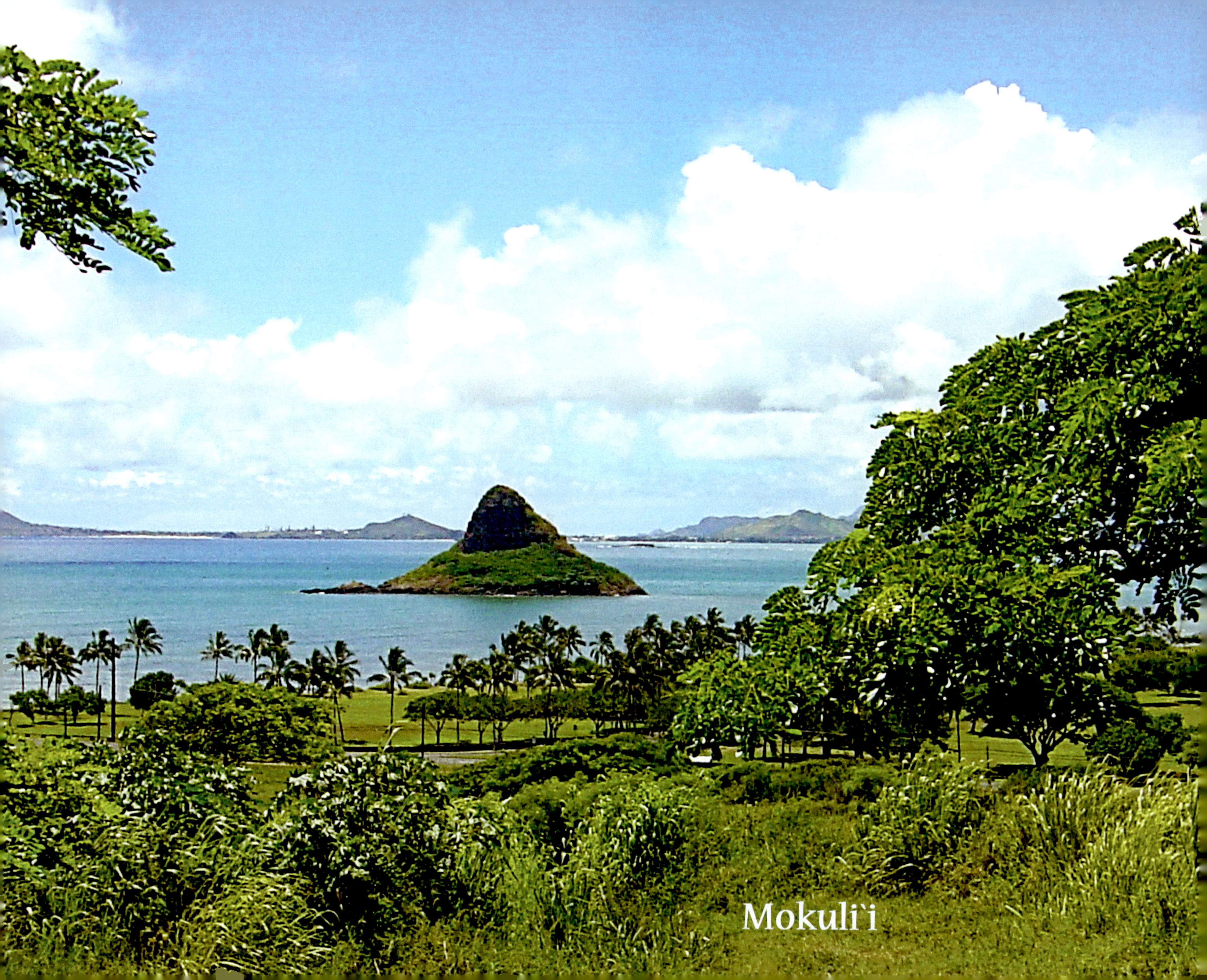
Mokuli`i

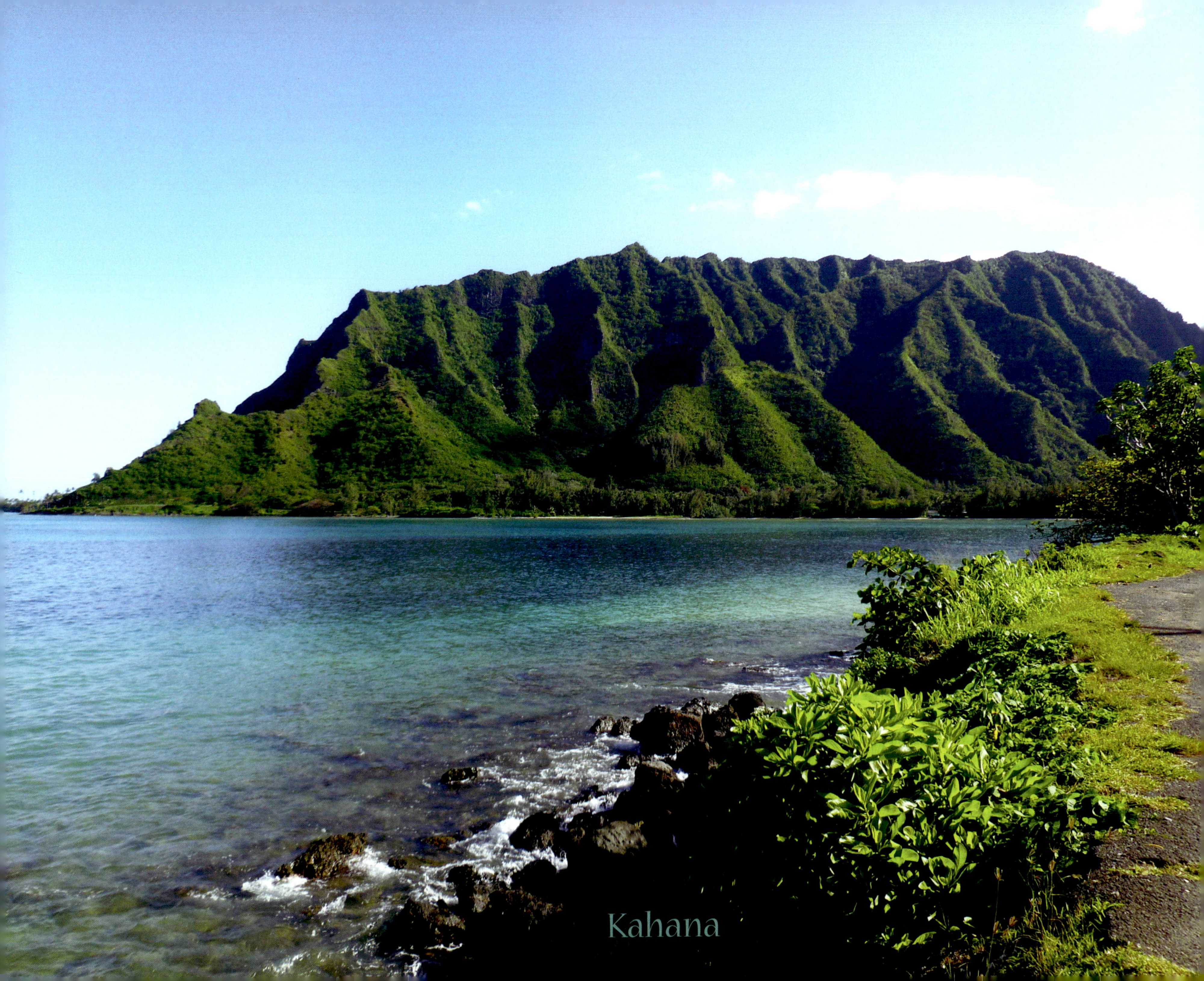

Kahana

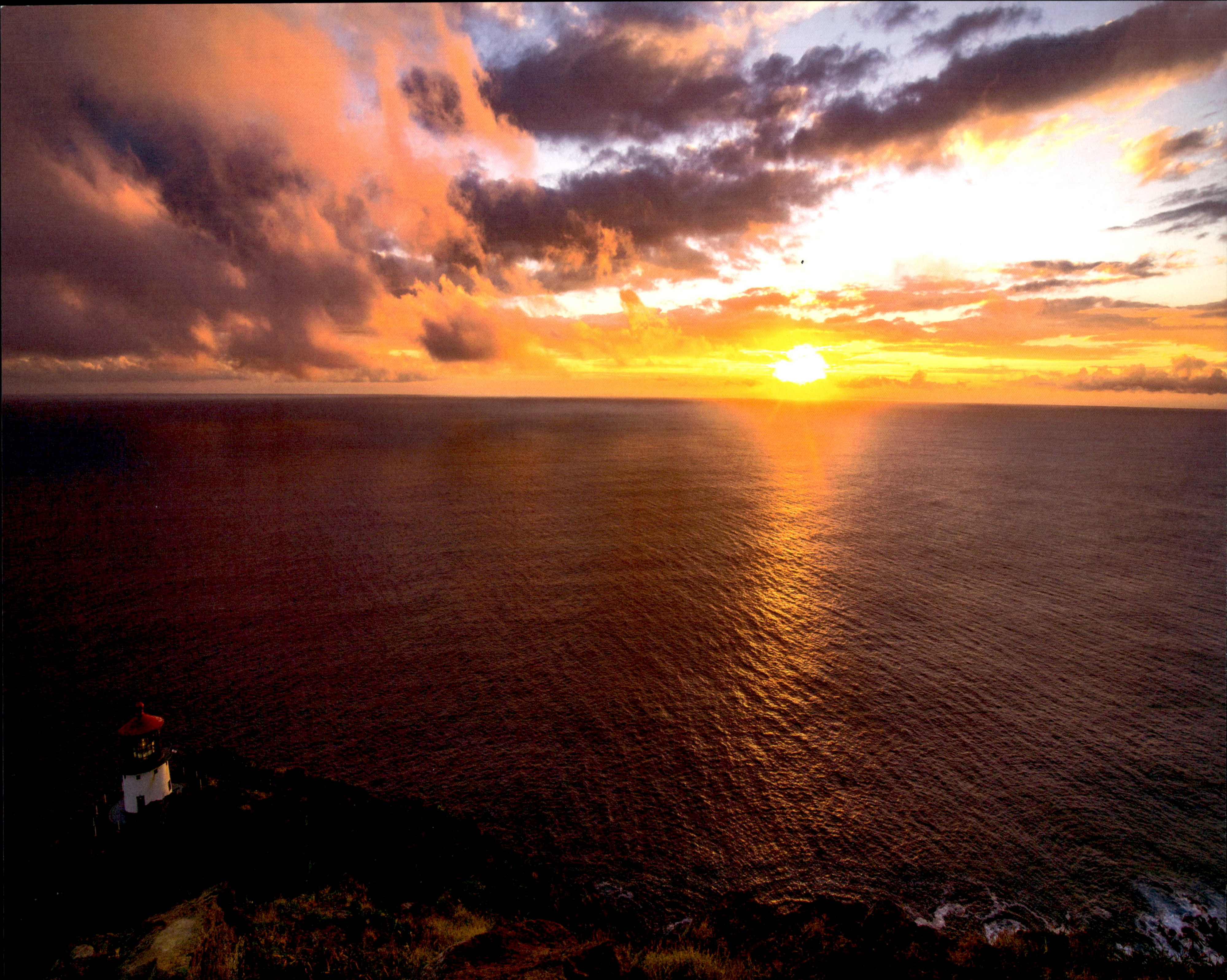

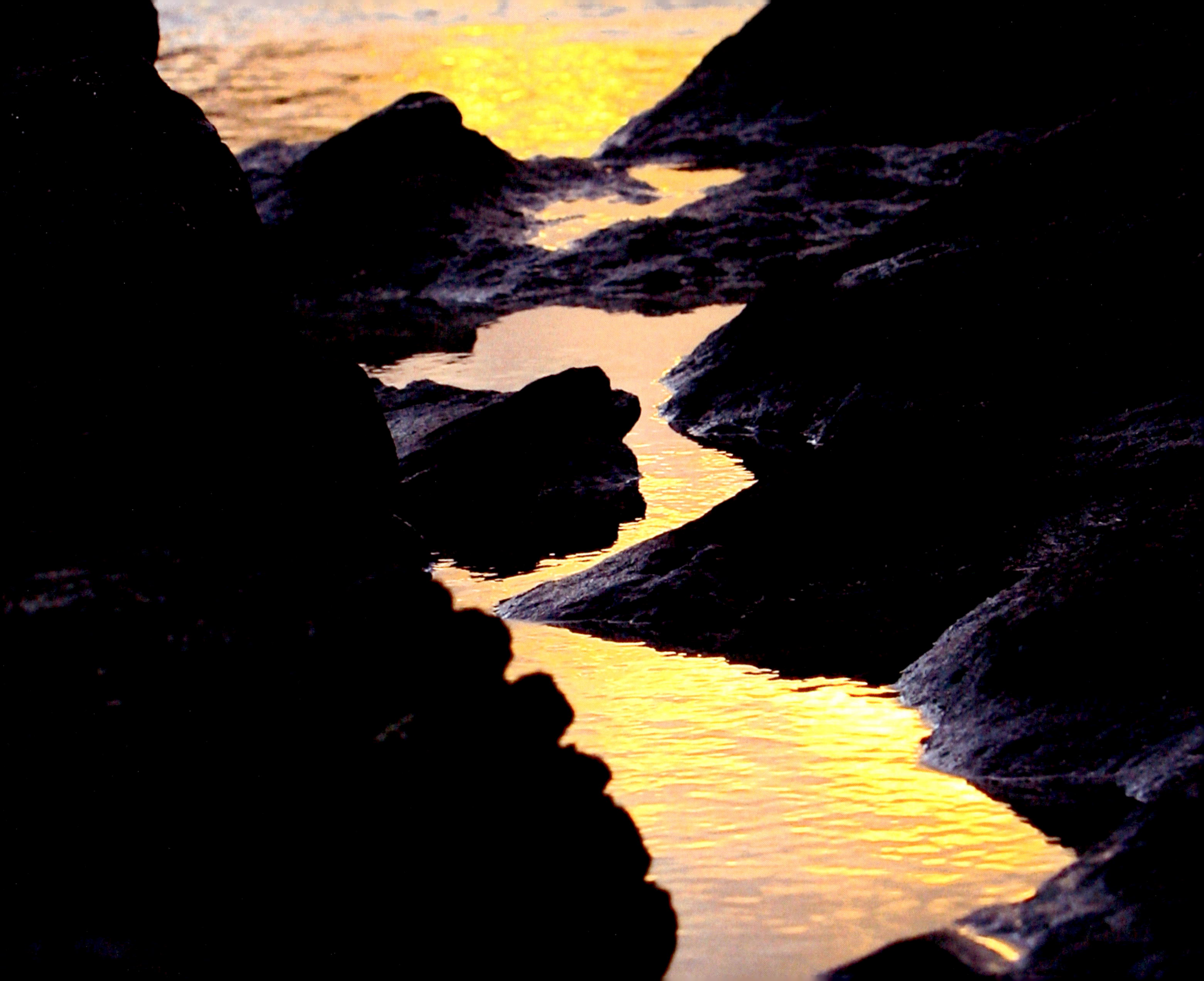

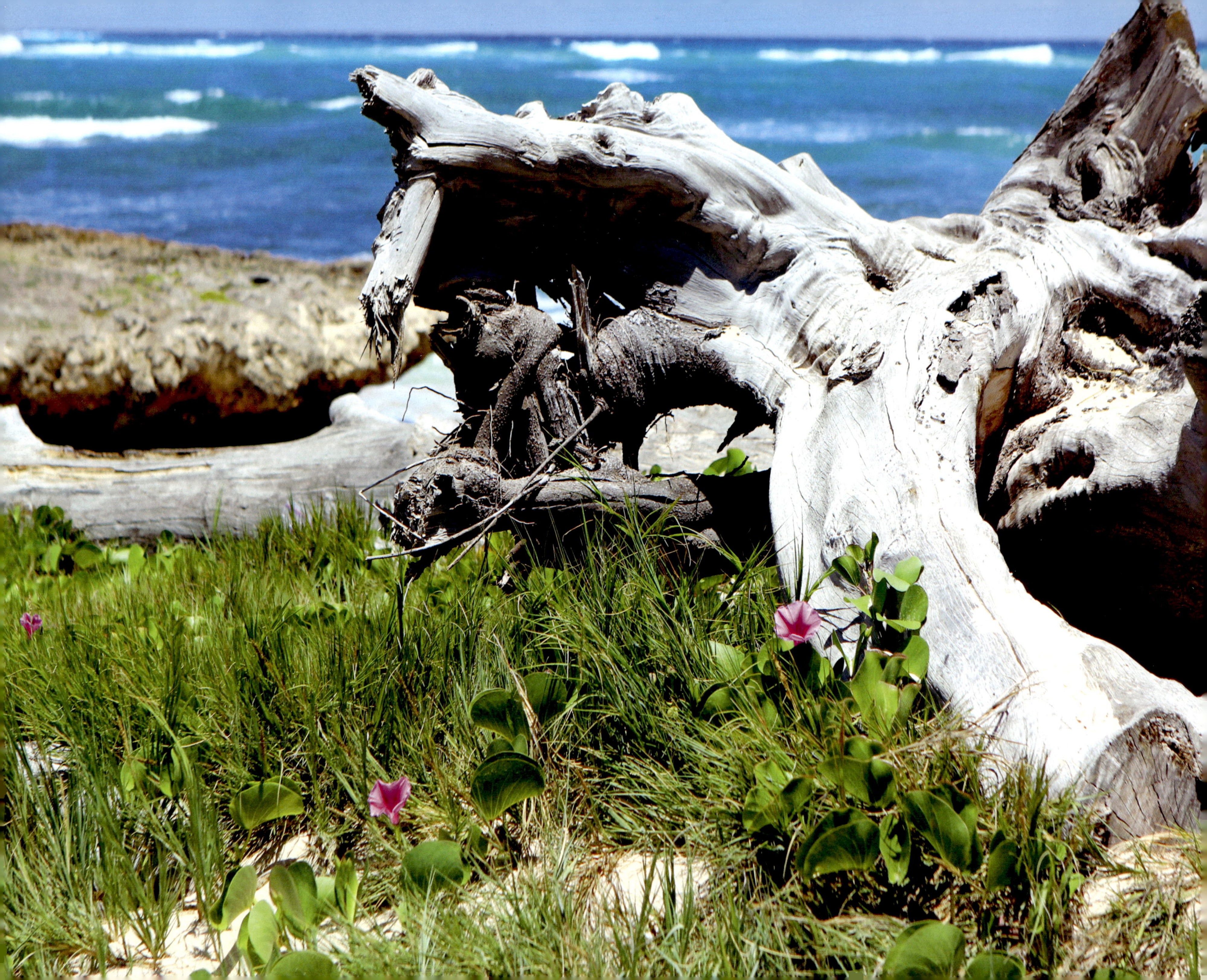

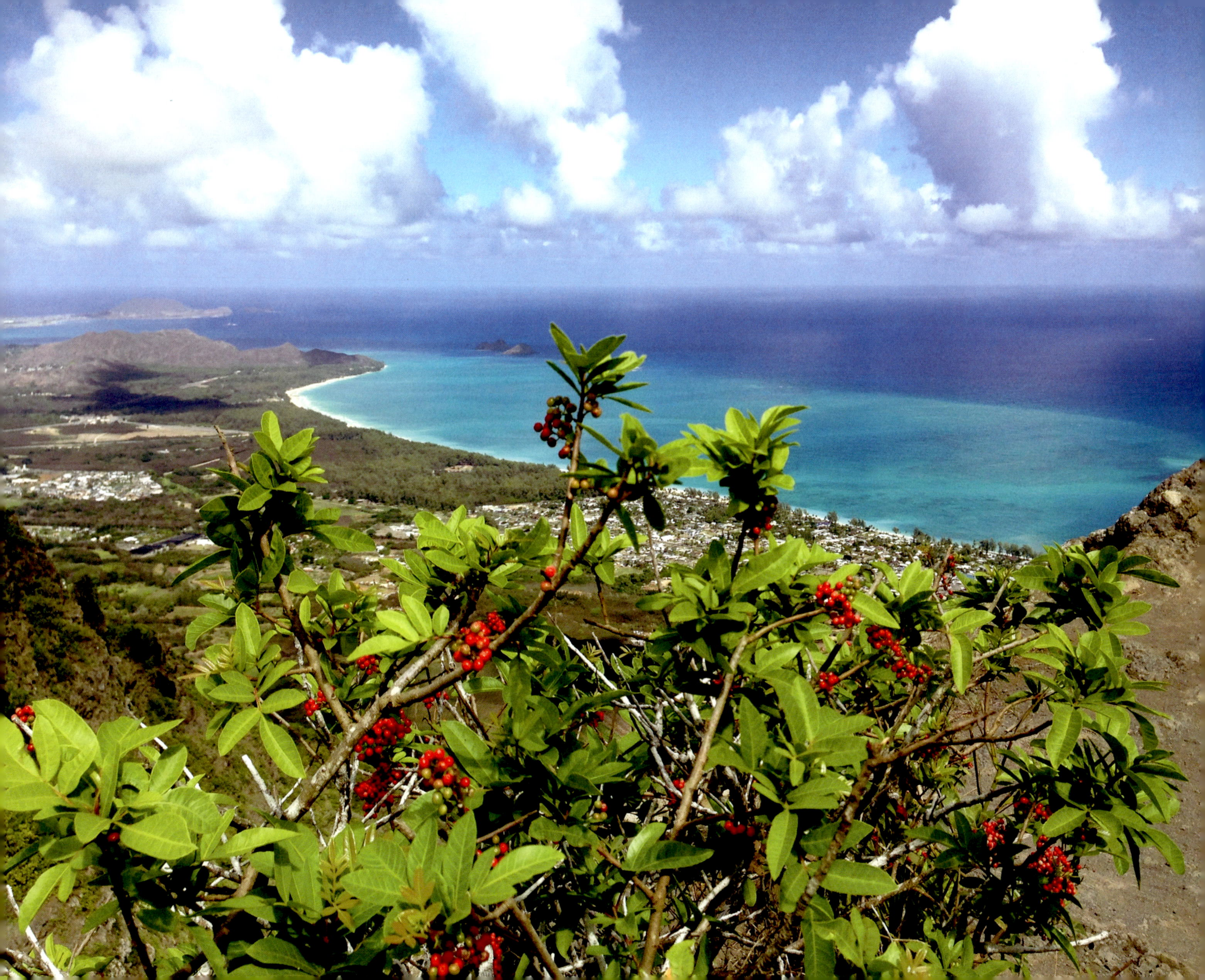

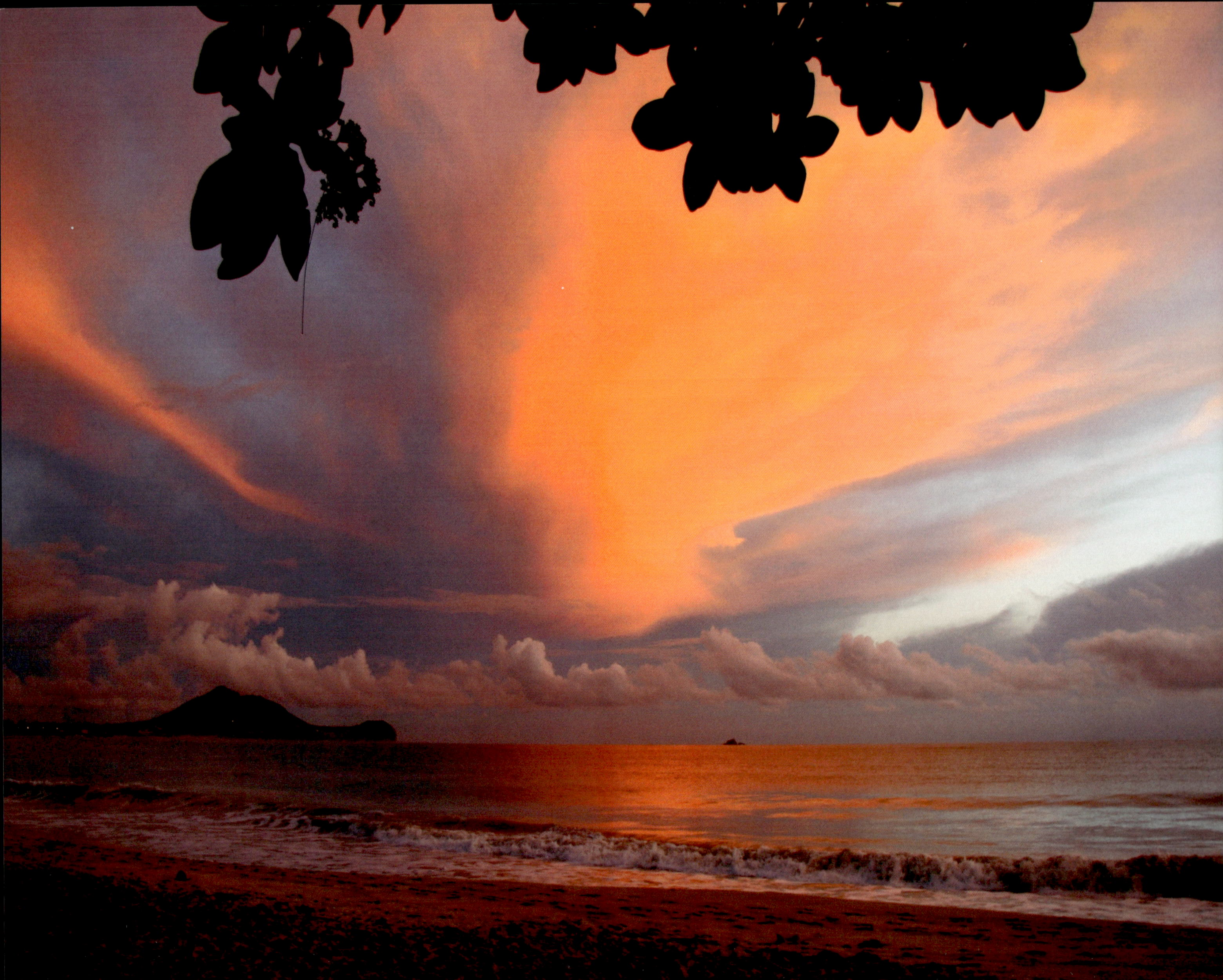

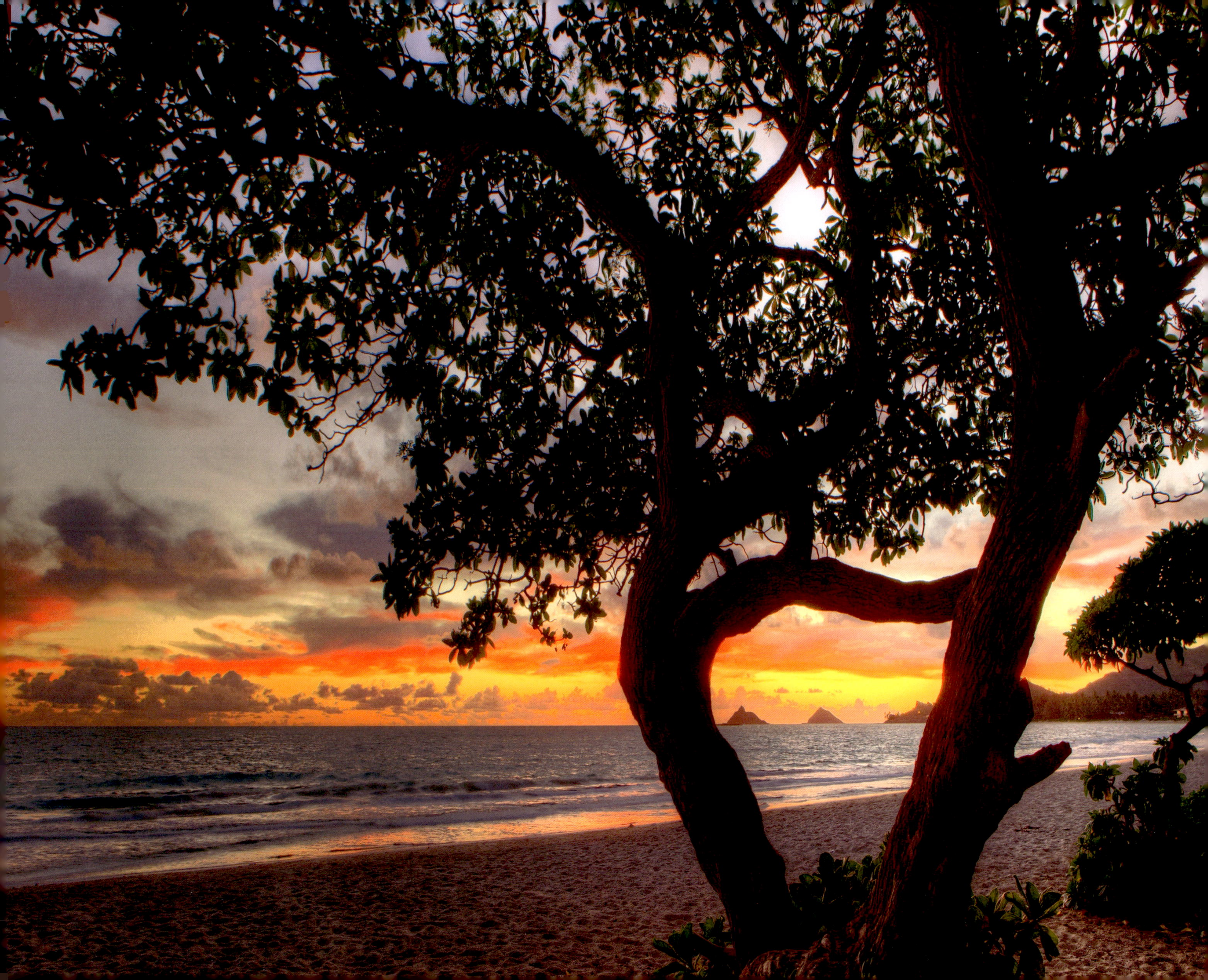

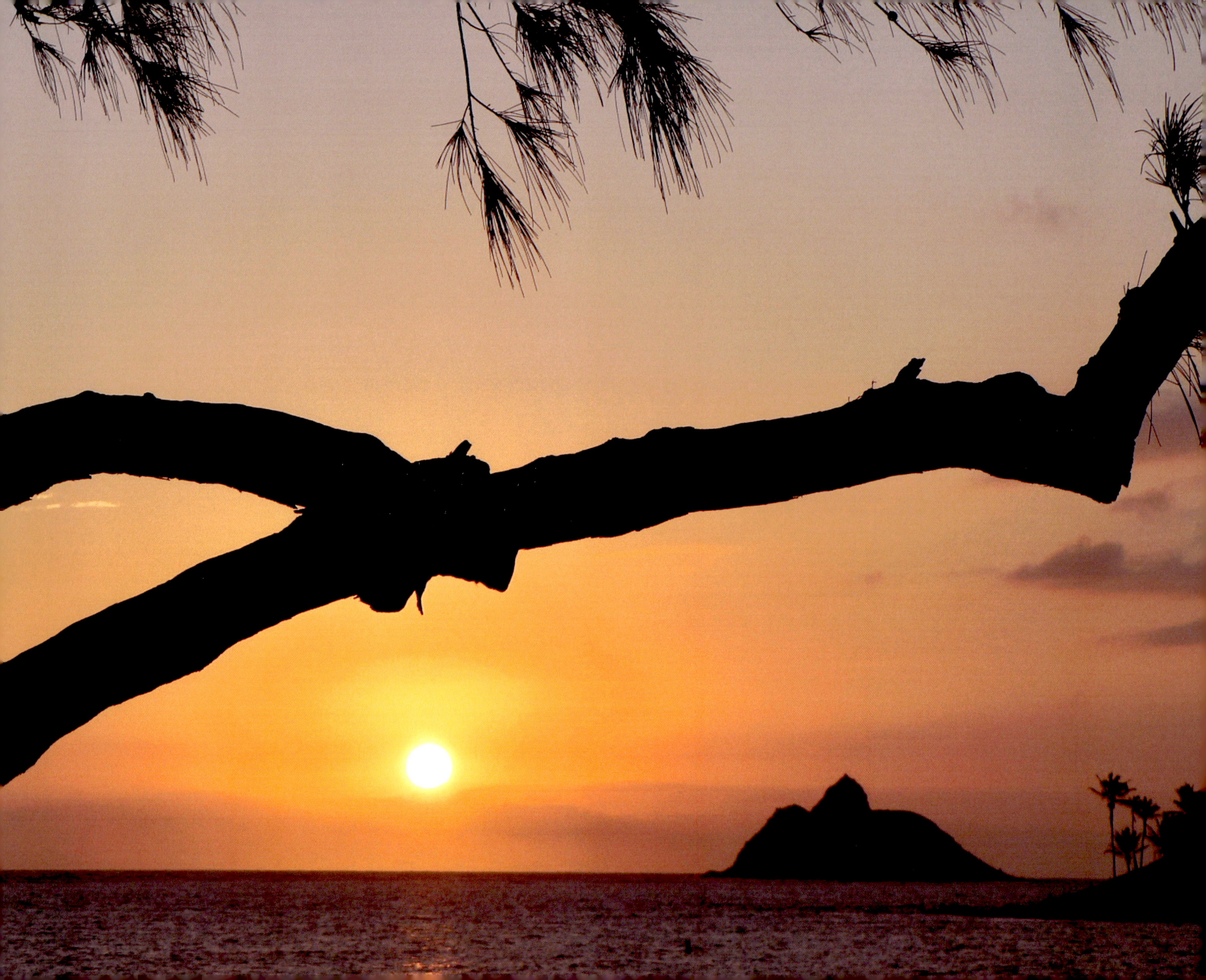

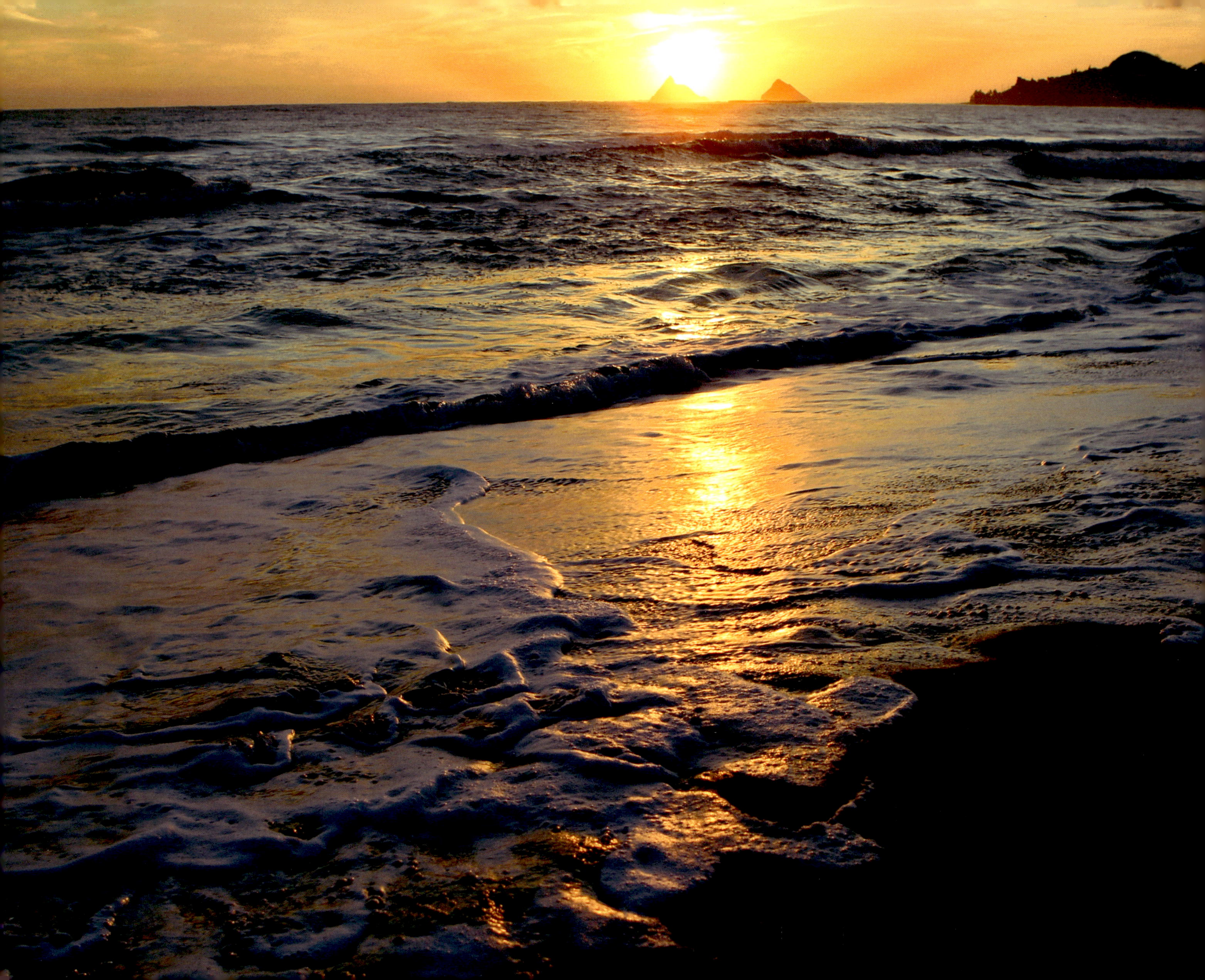

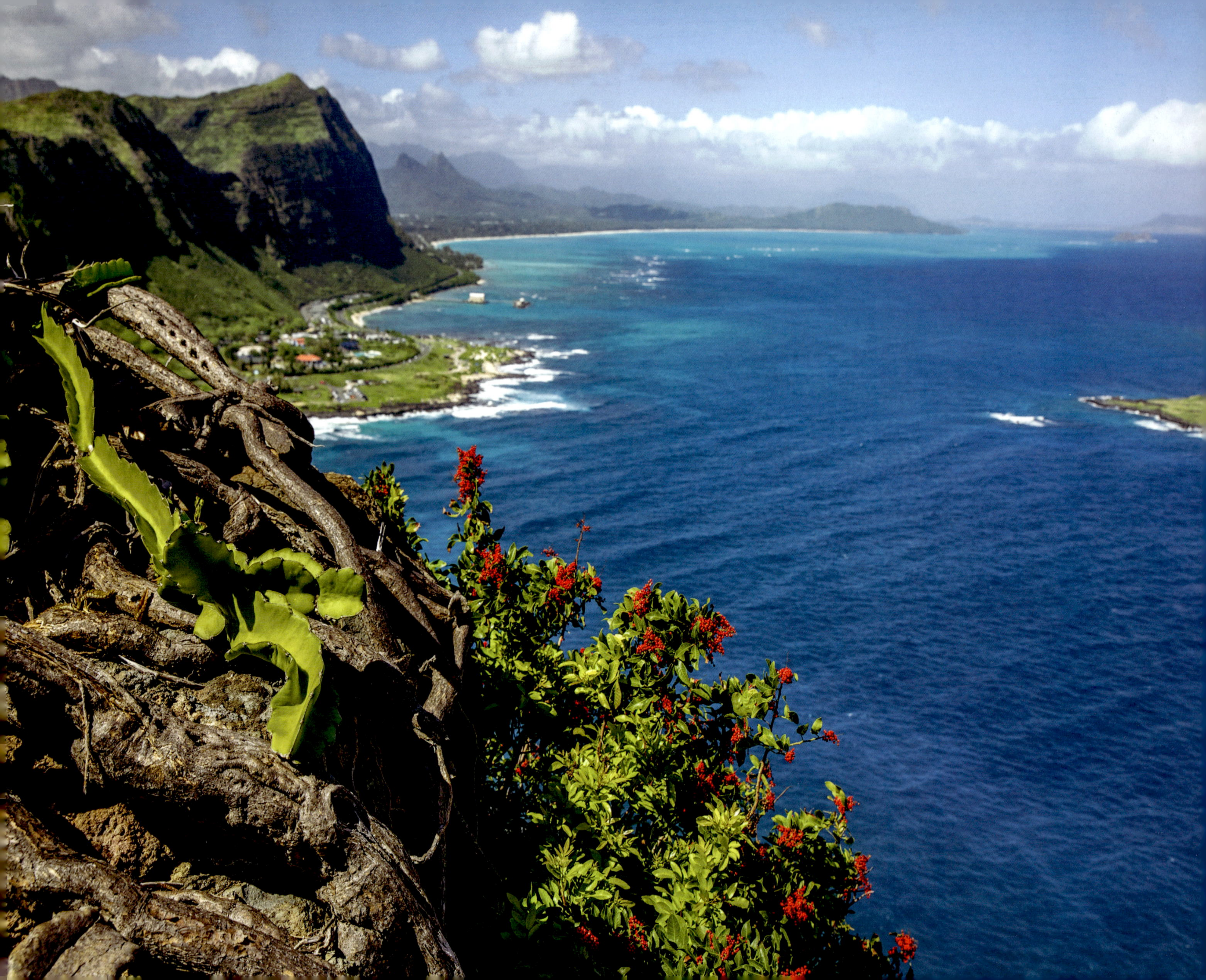

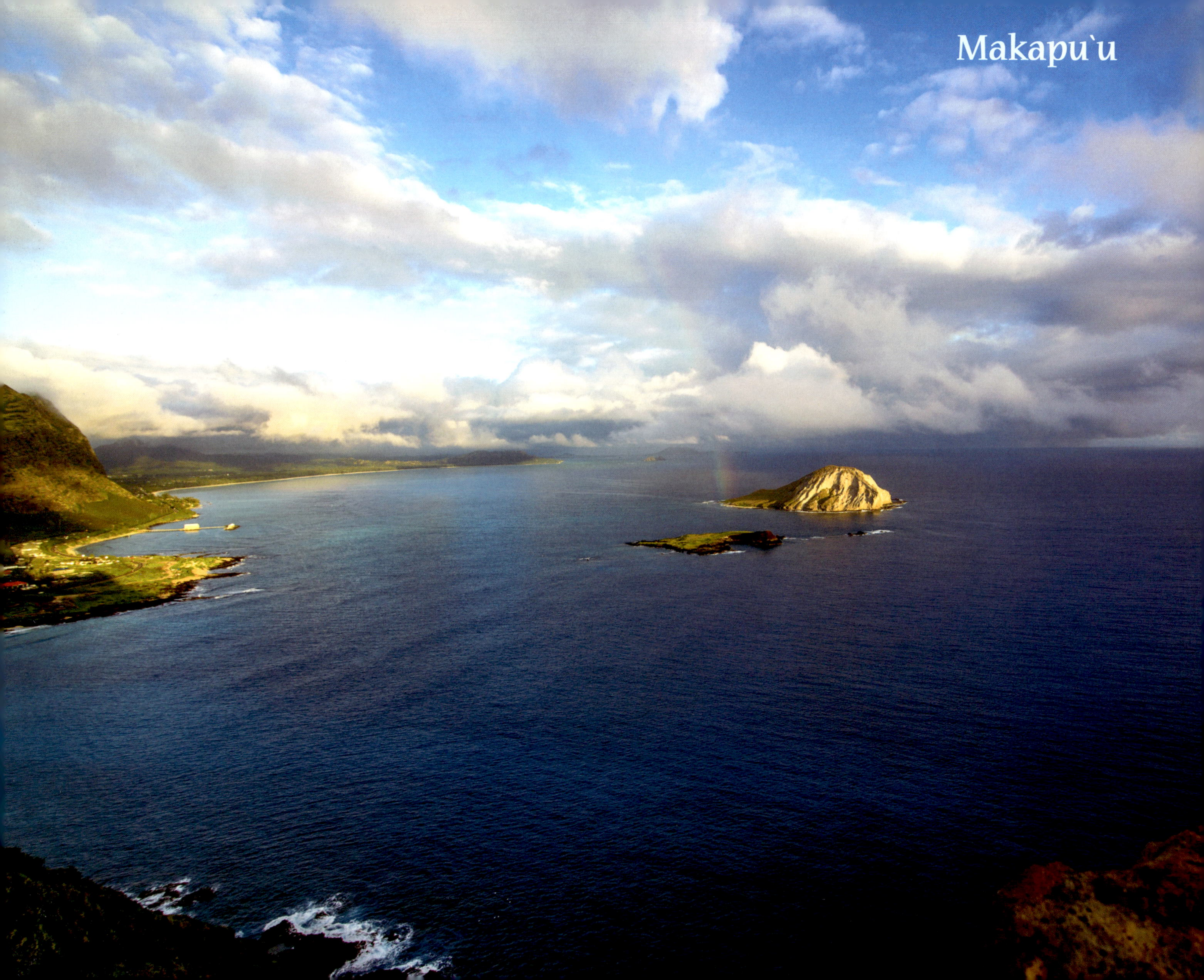

Makapu`u

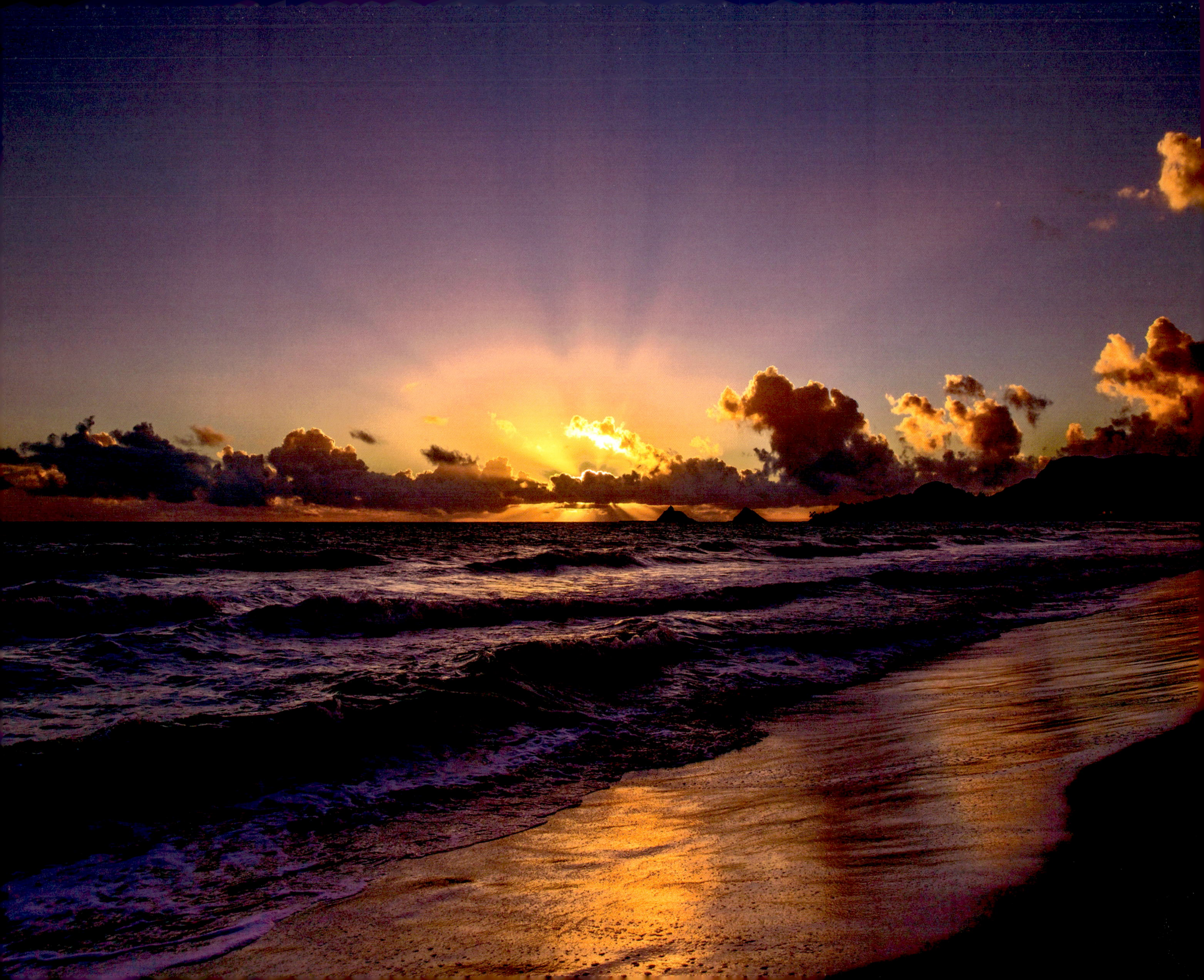

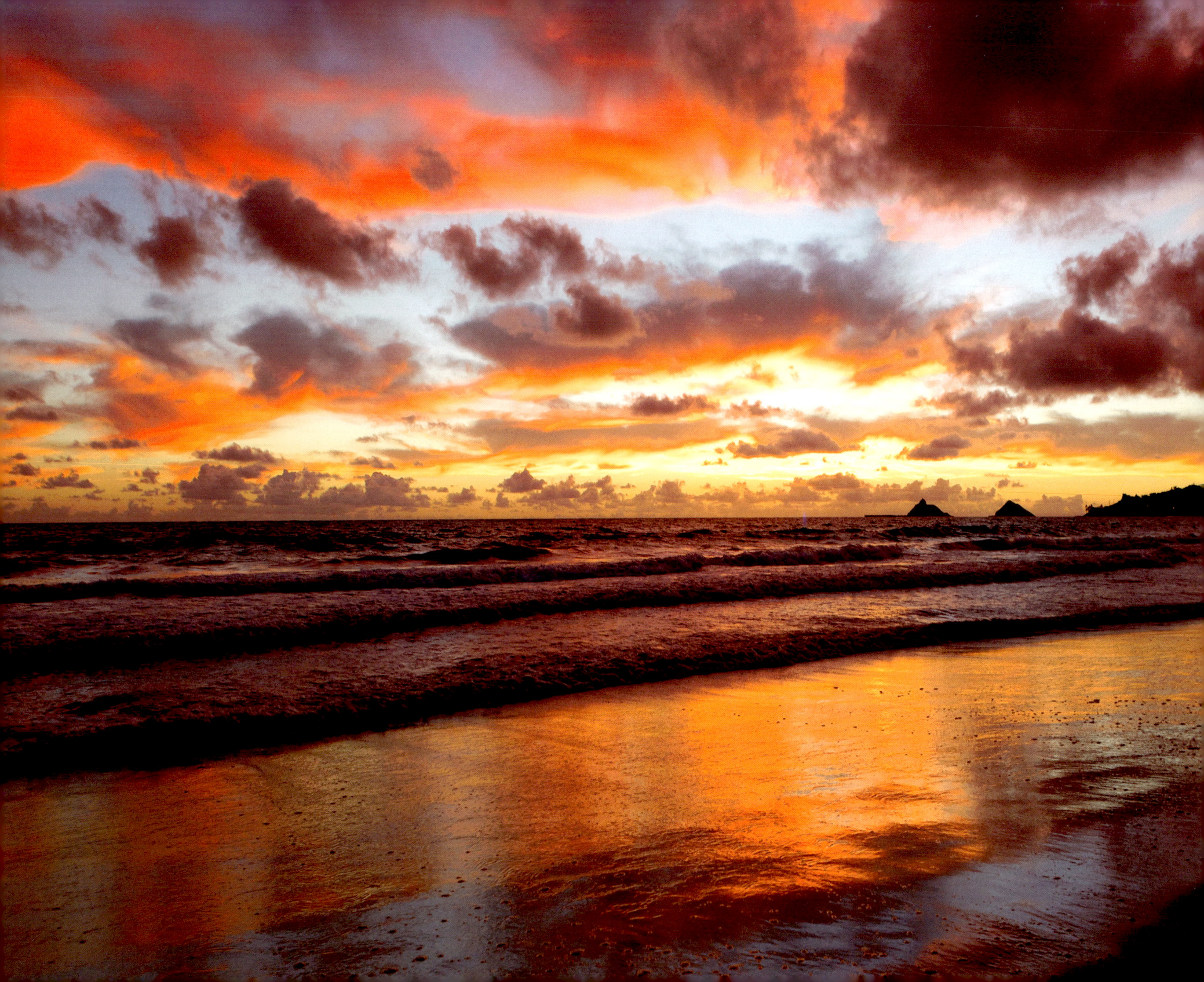

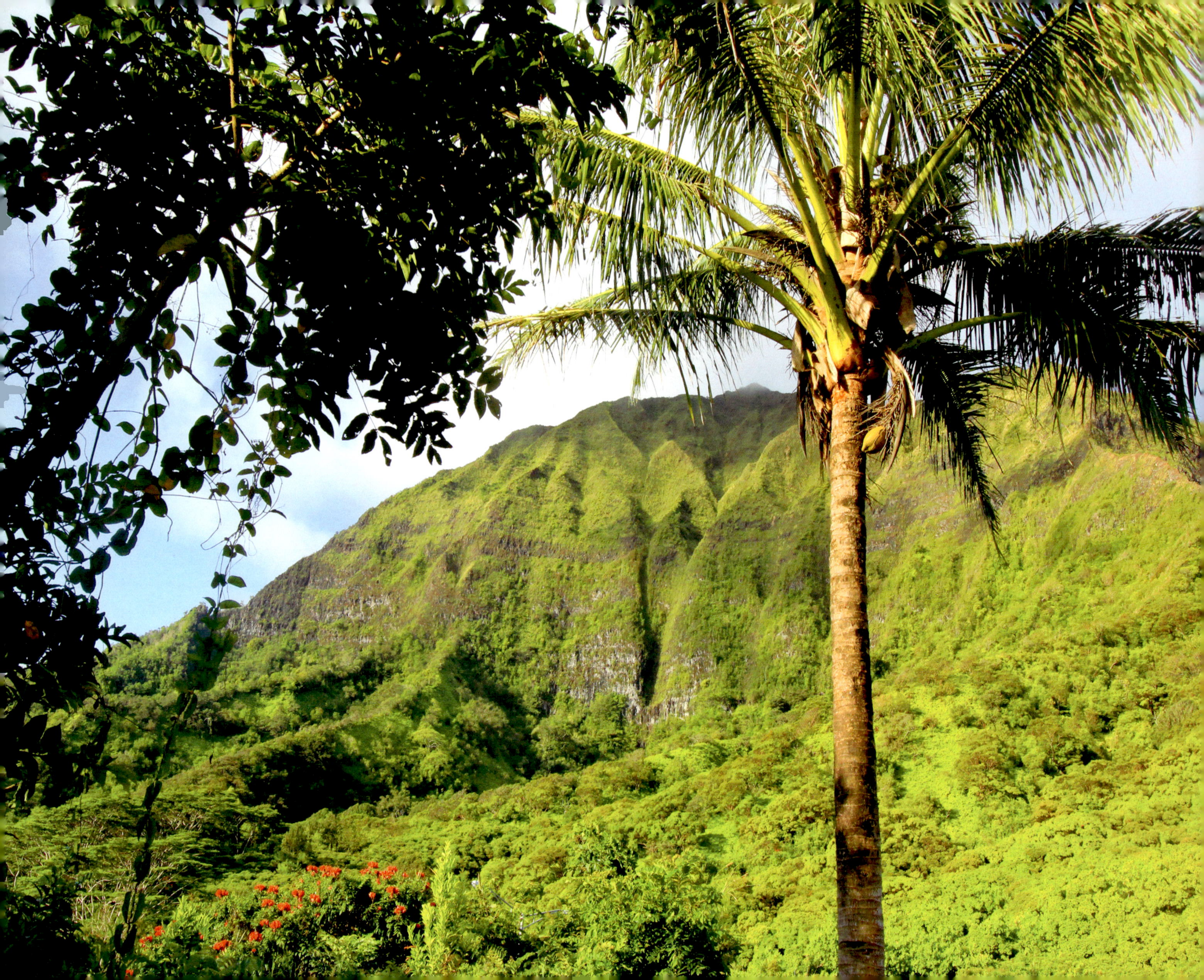

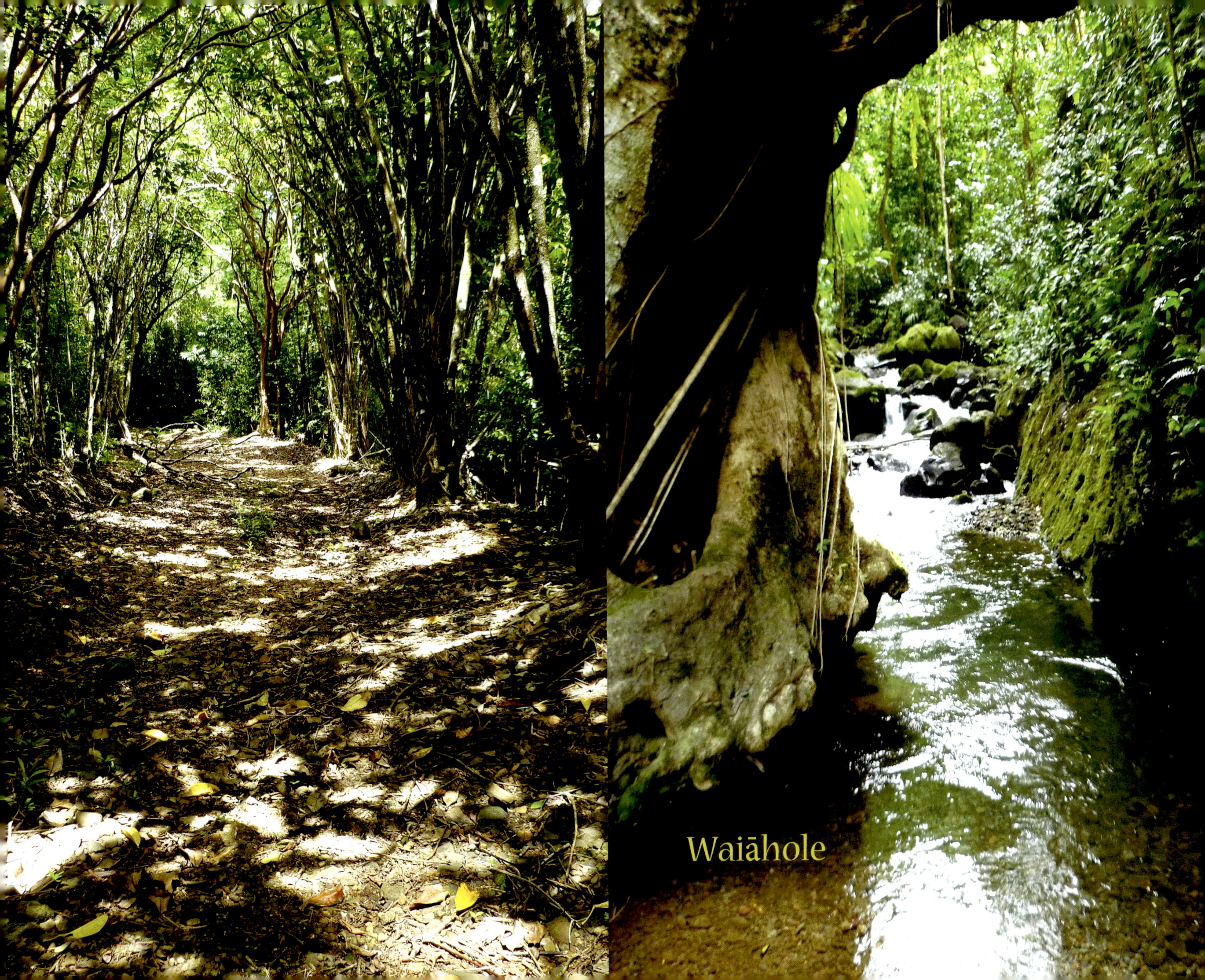
Waiāhole

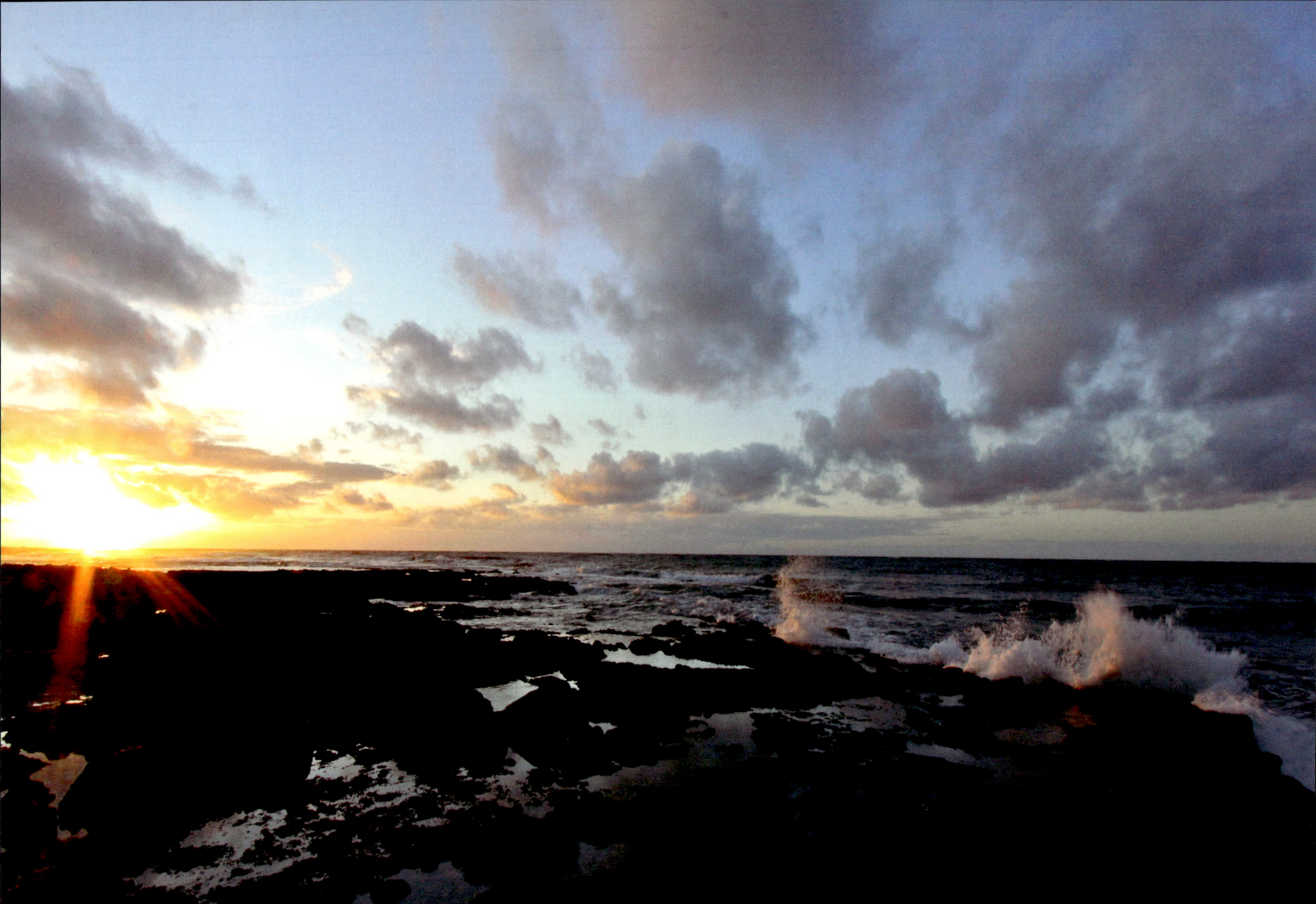

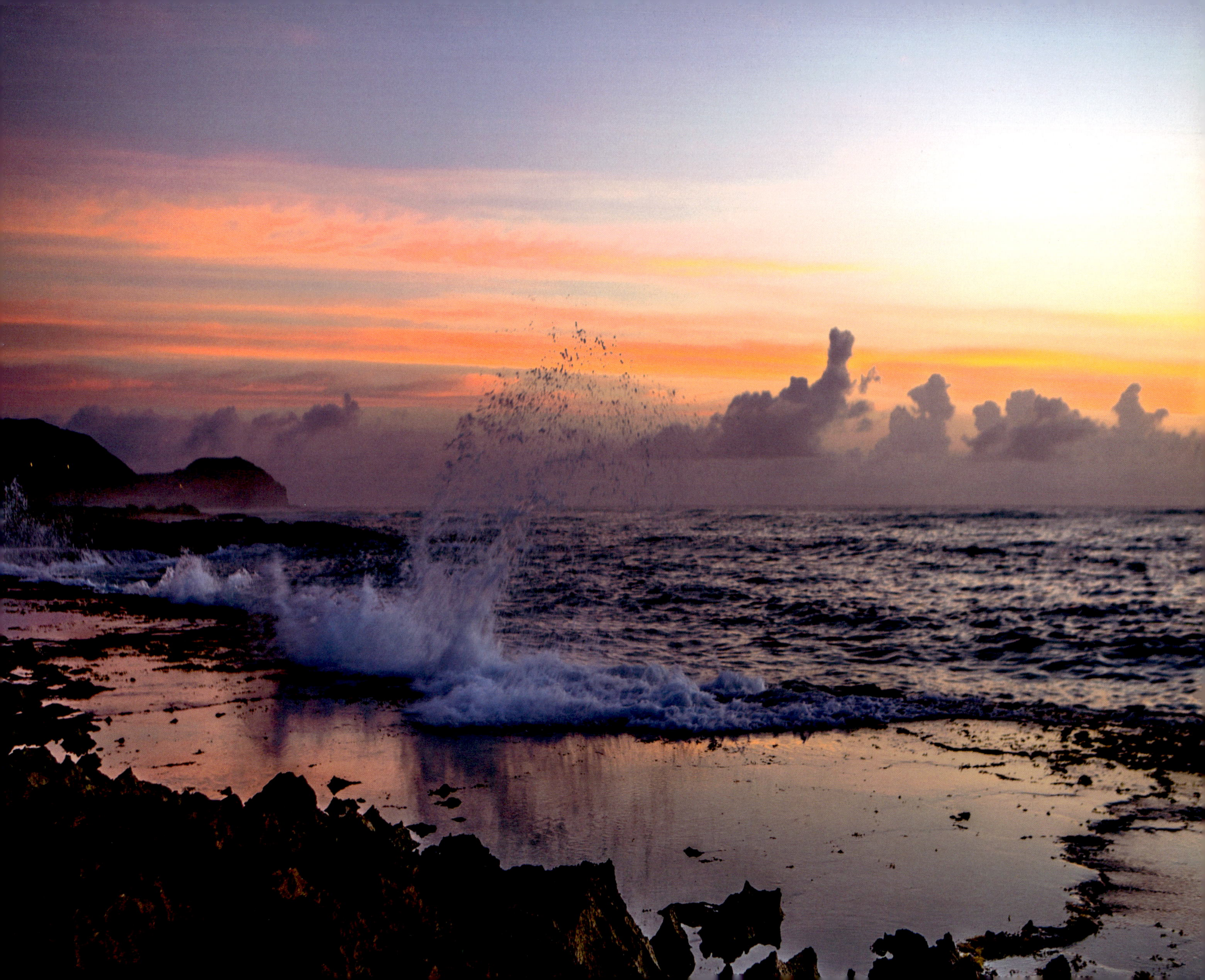

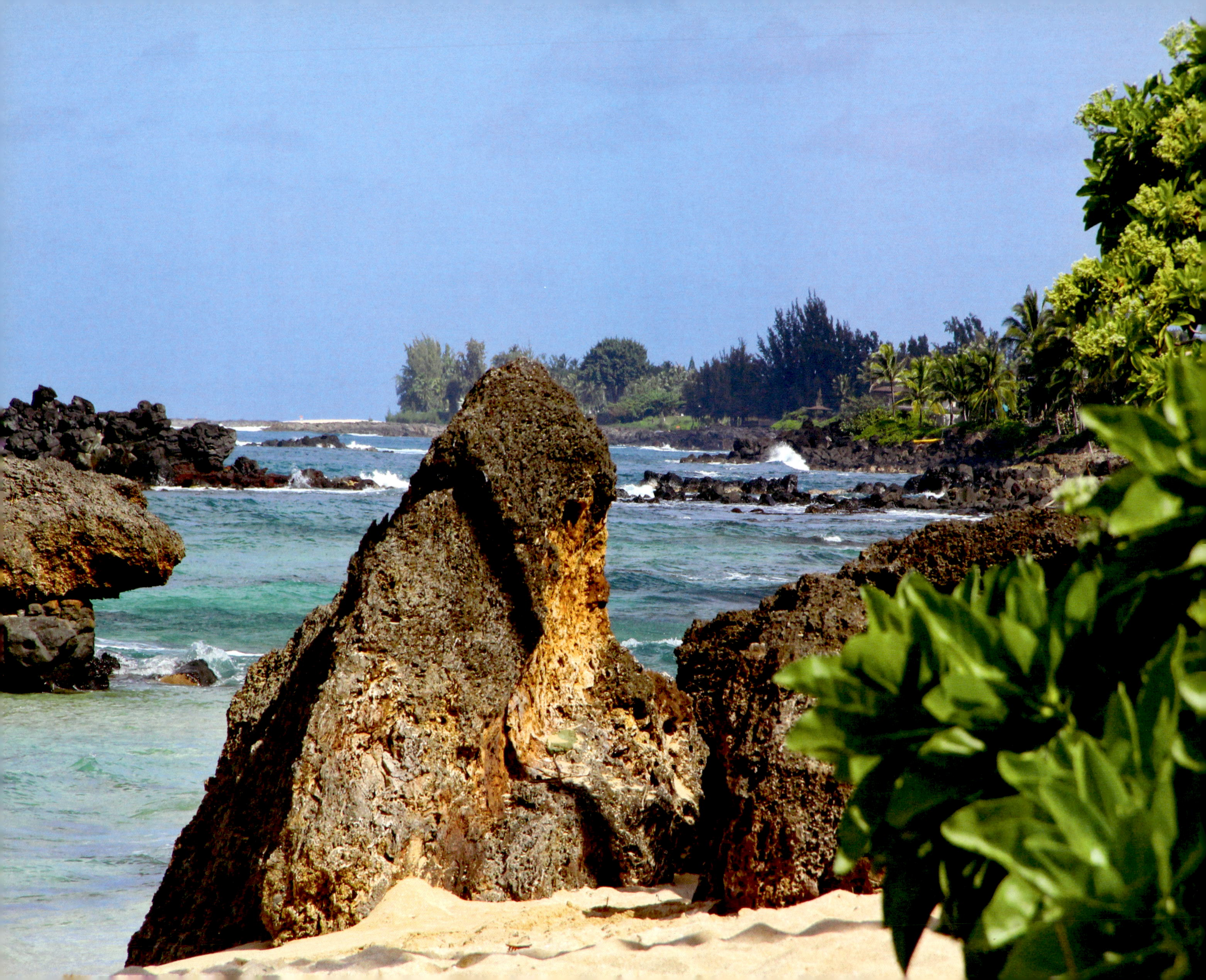

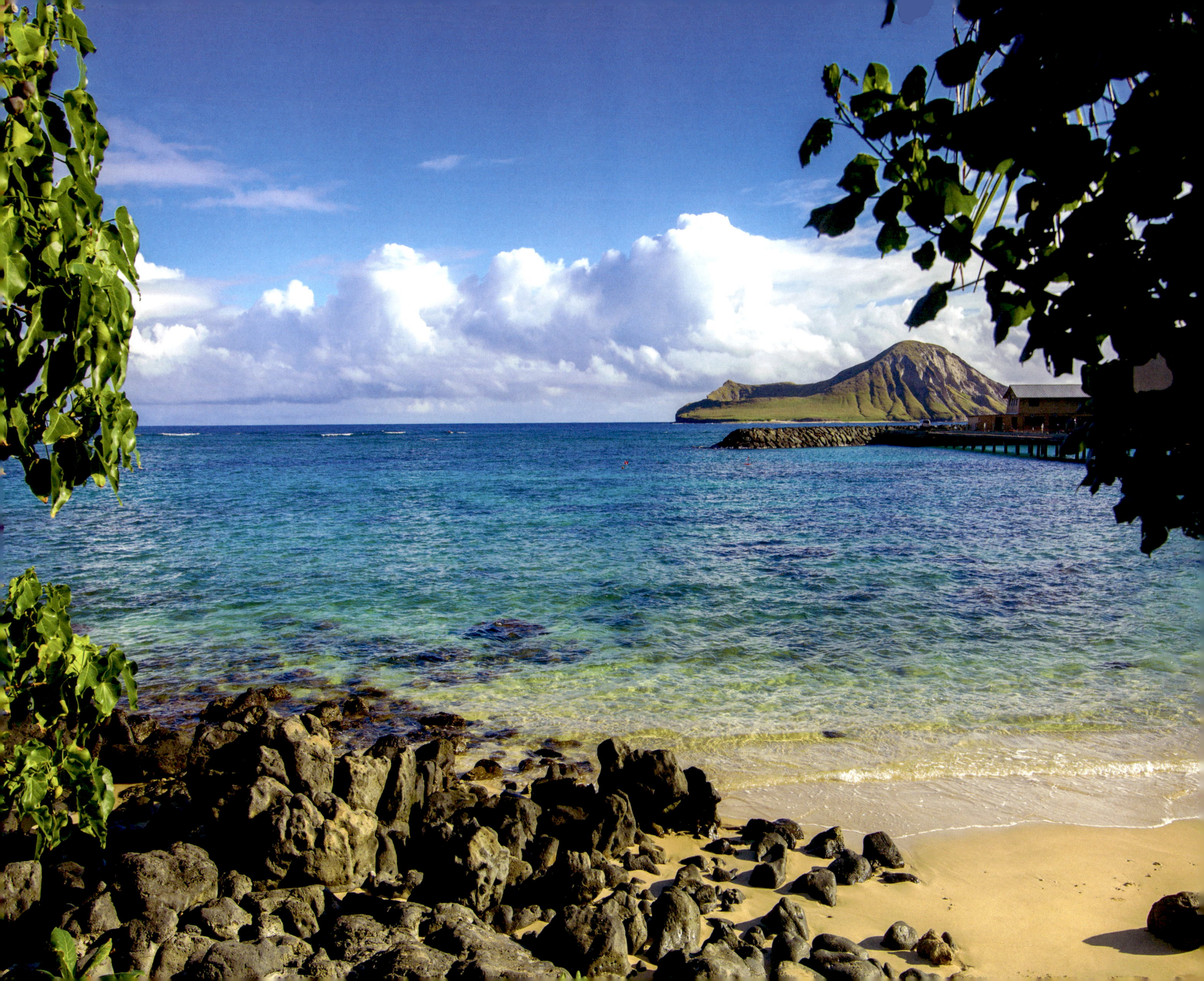

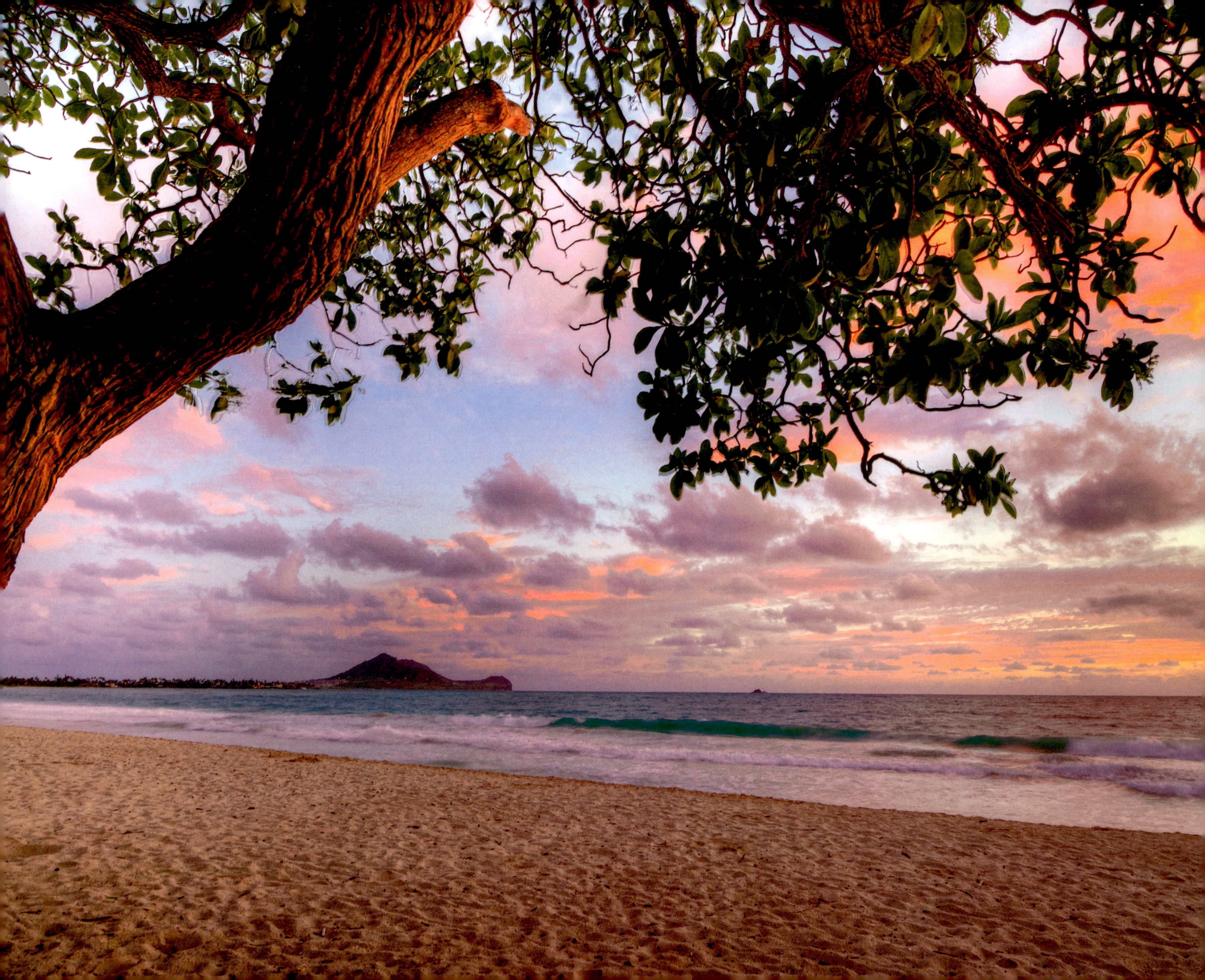

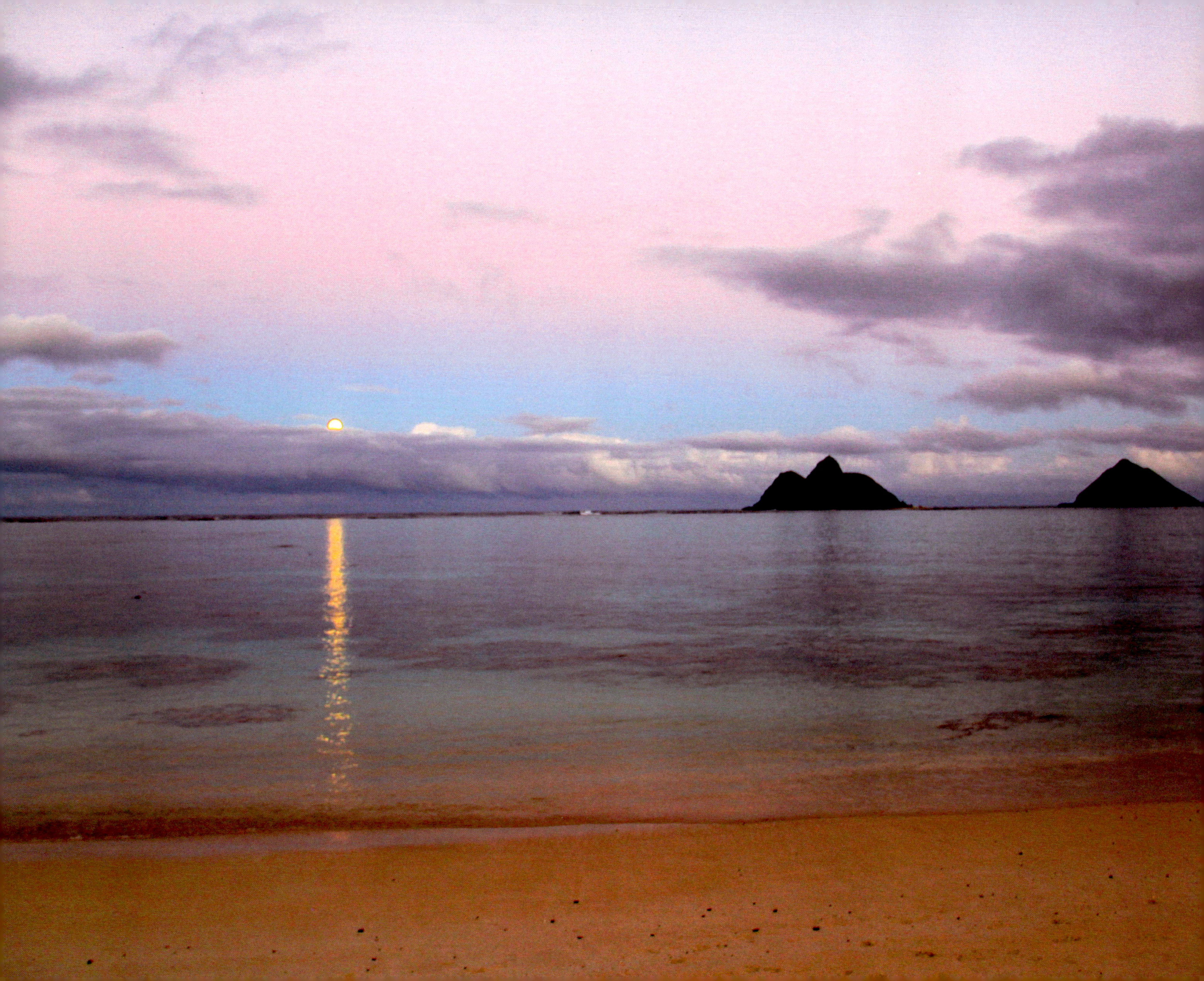

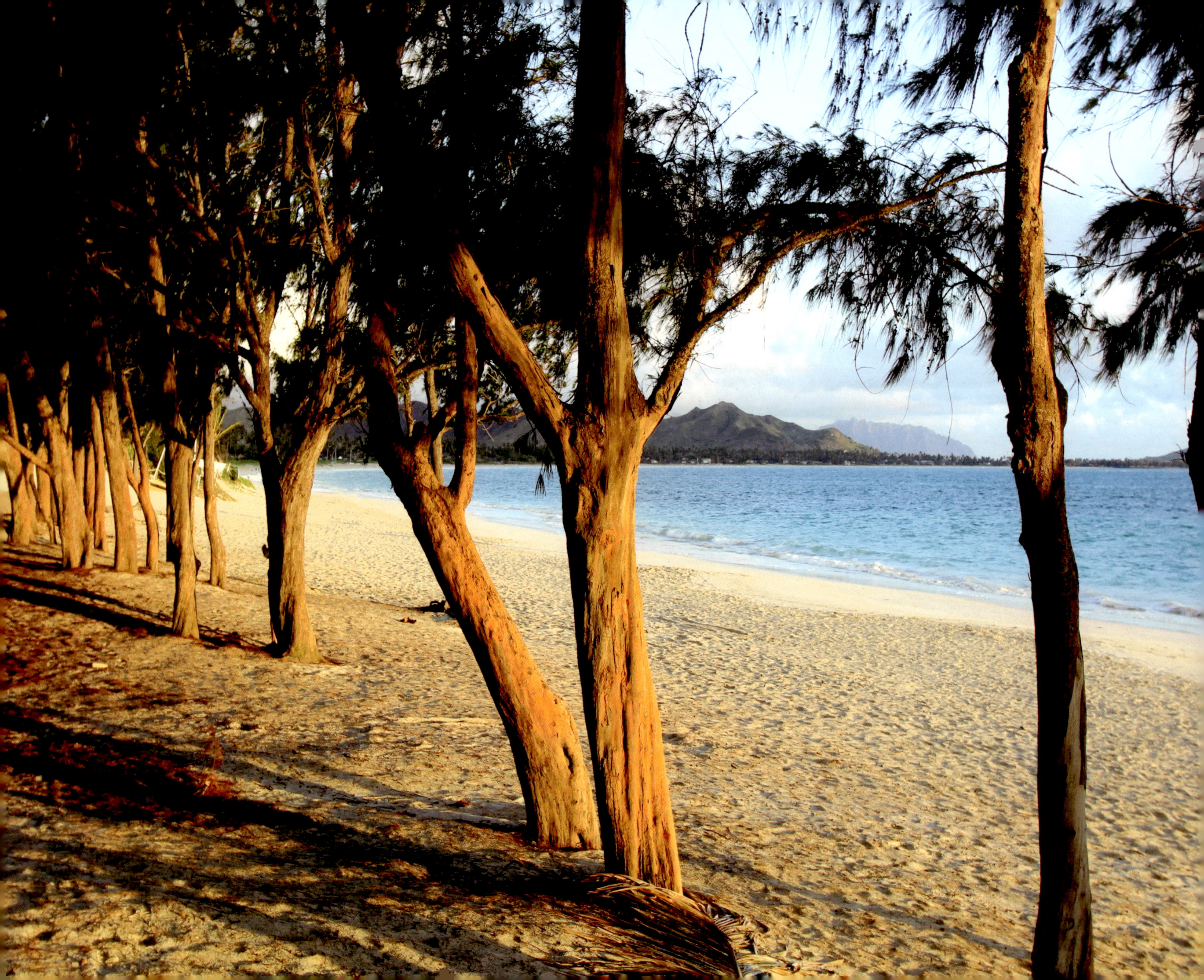

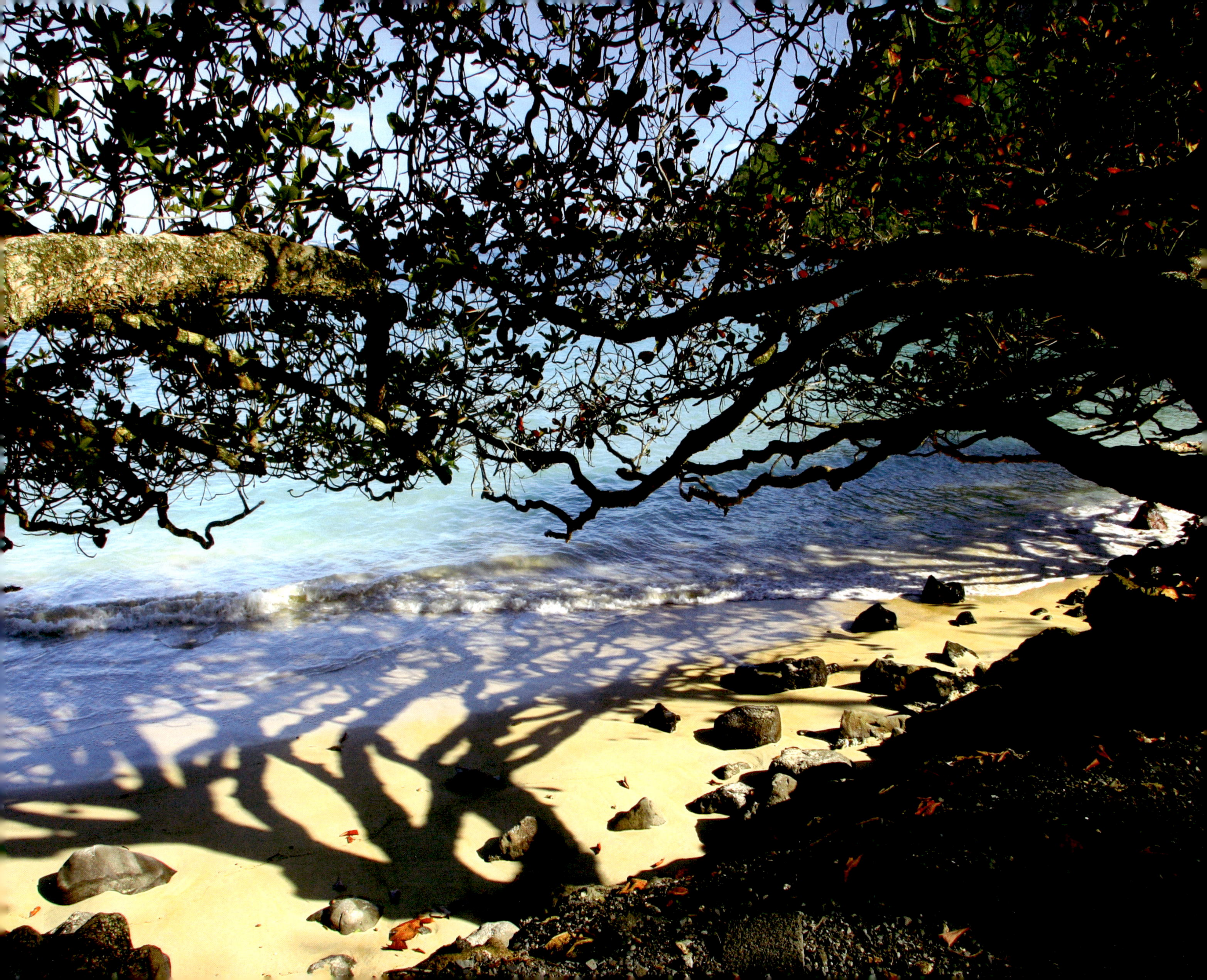

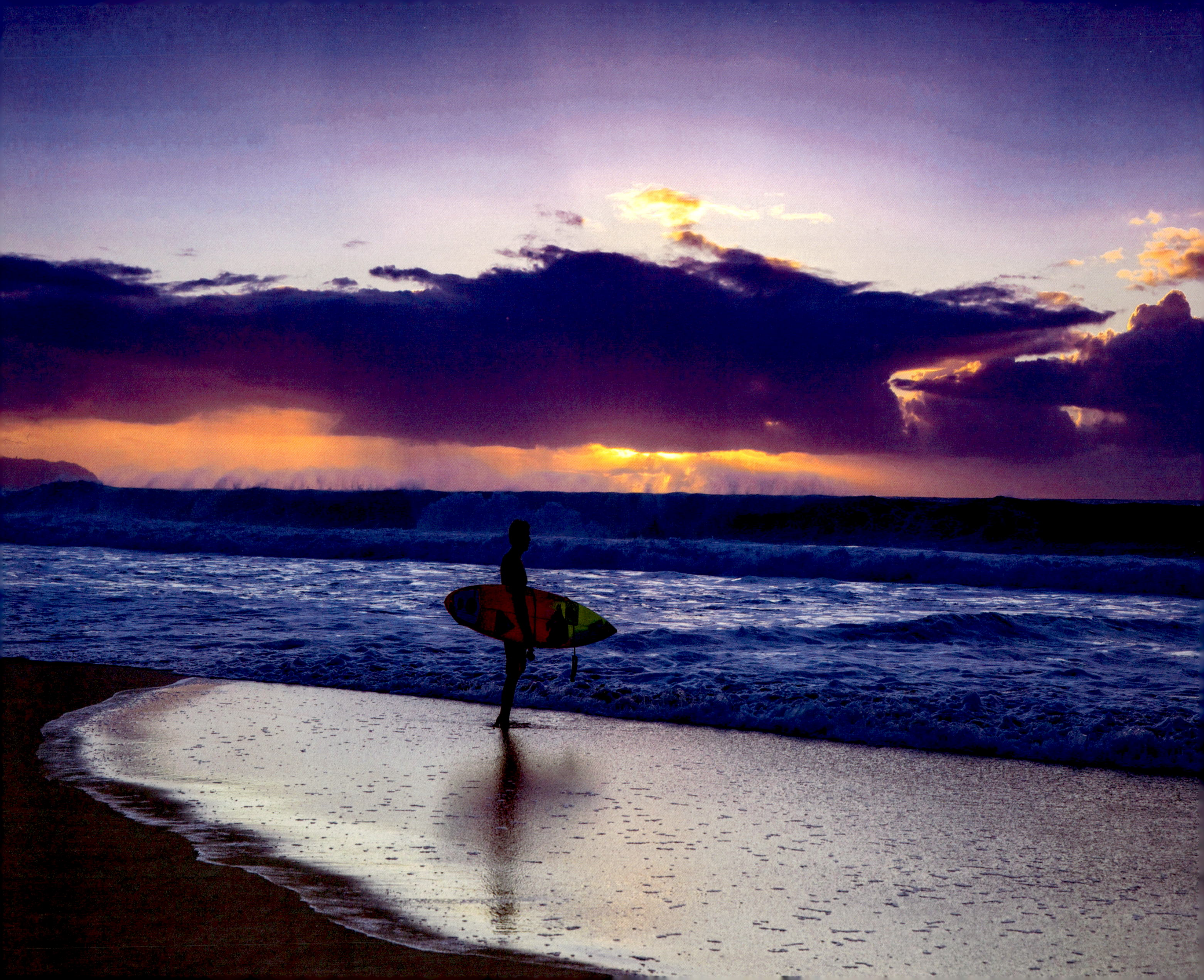

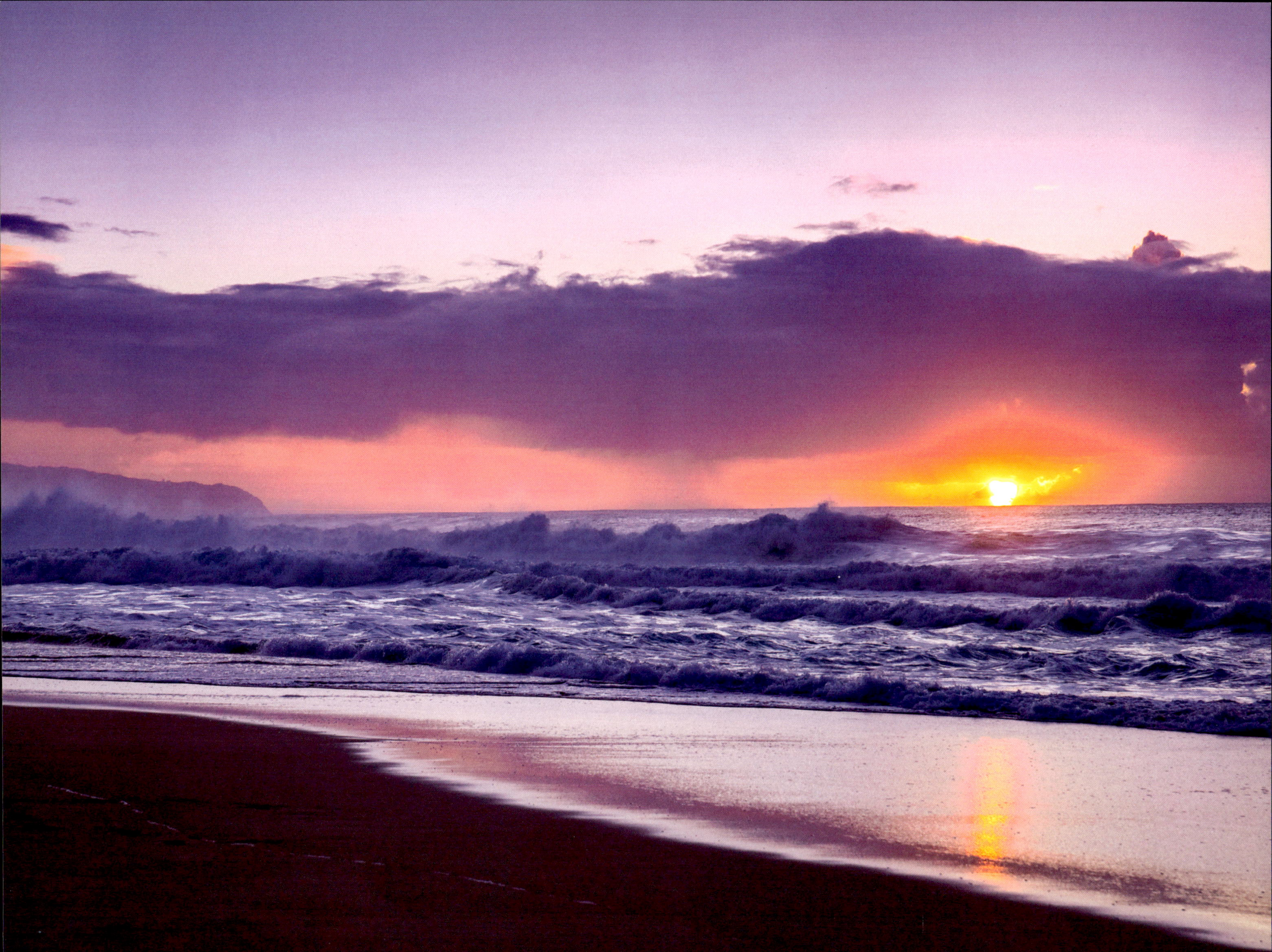

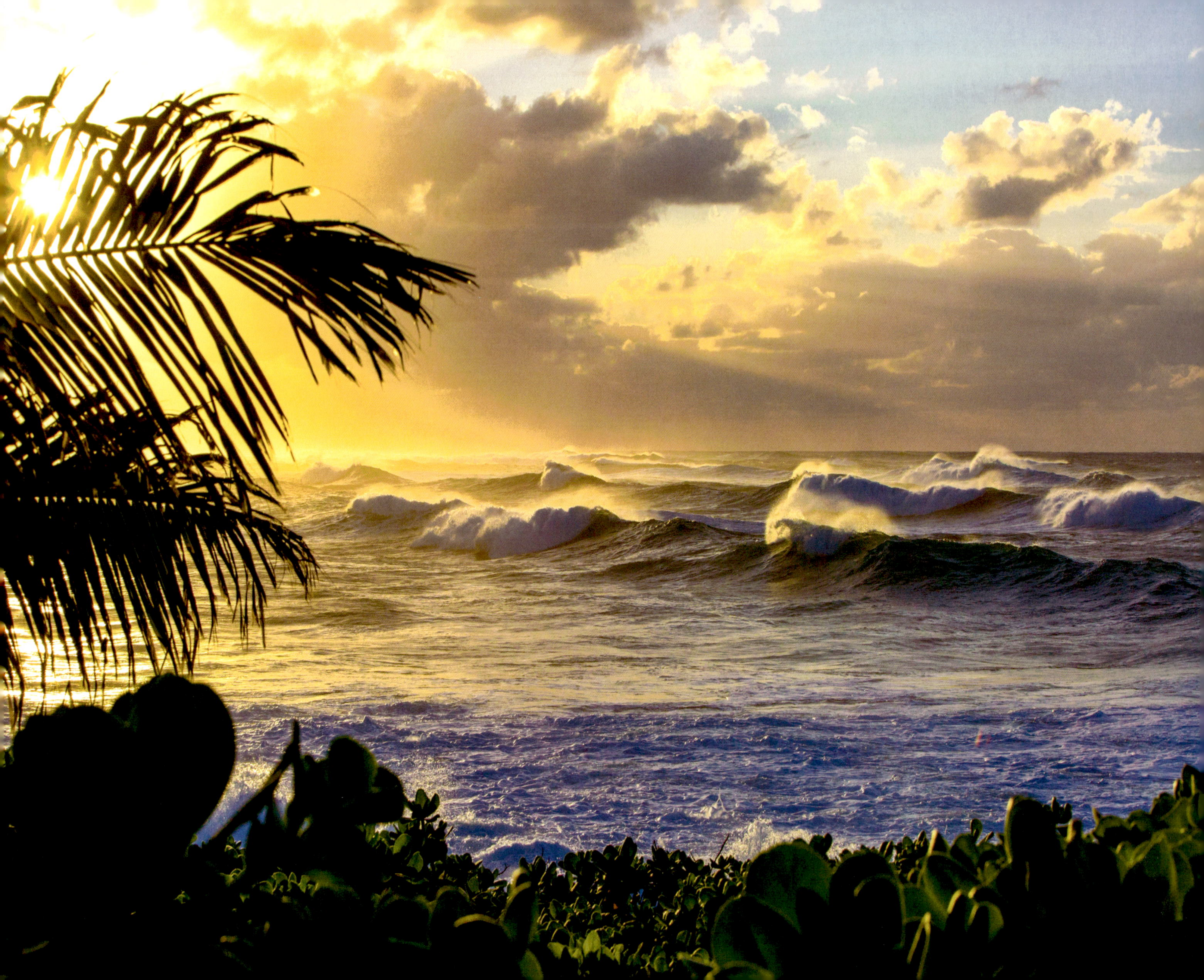

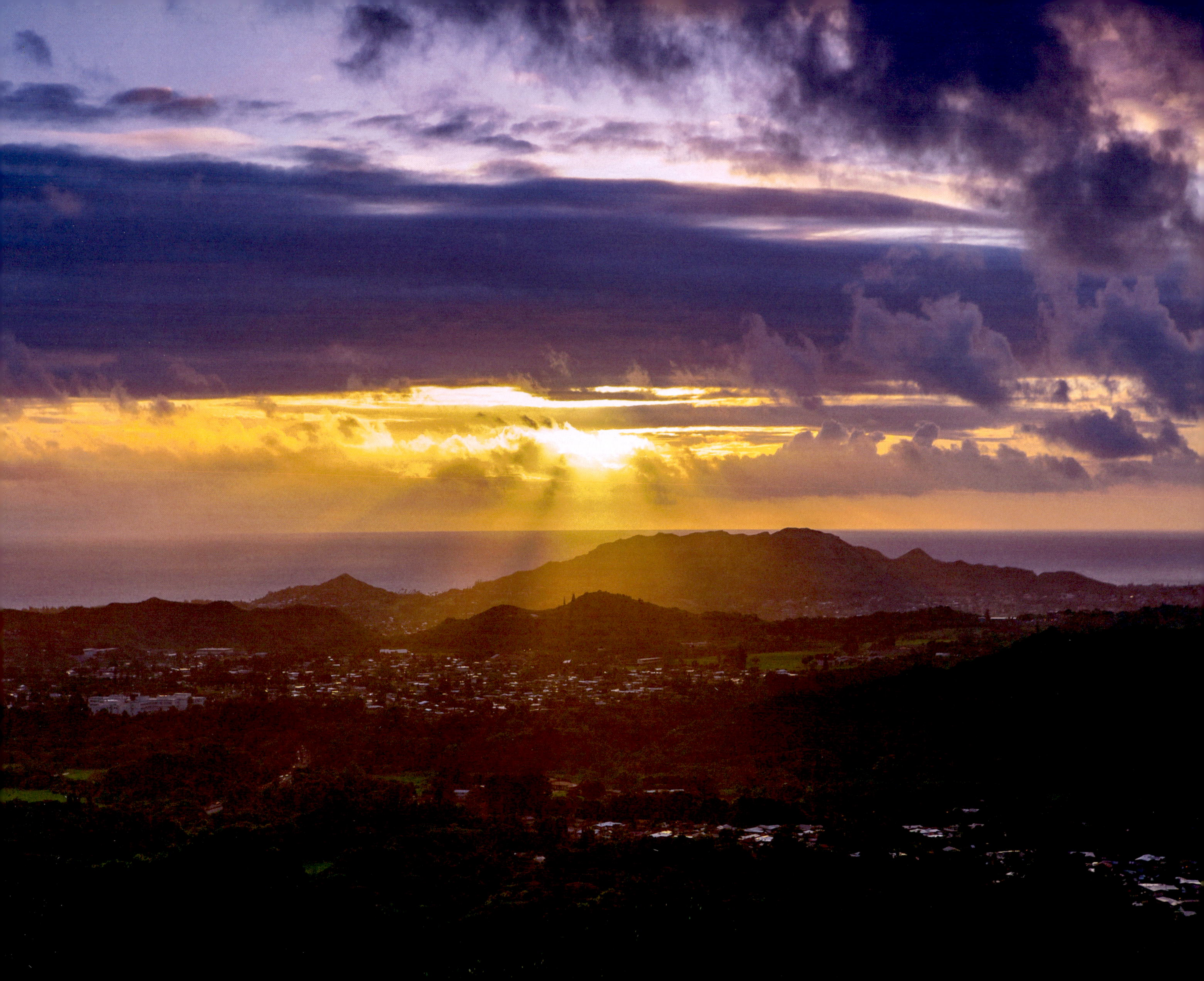

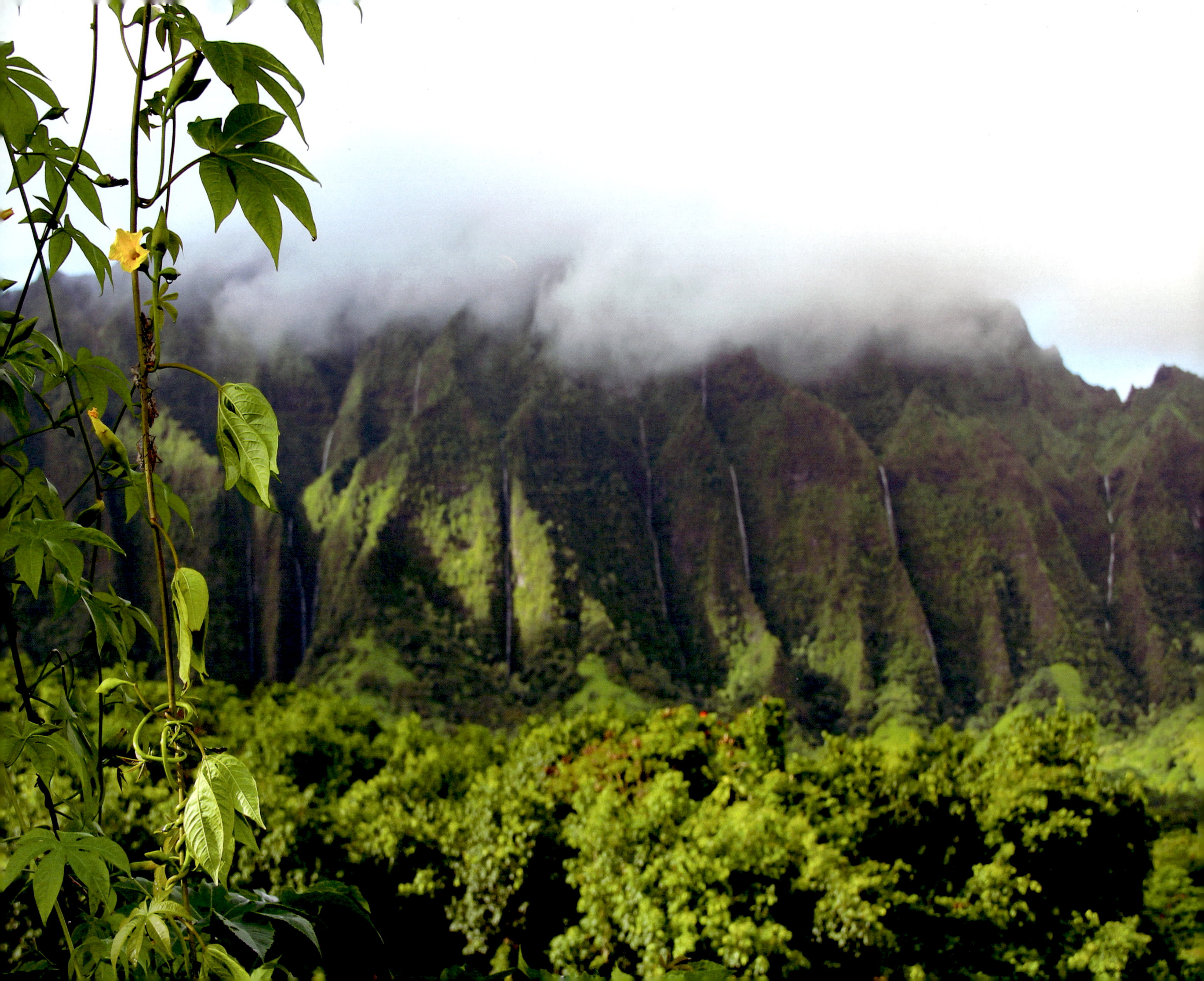

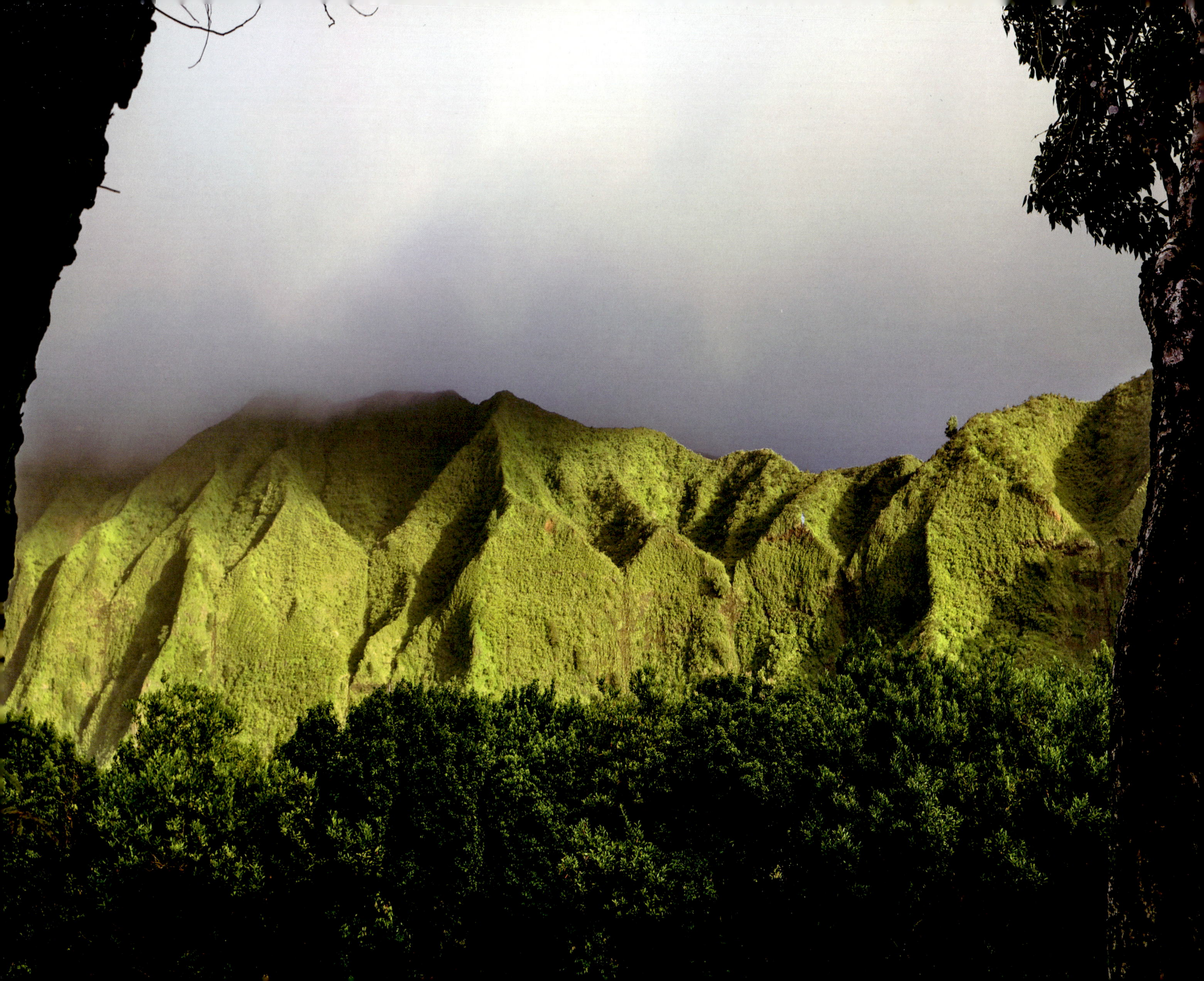

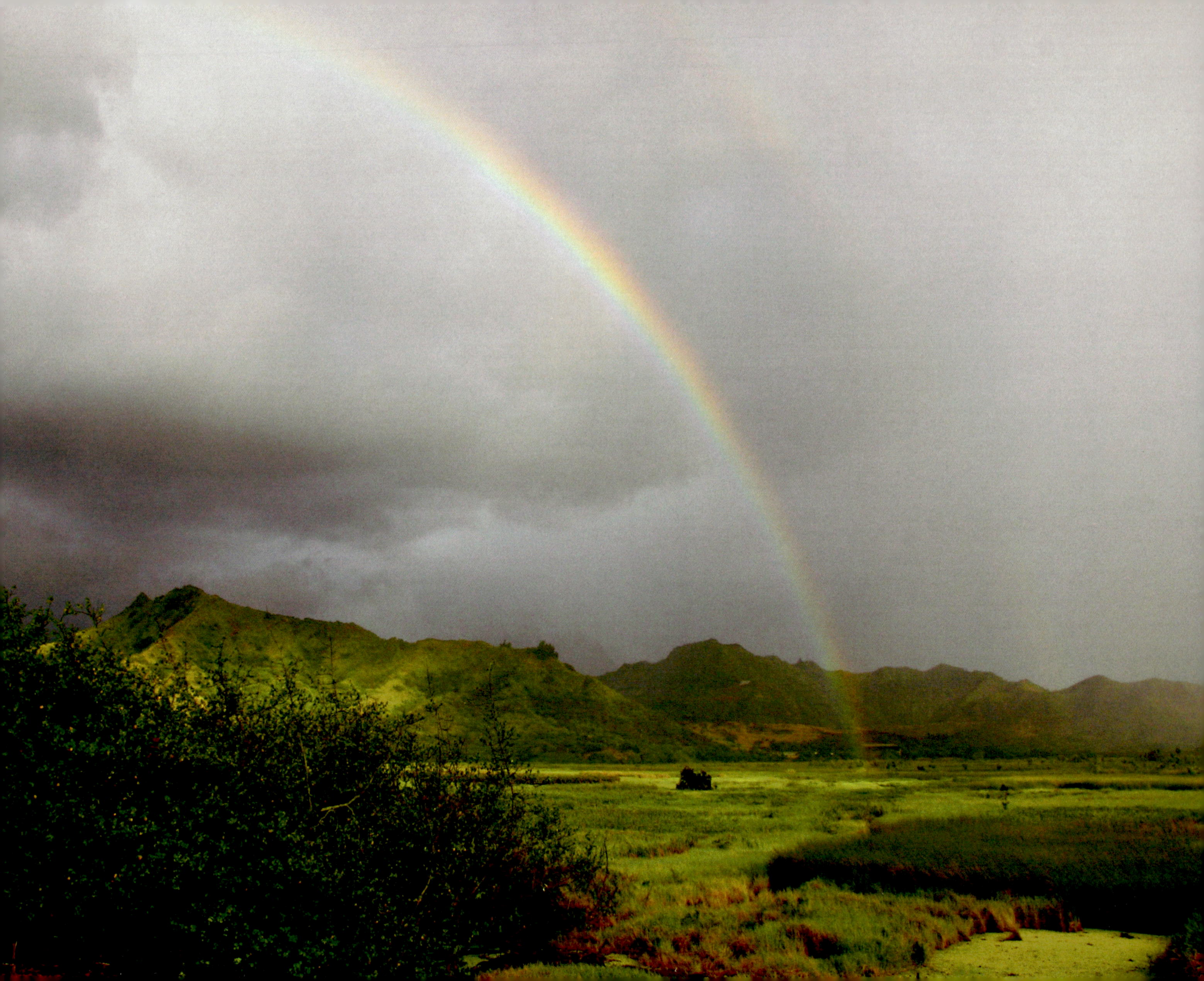

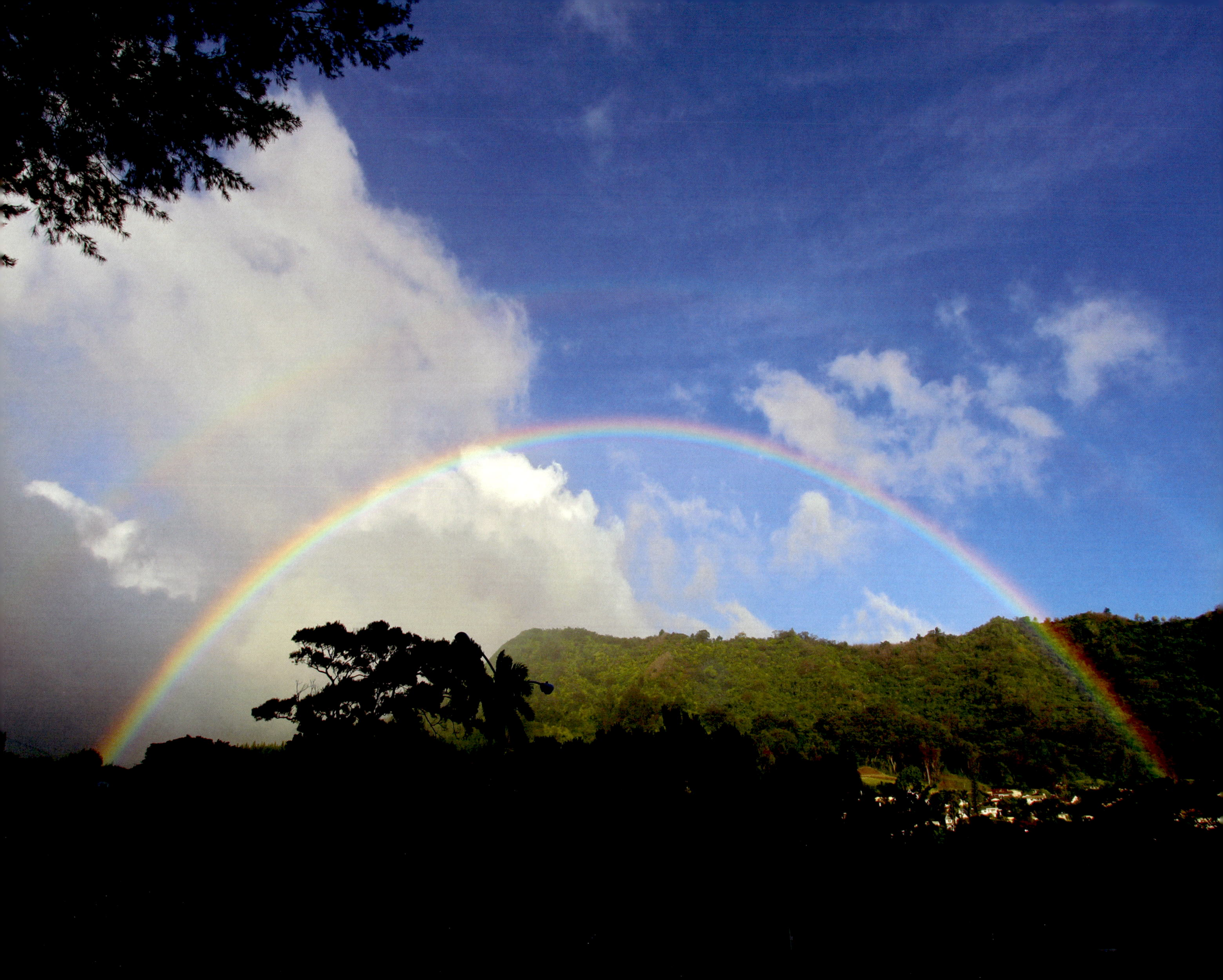

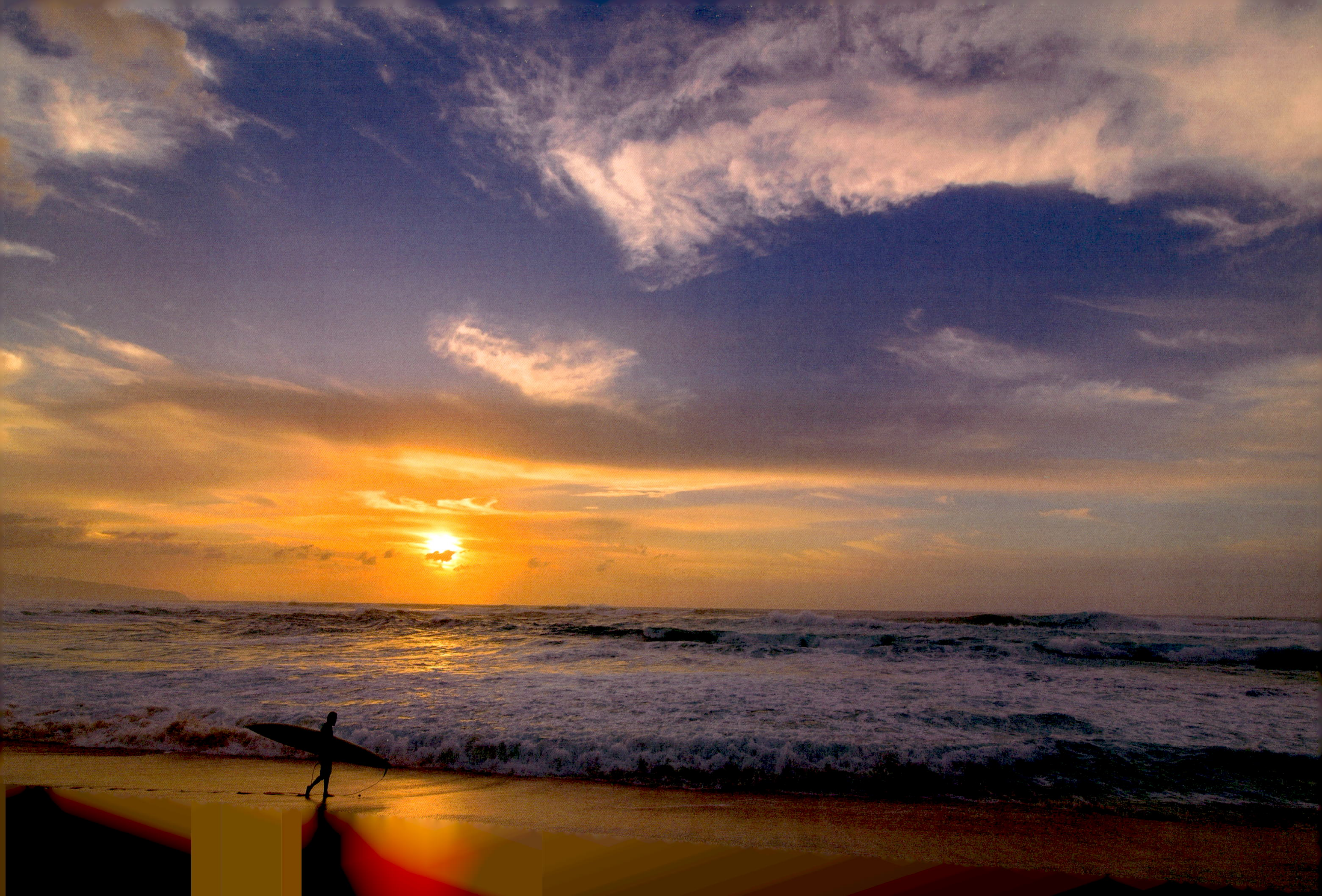

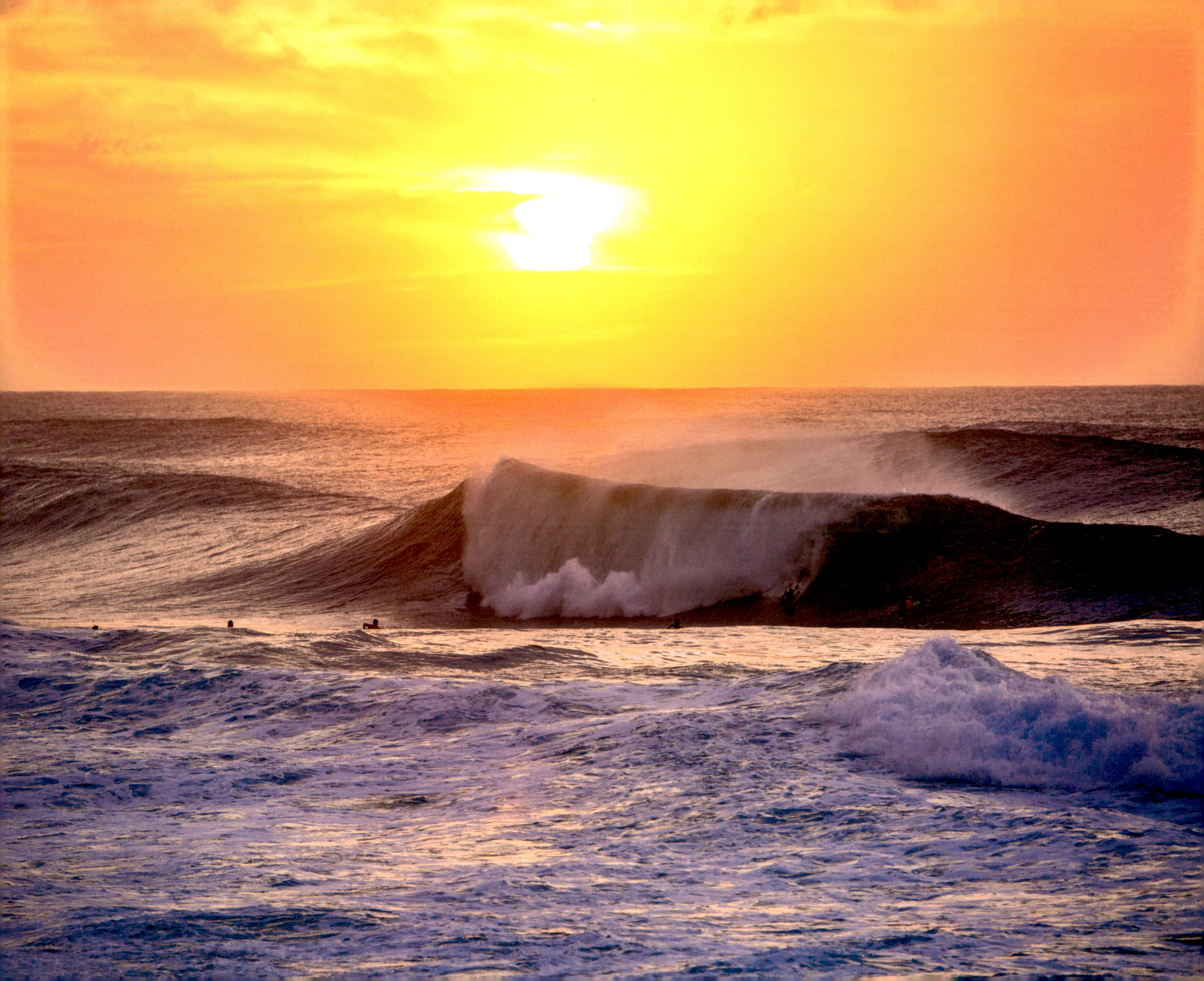

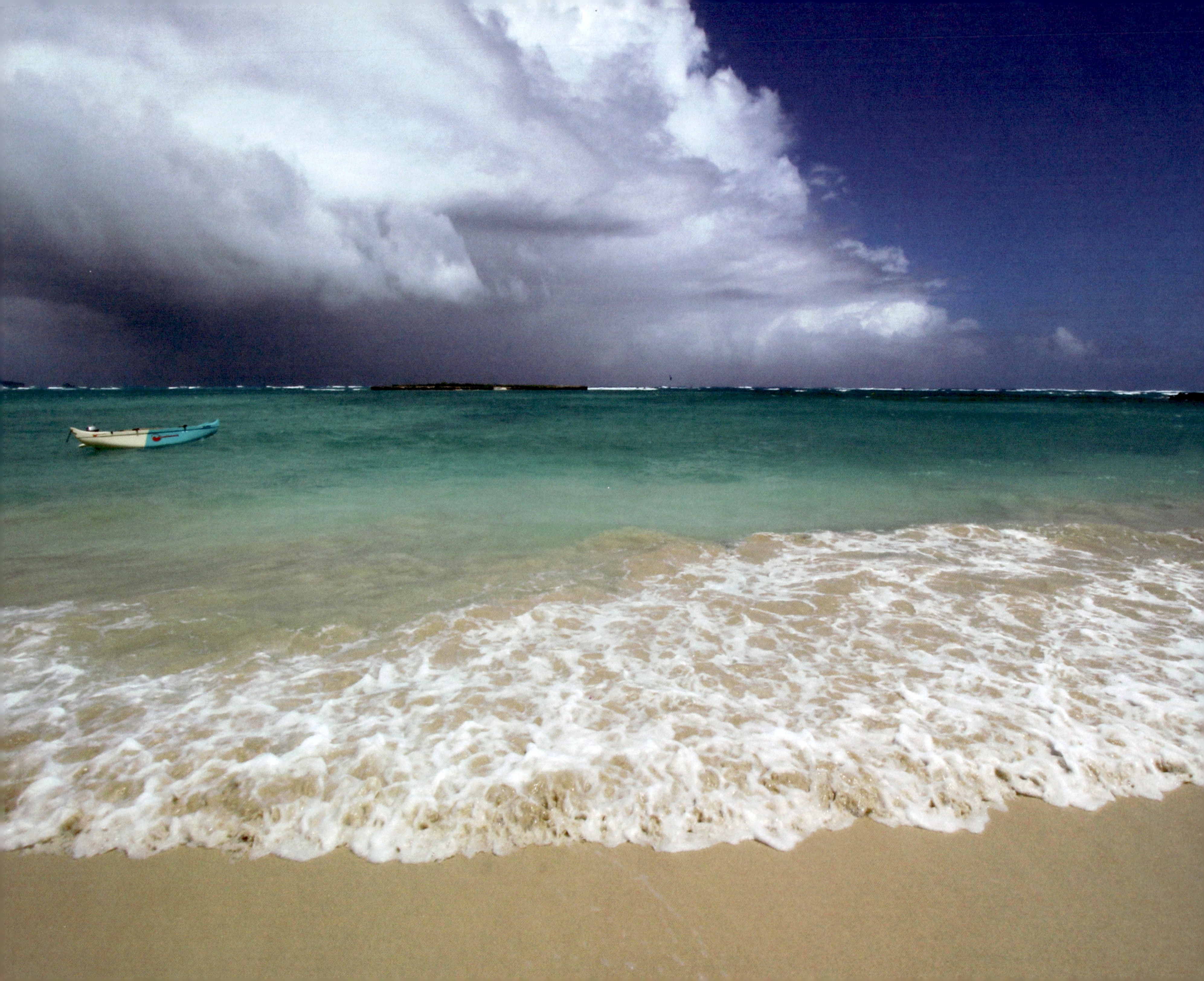

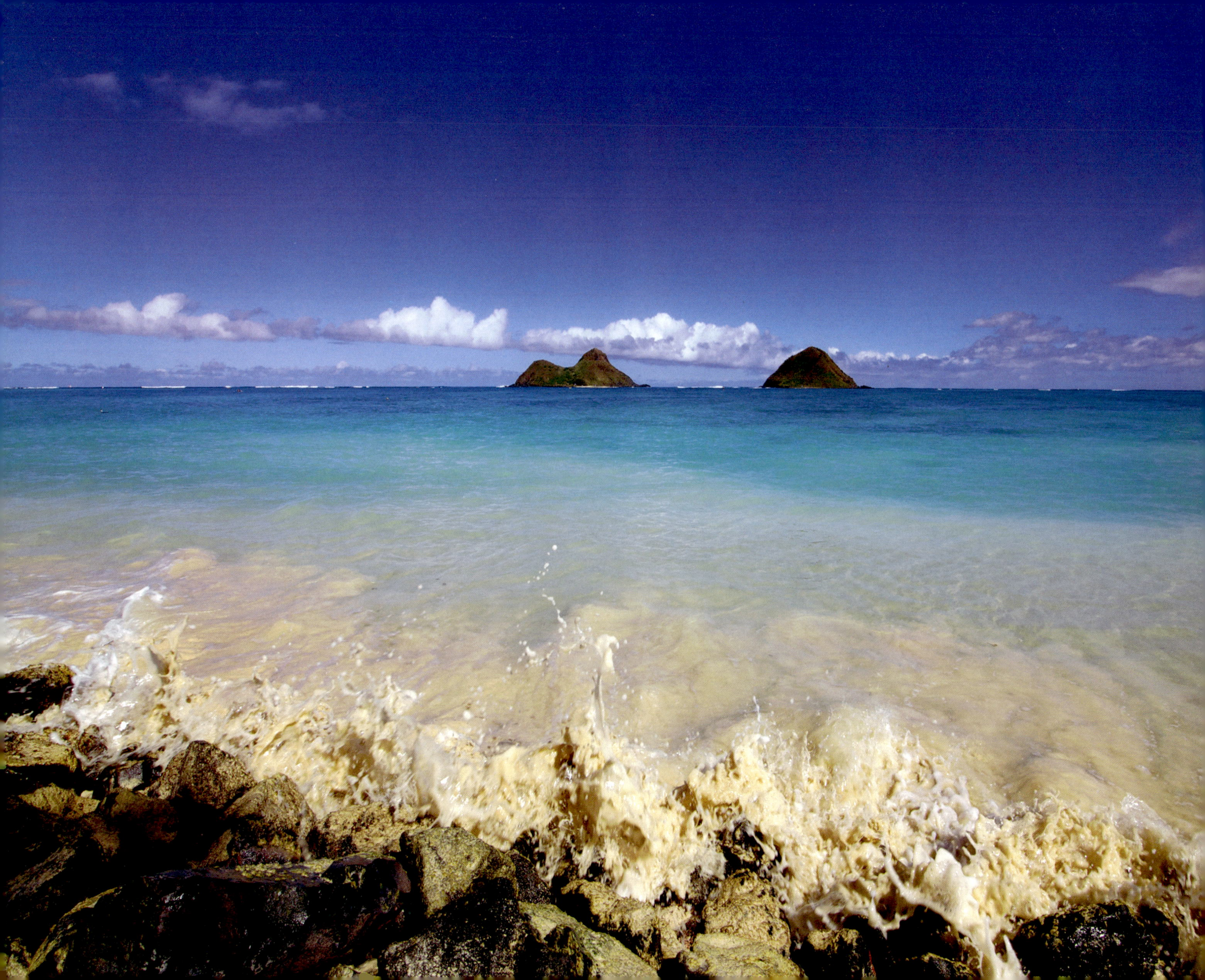

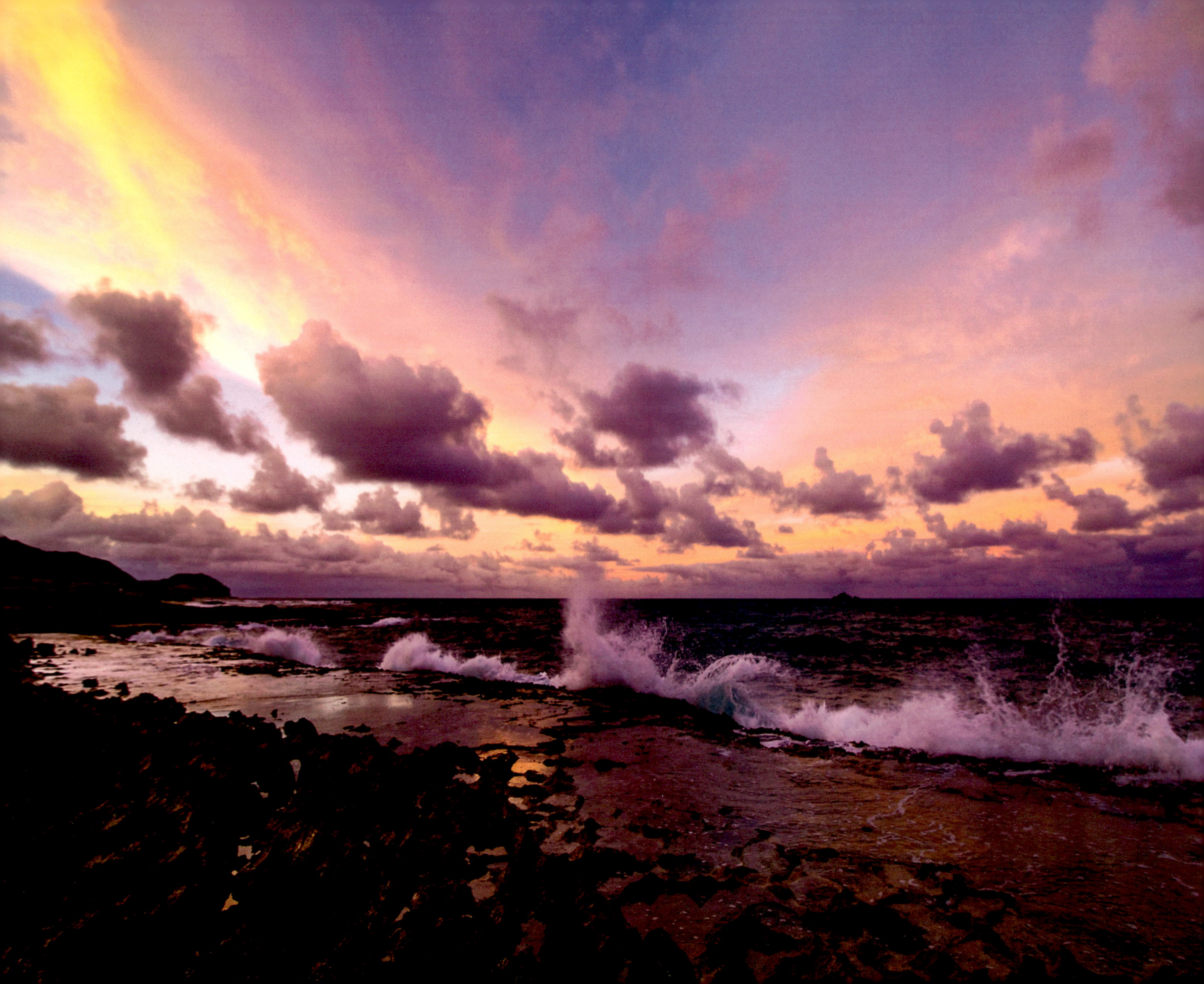

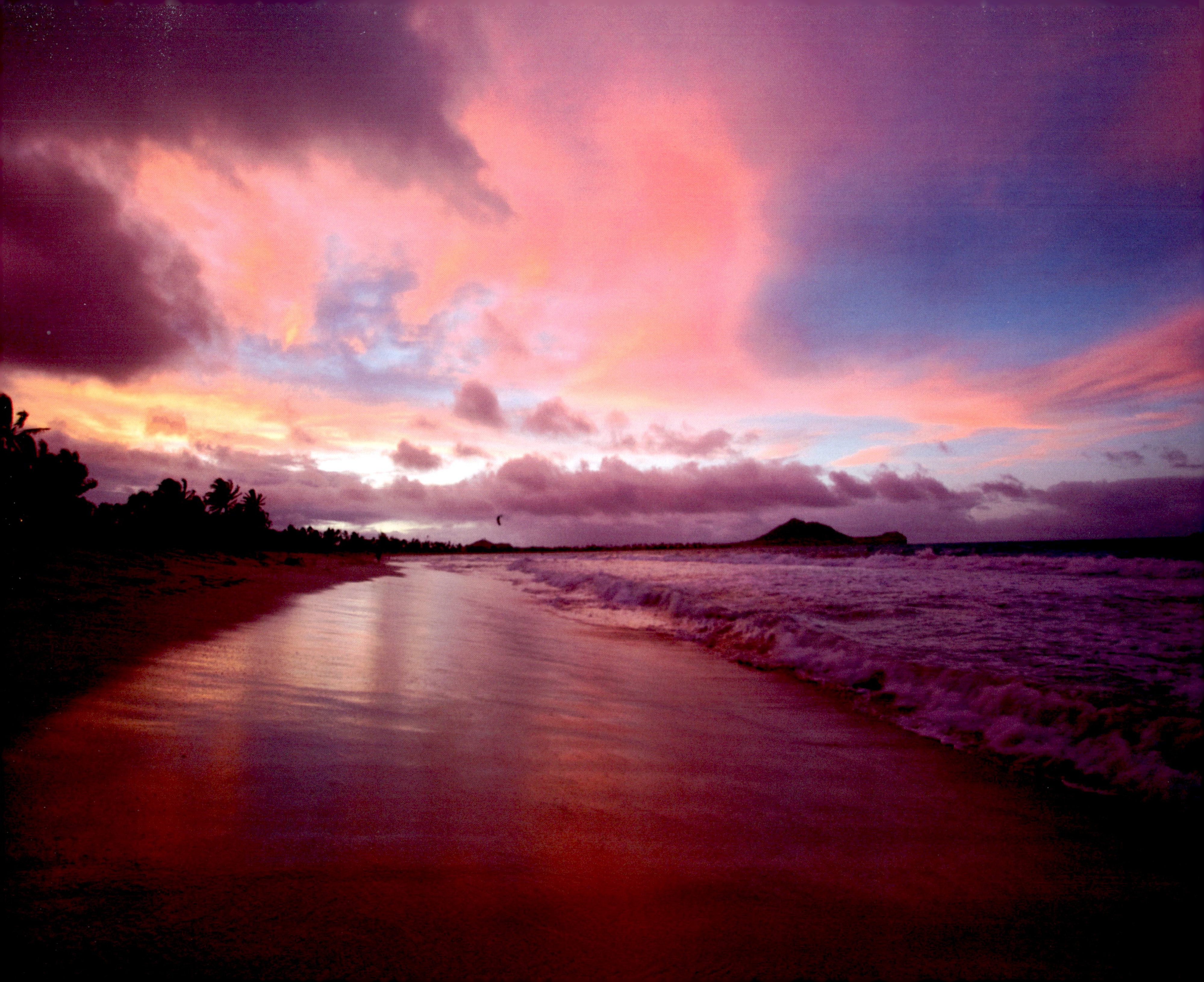

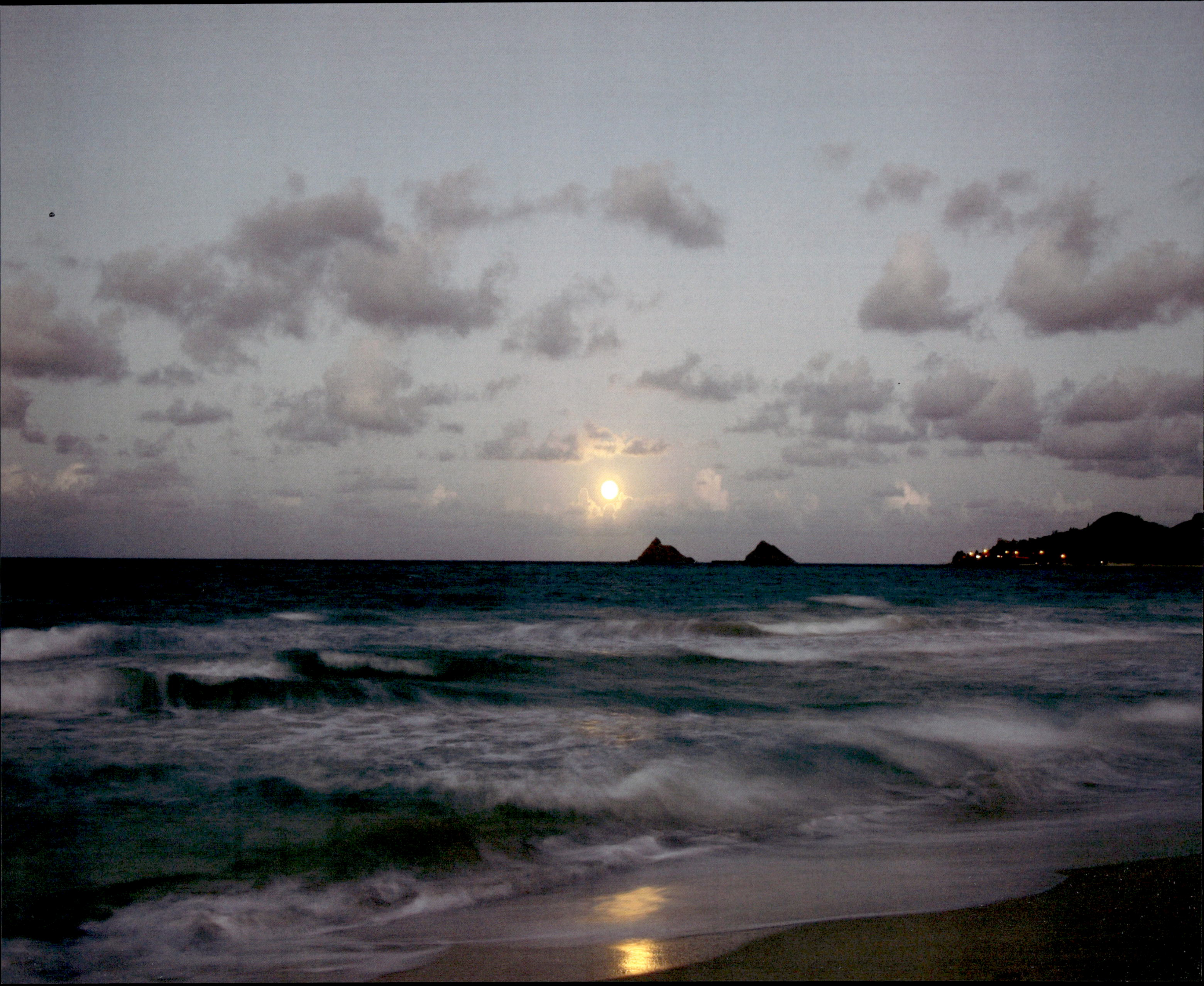

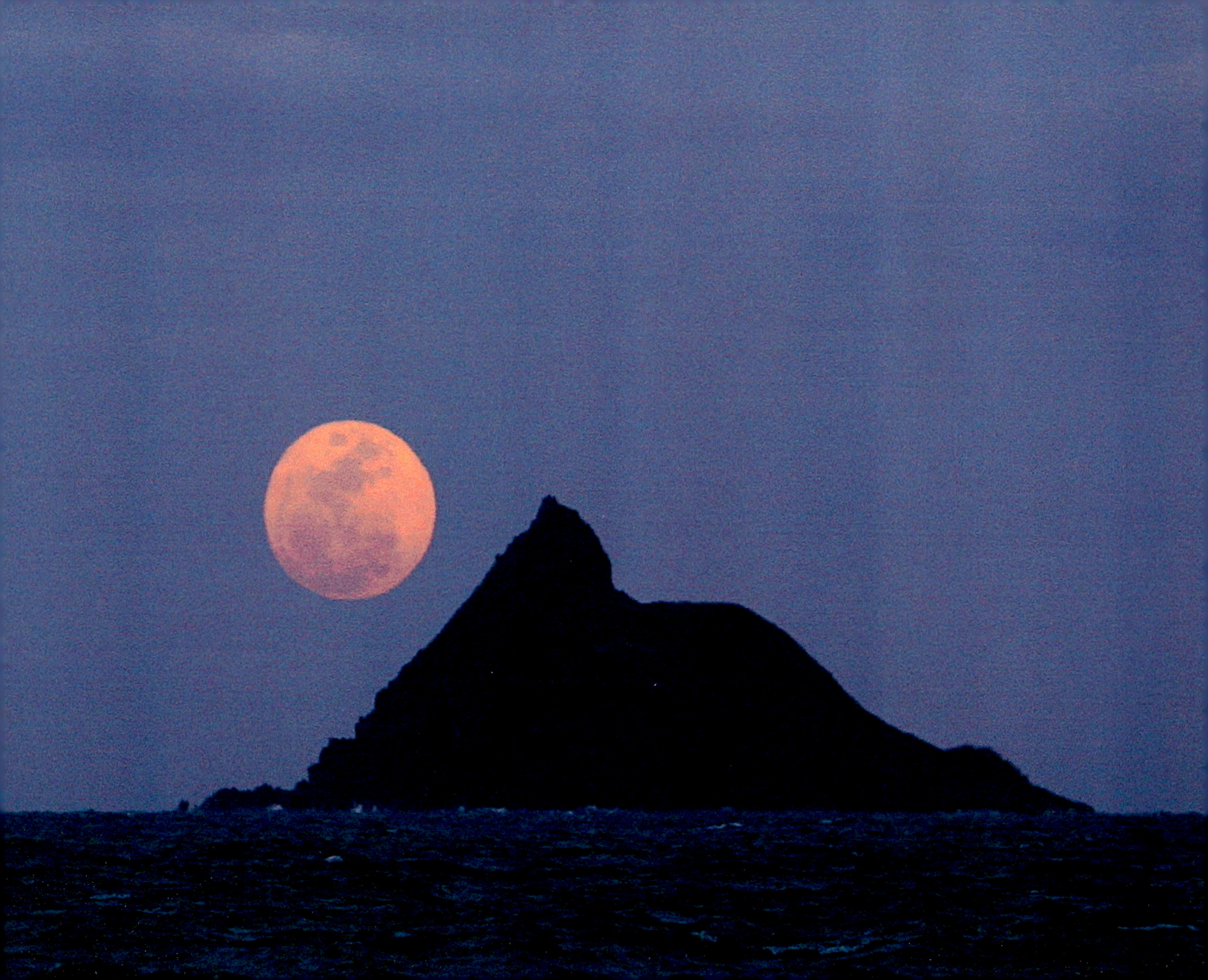

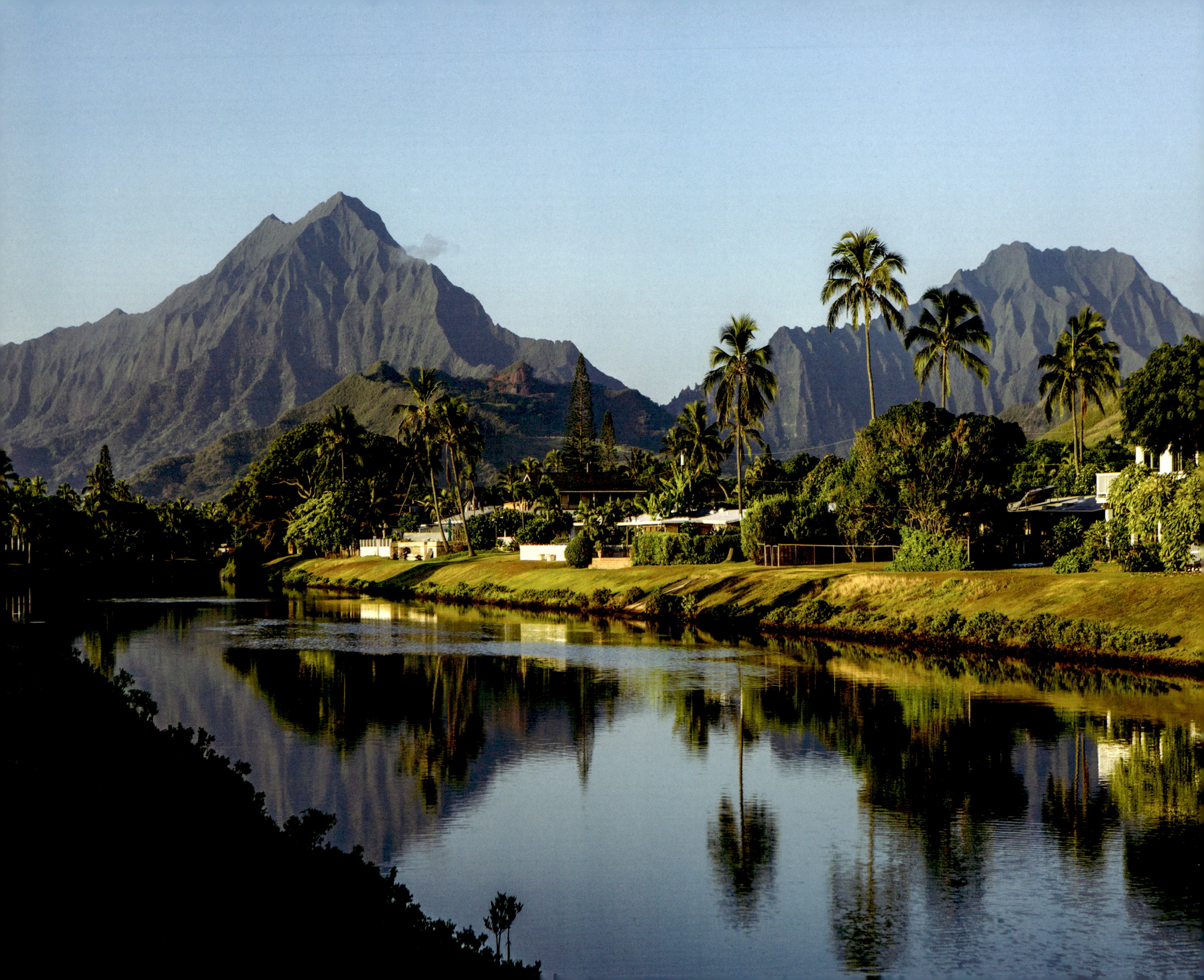

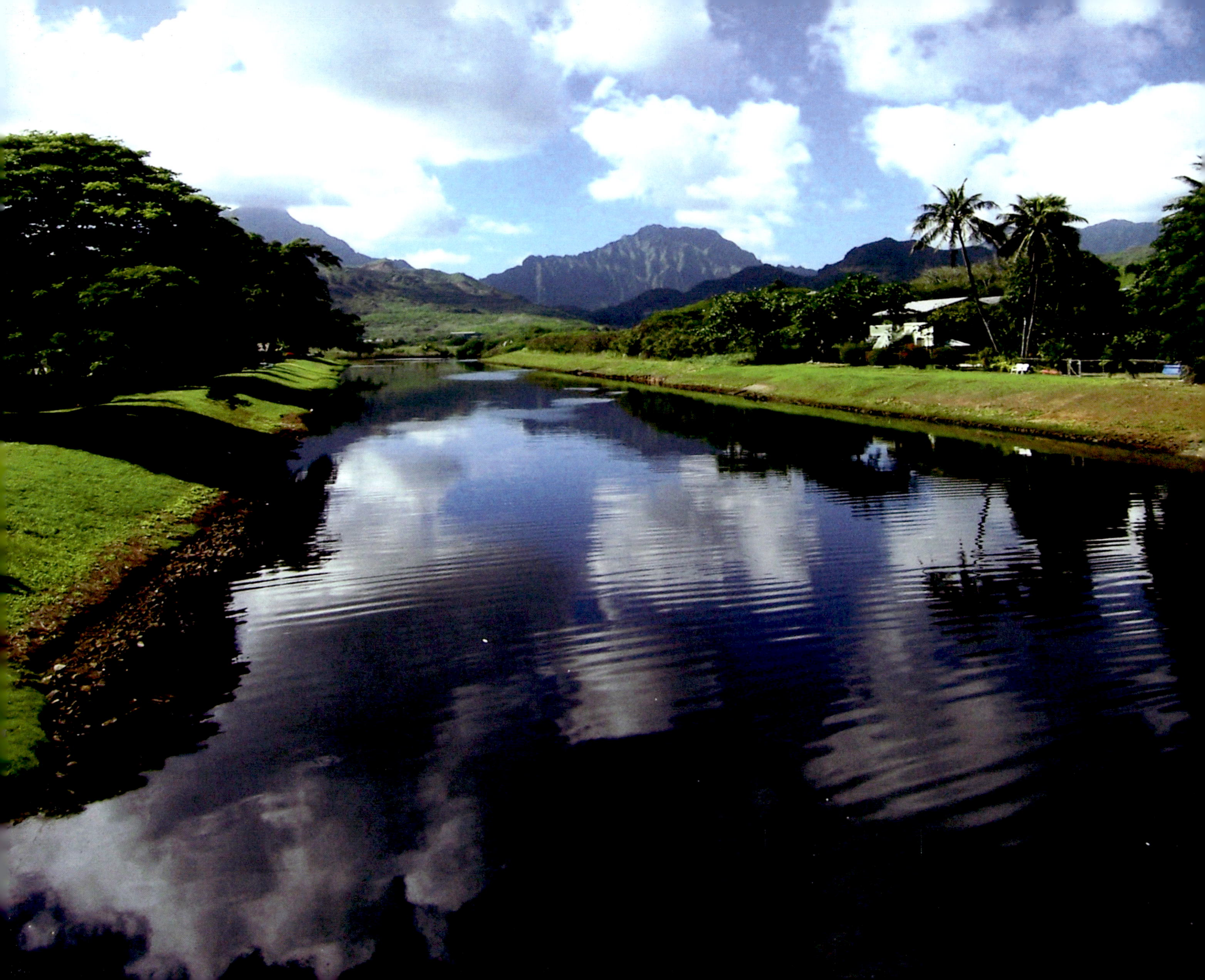

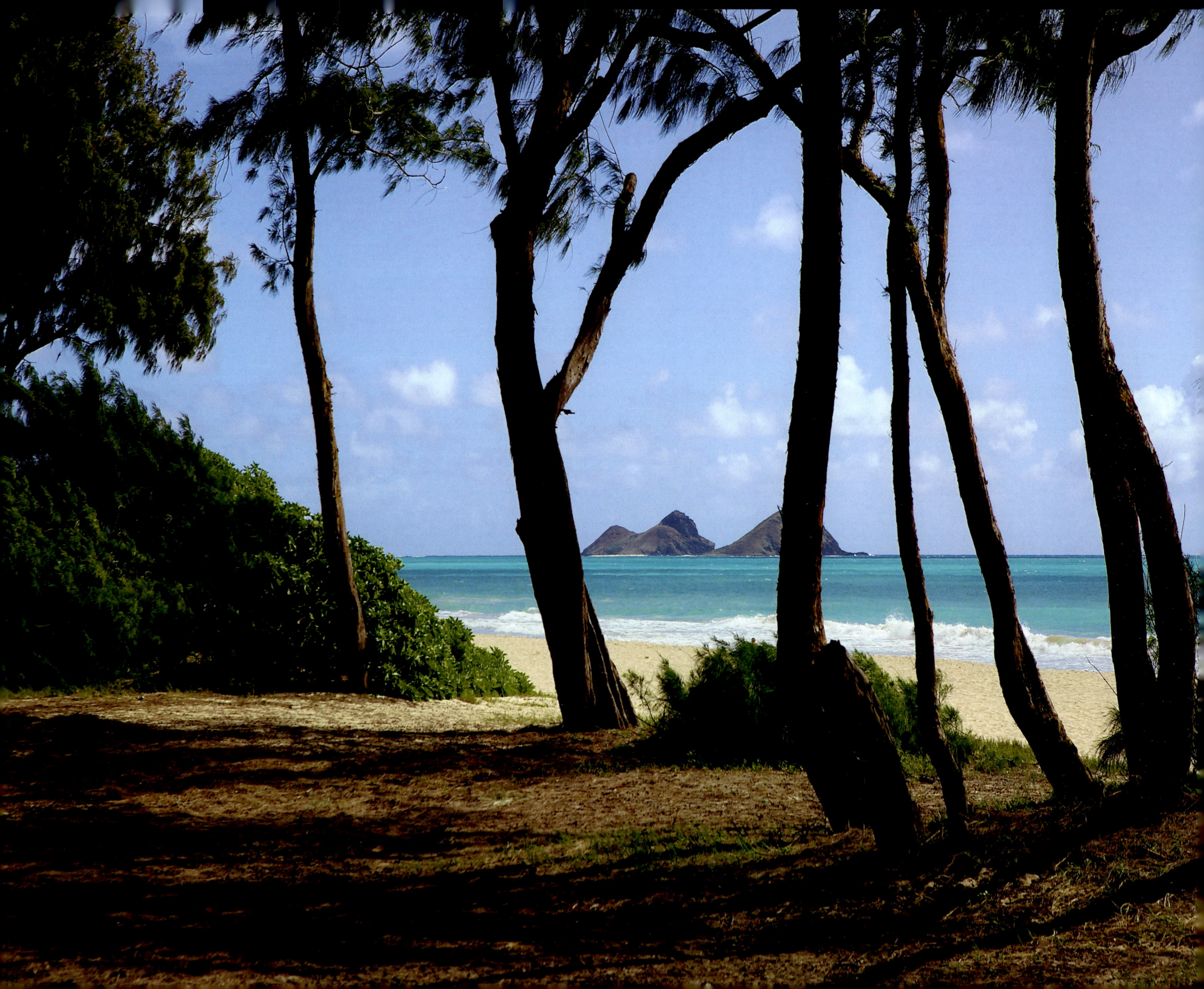

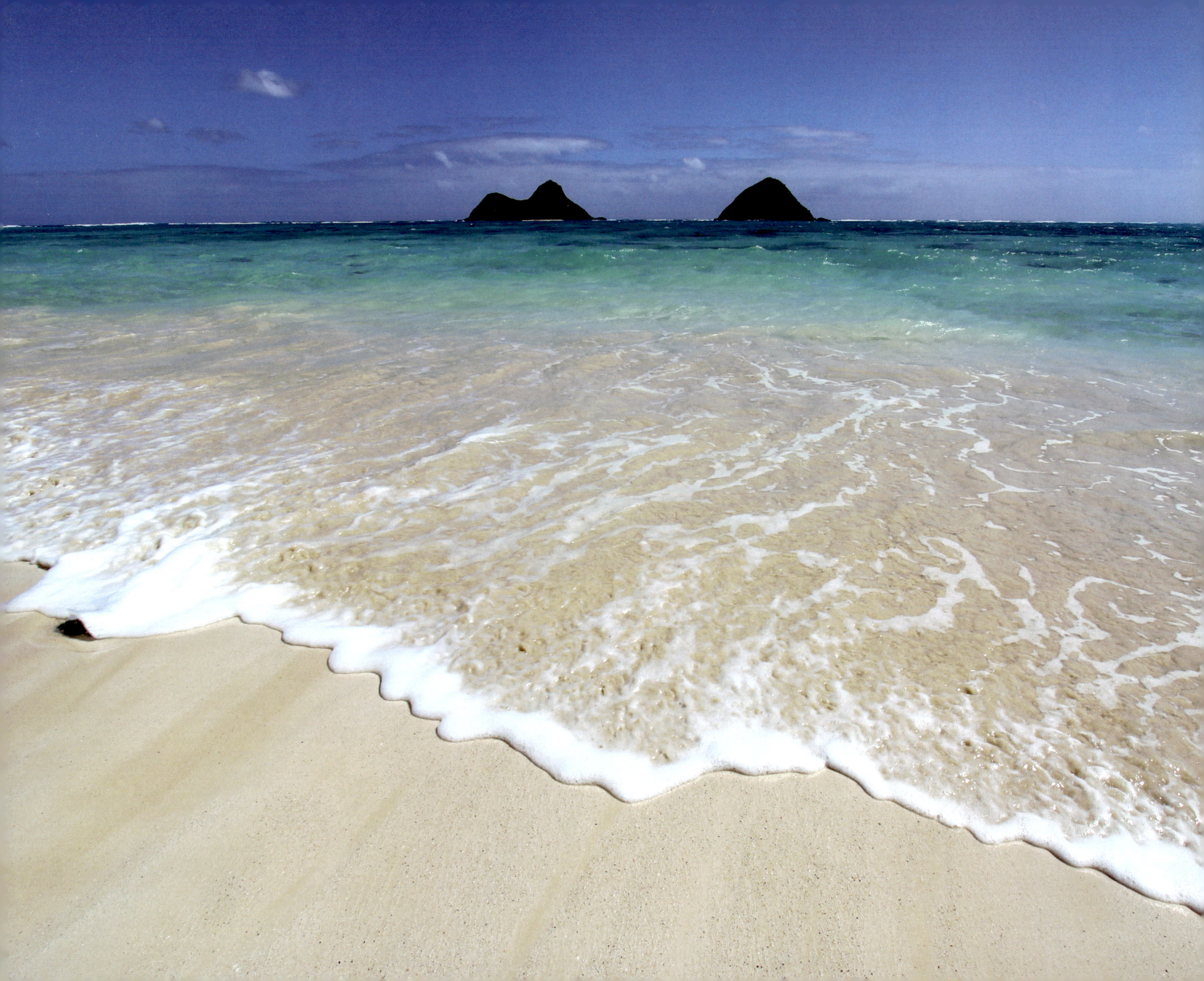

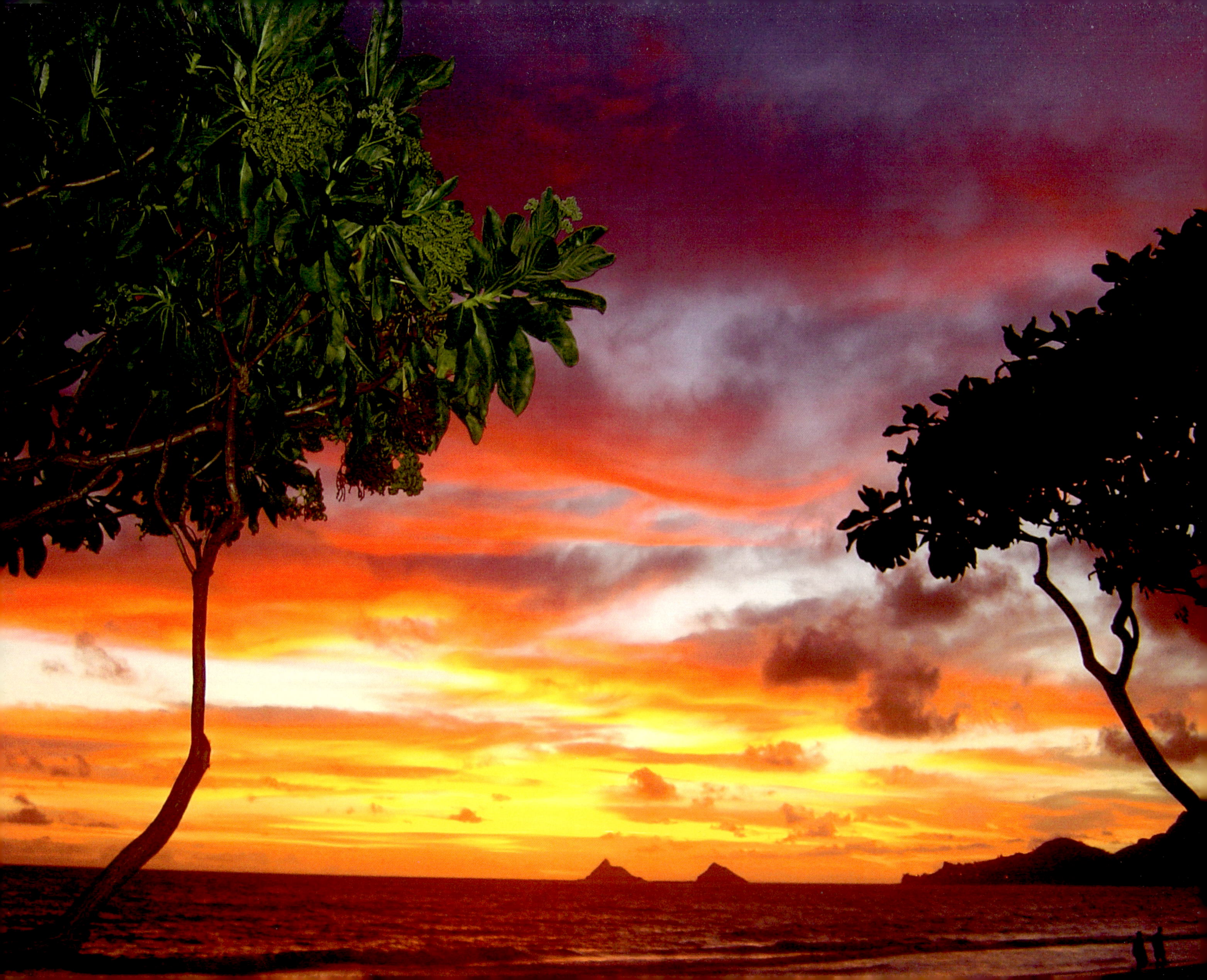

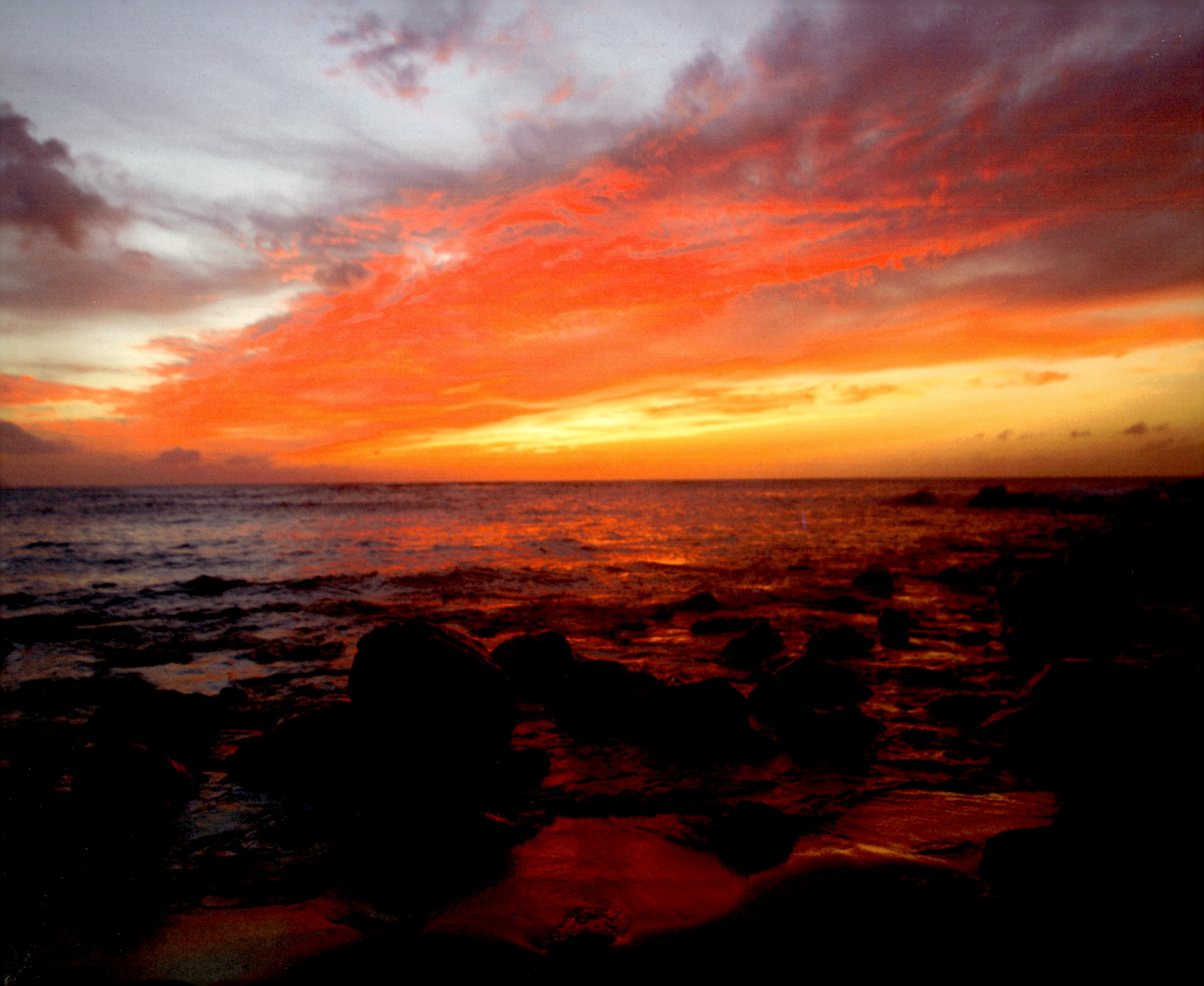

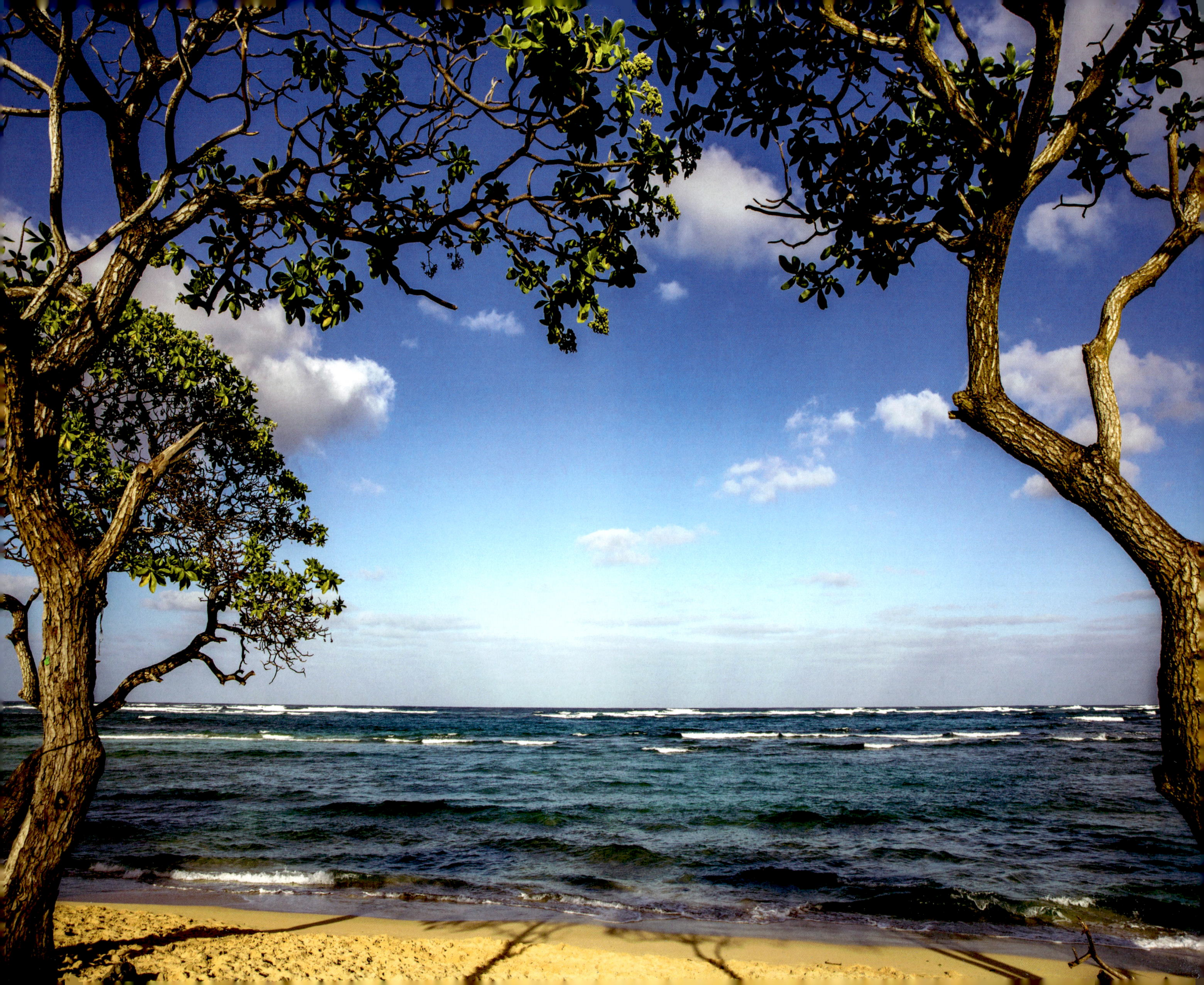

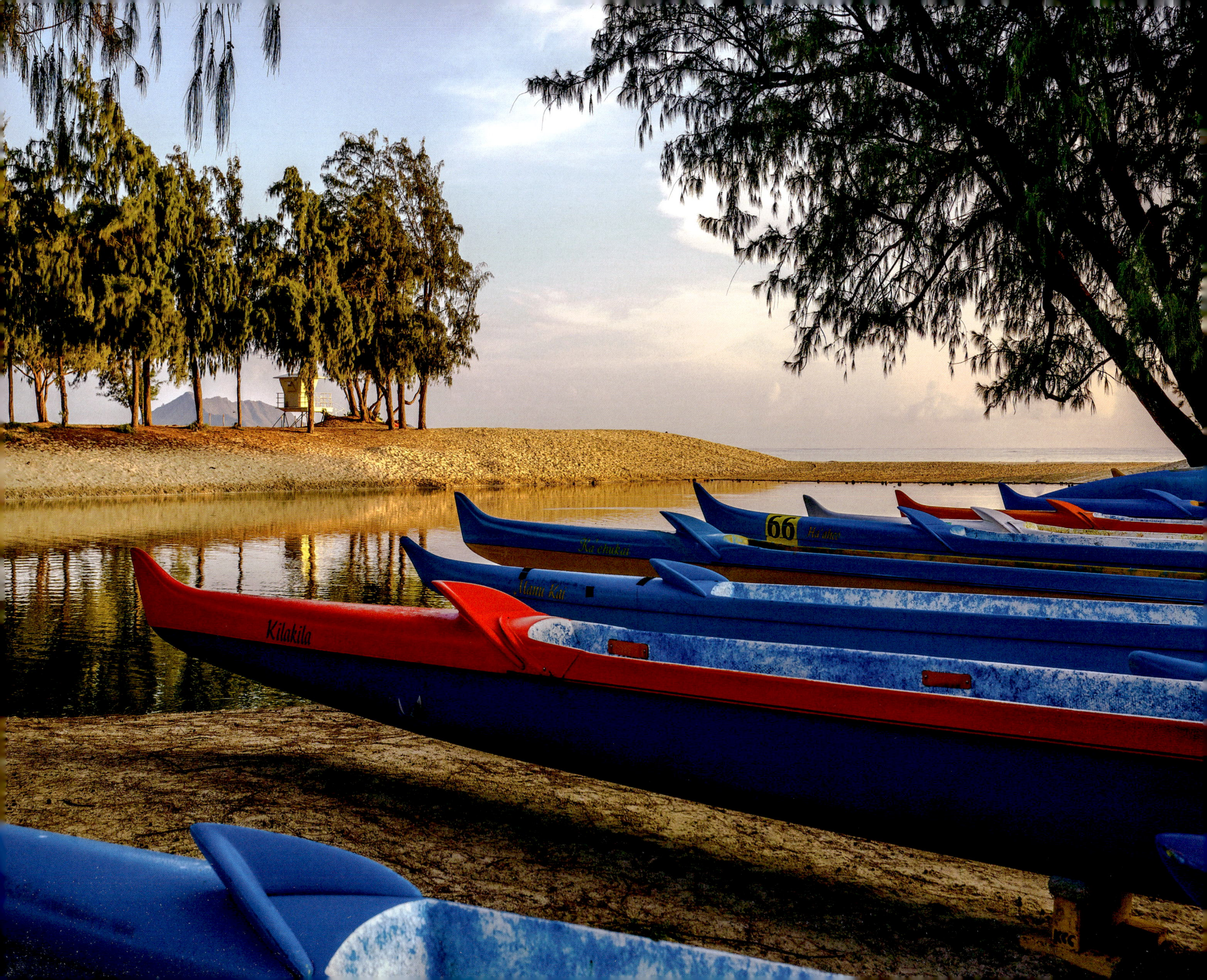
Kilakila
Manu Kai
Ka'ehukai
66
Ha'aheo

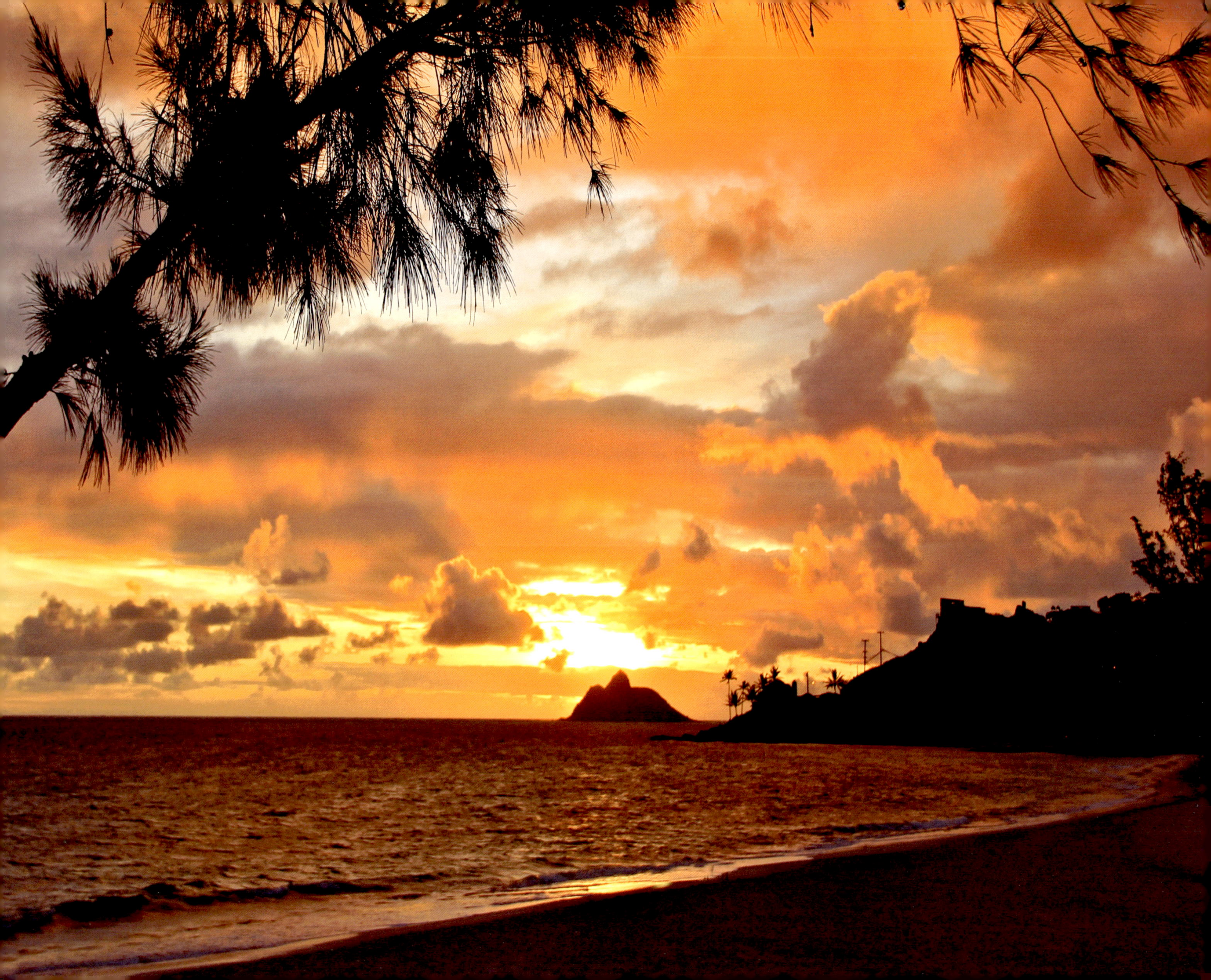

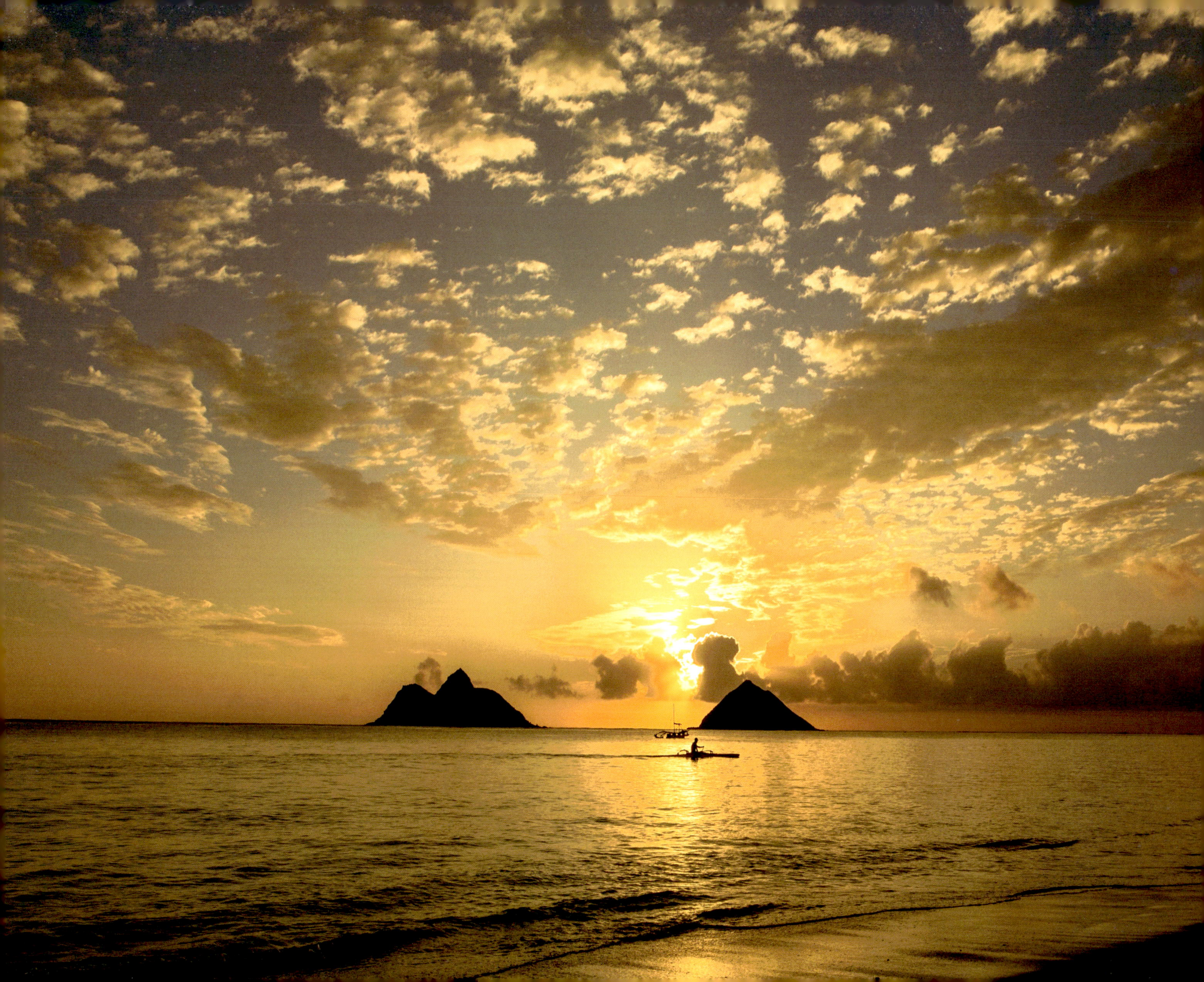

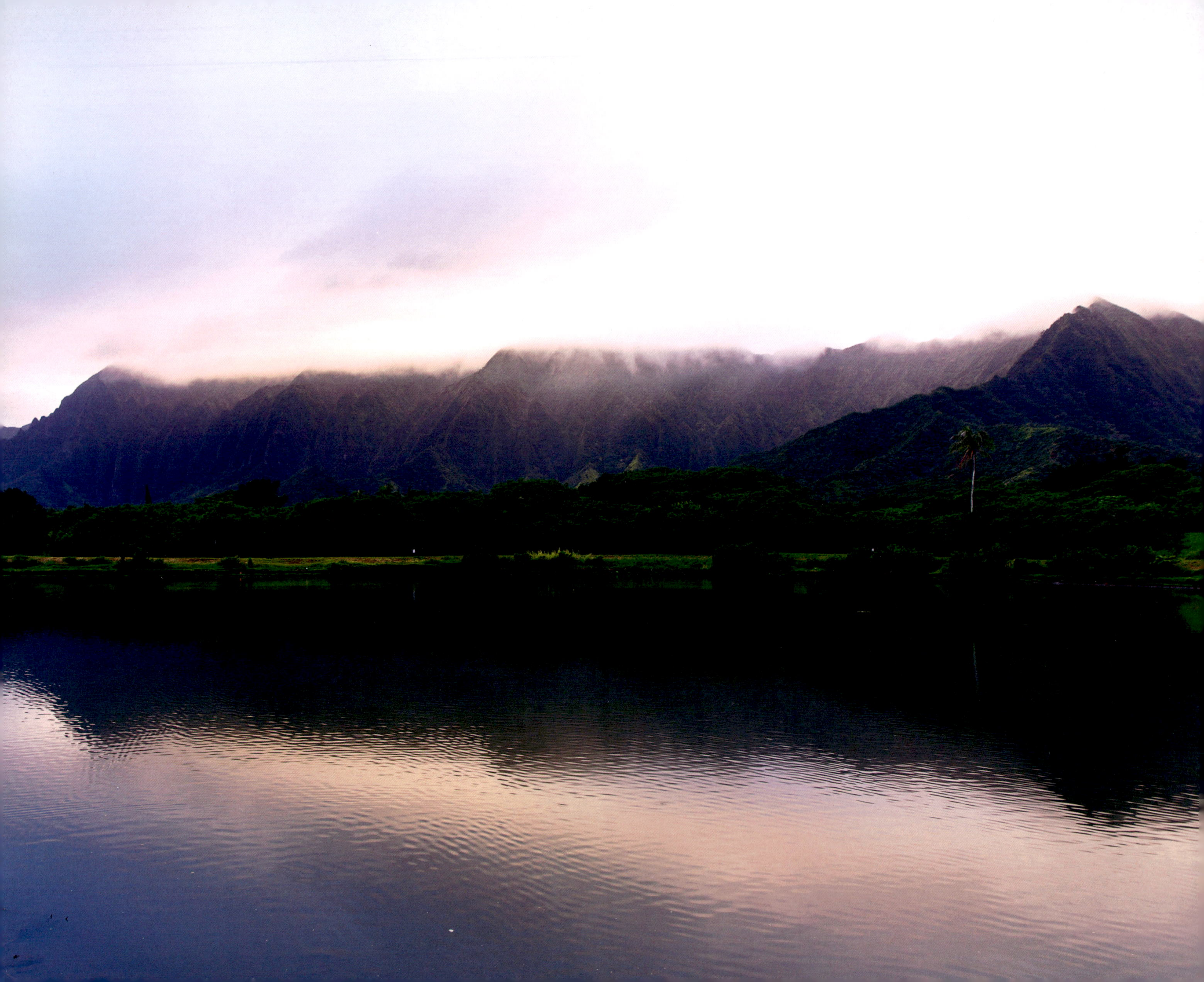

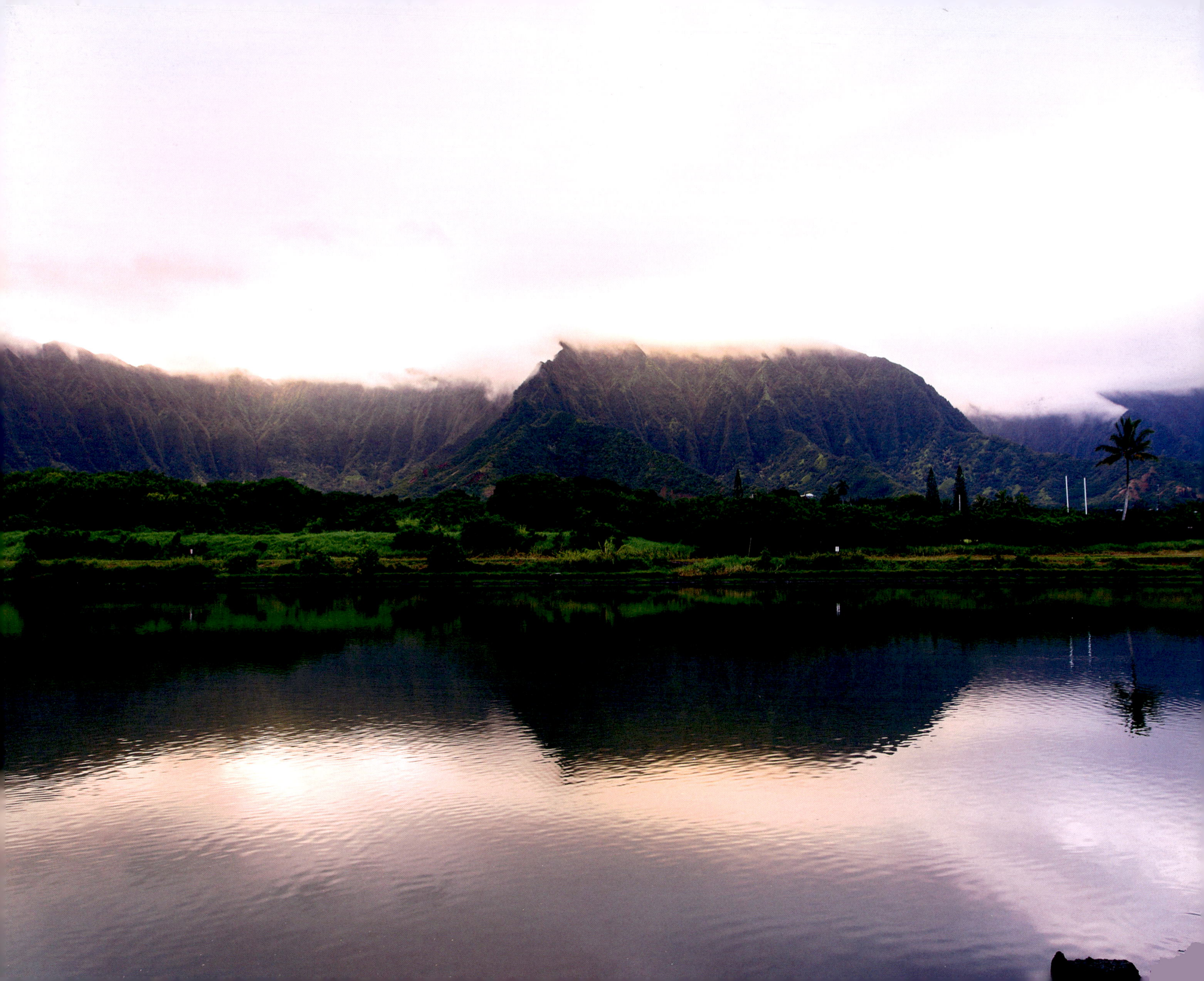

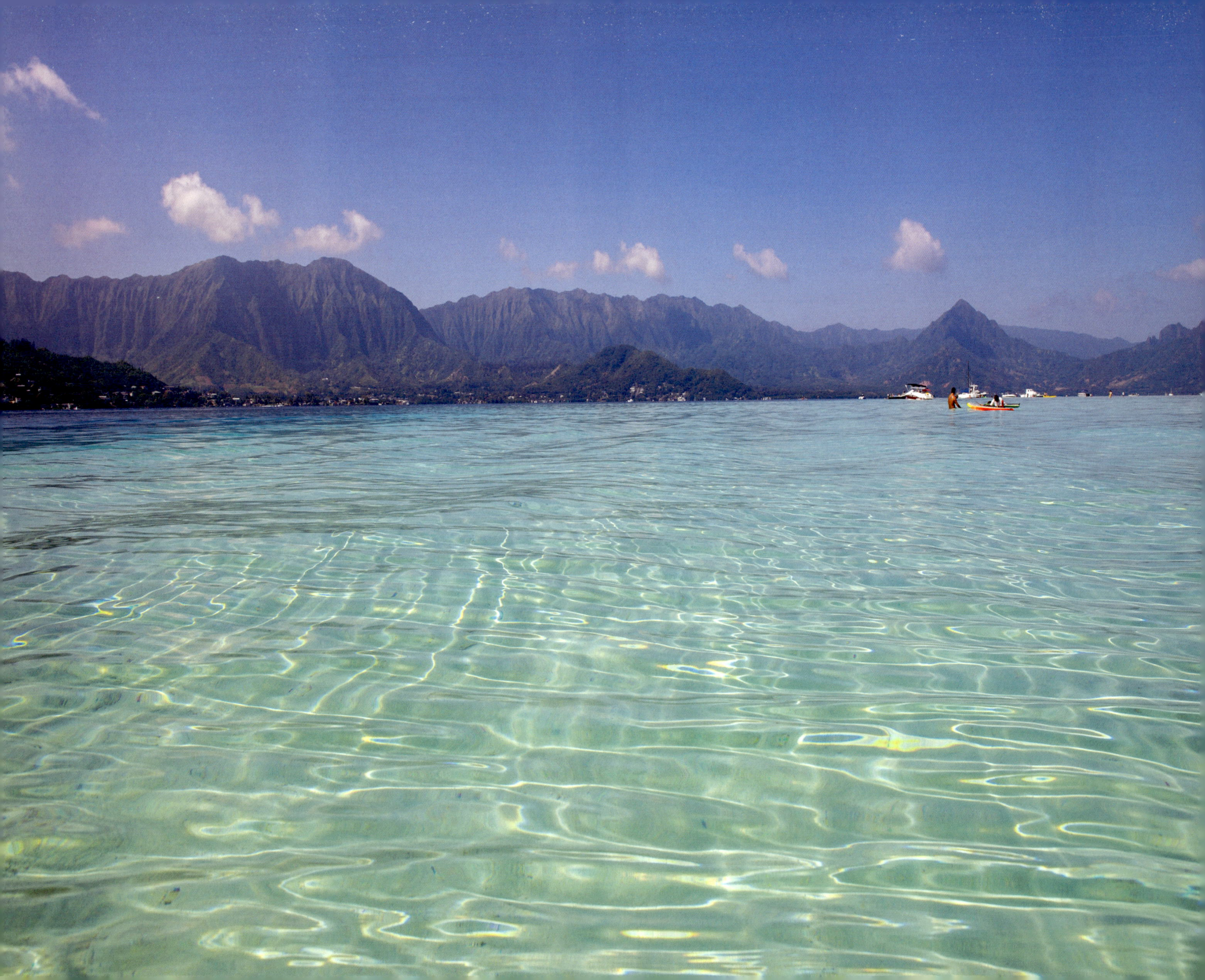

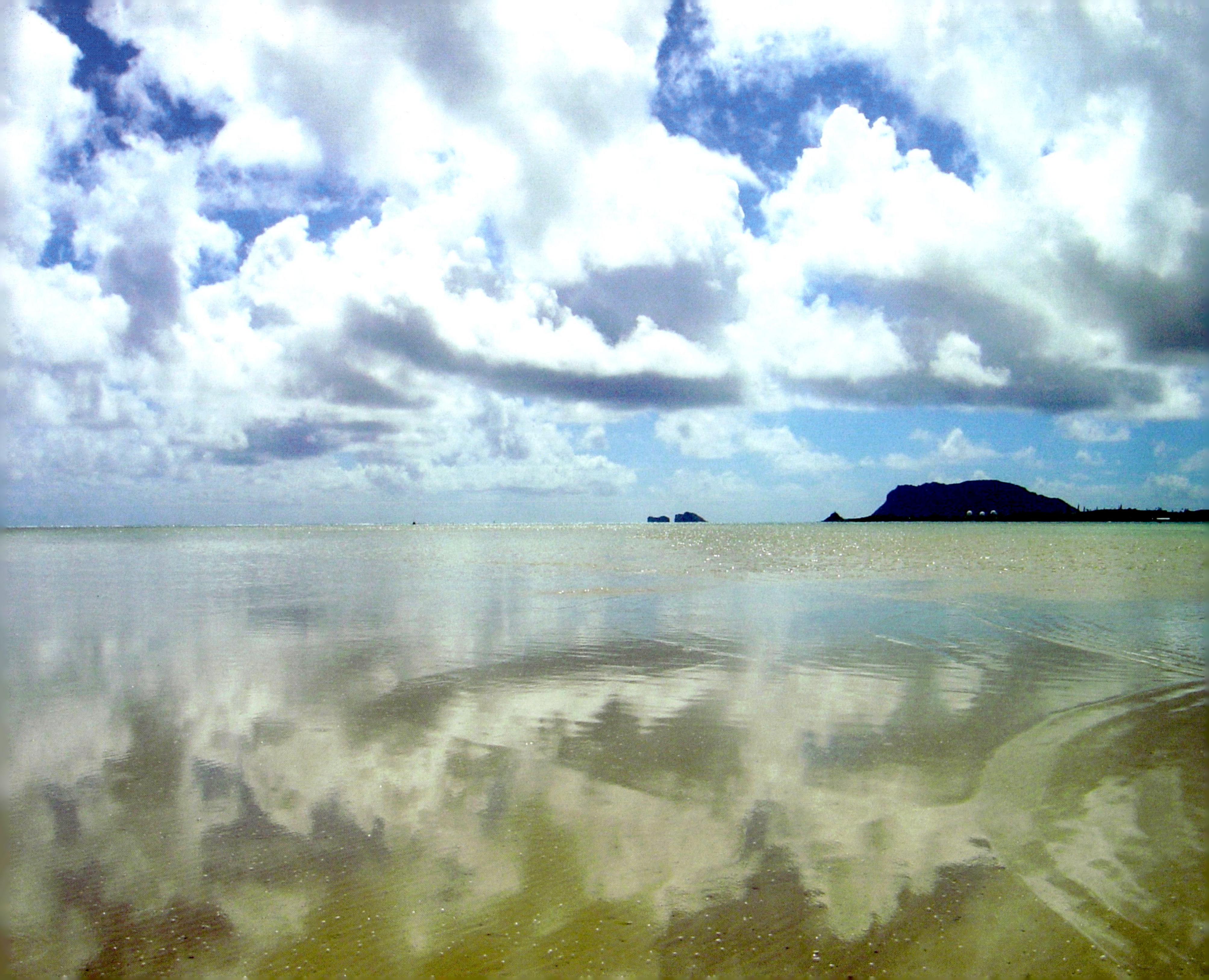

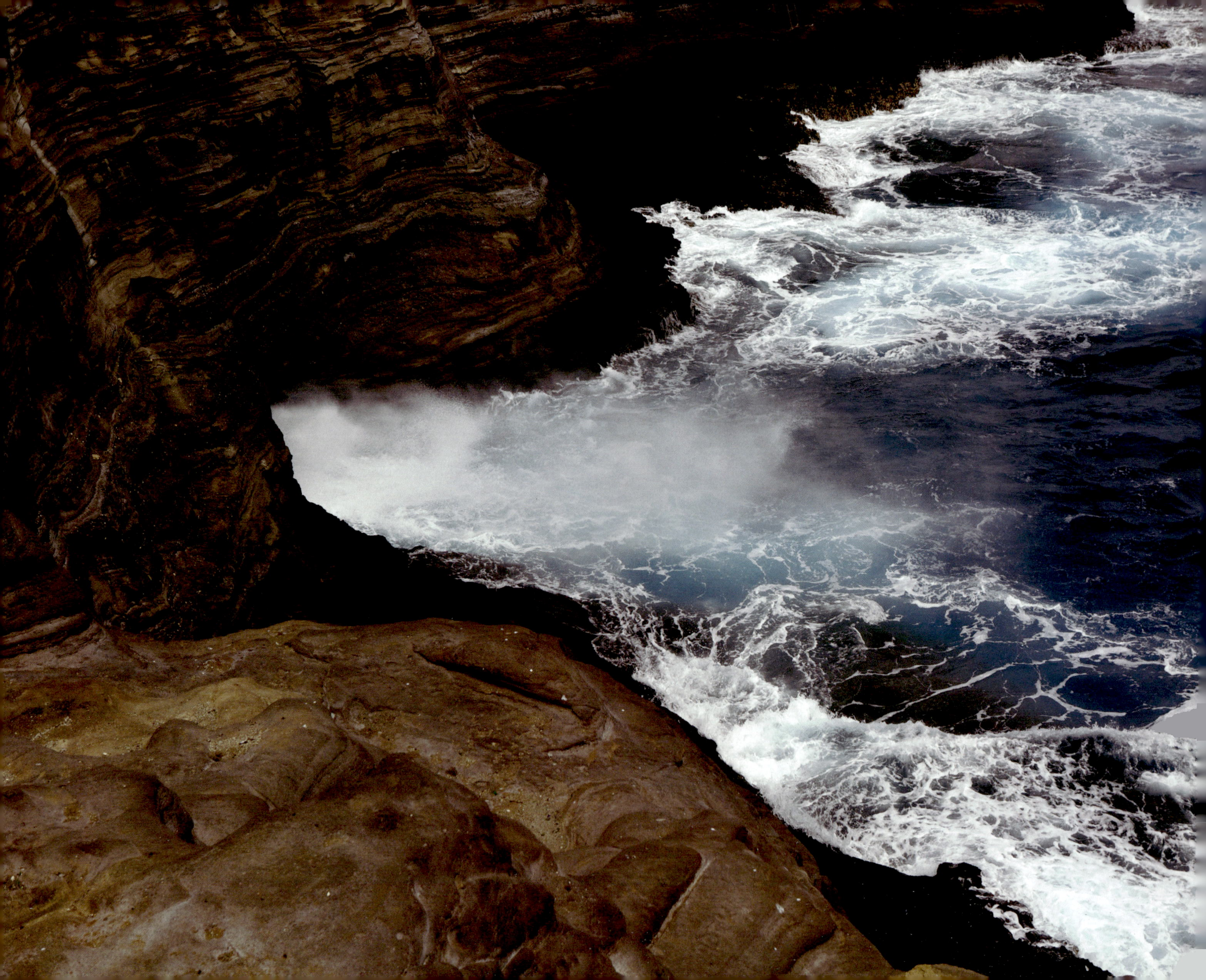

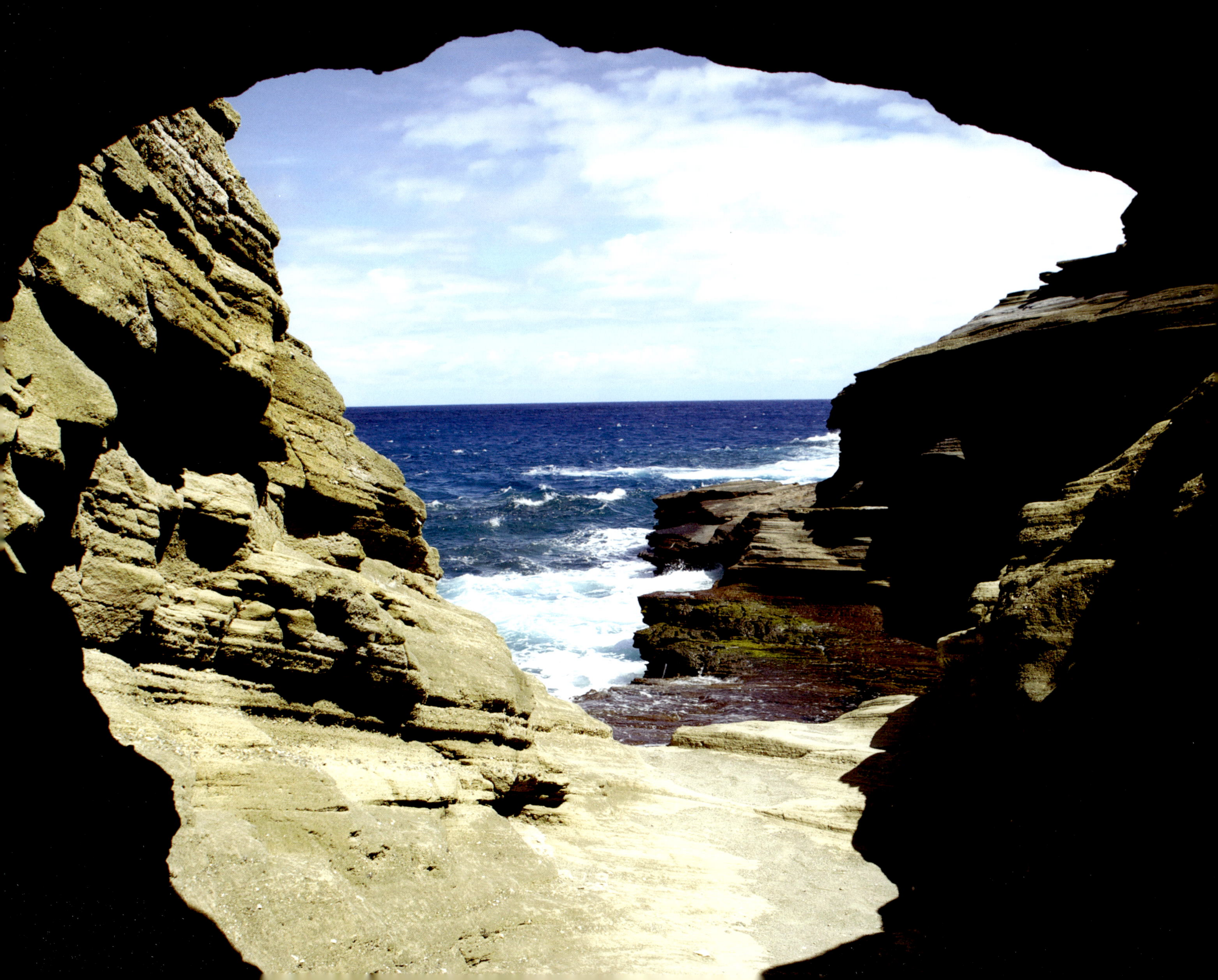

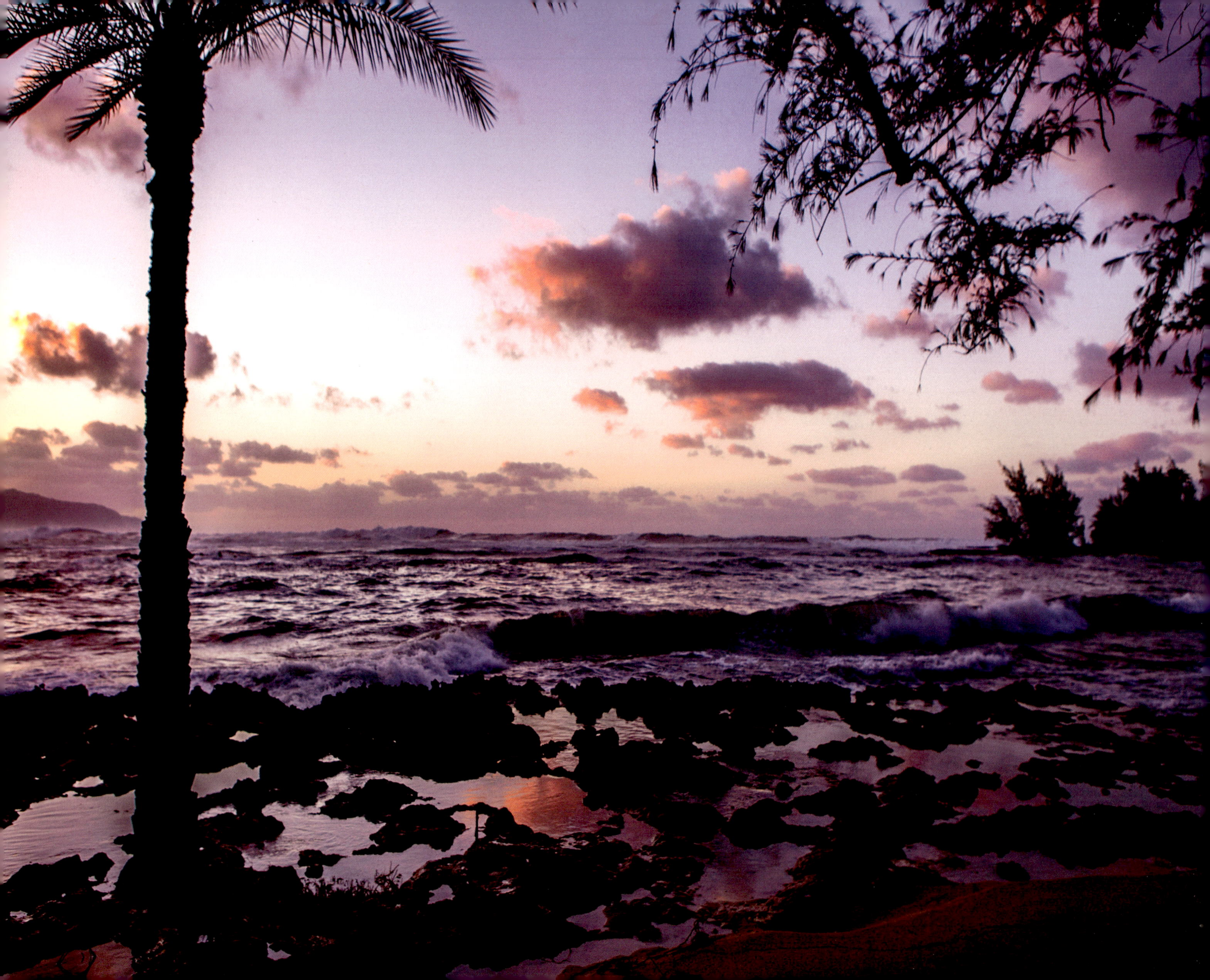

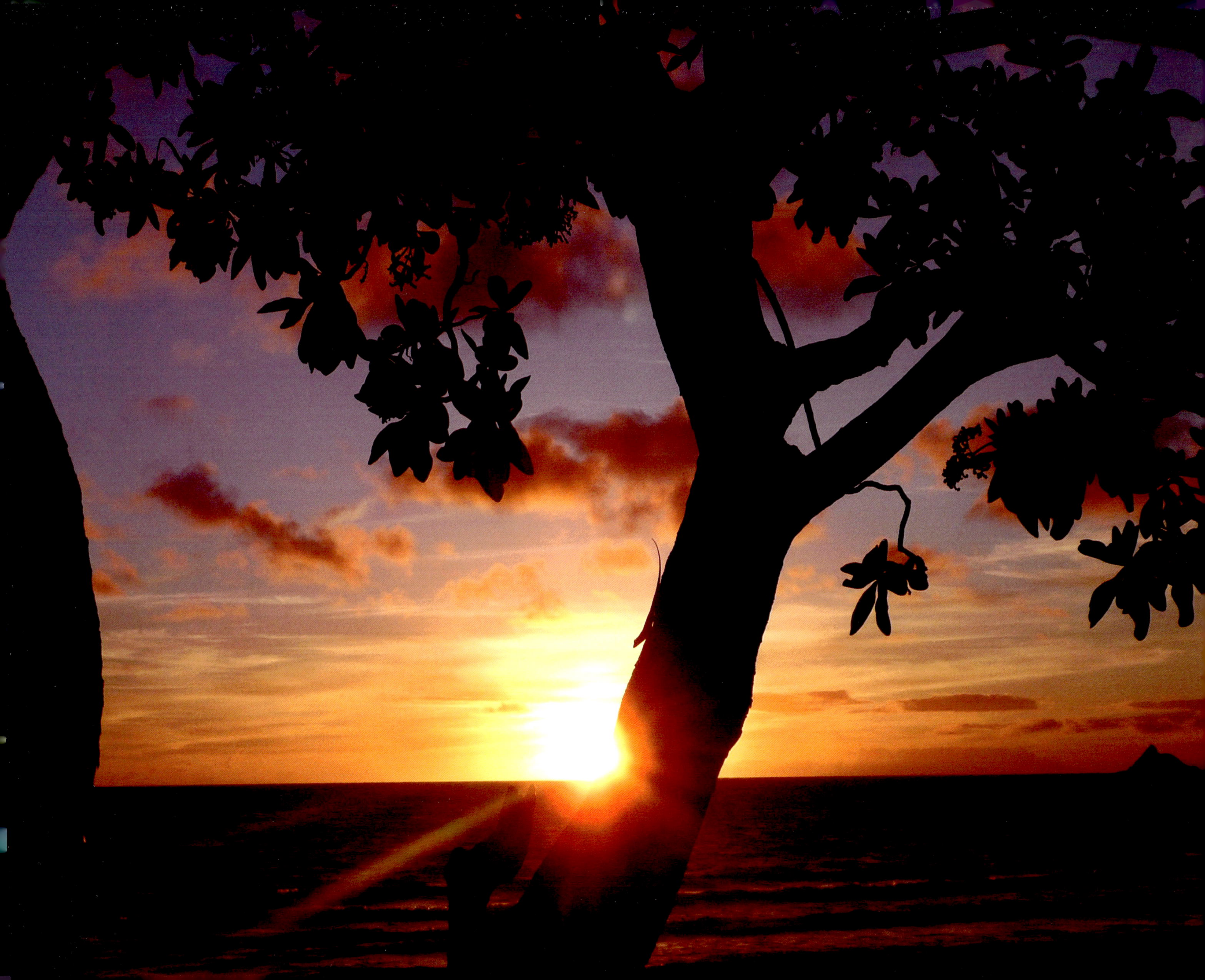

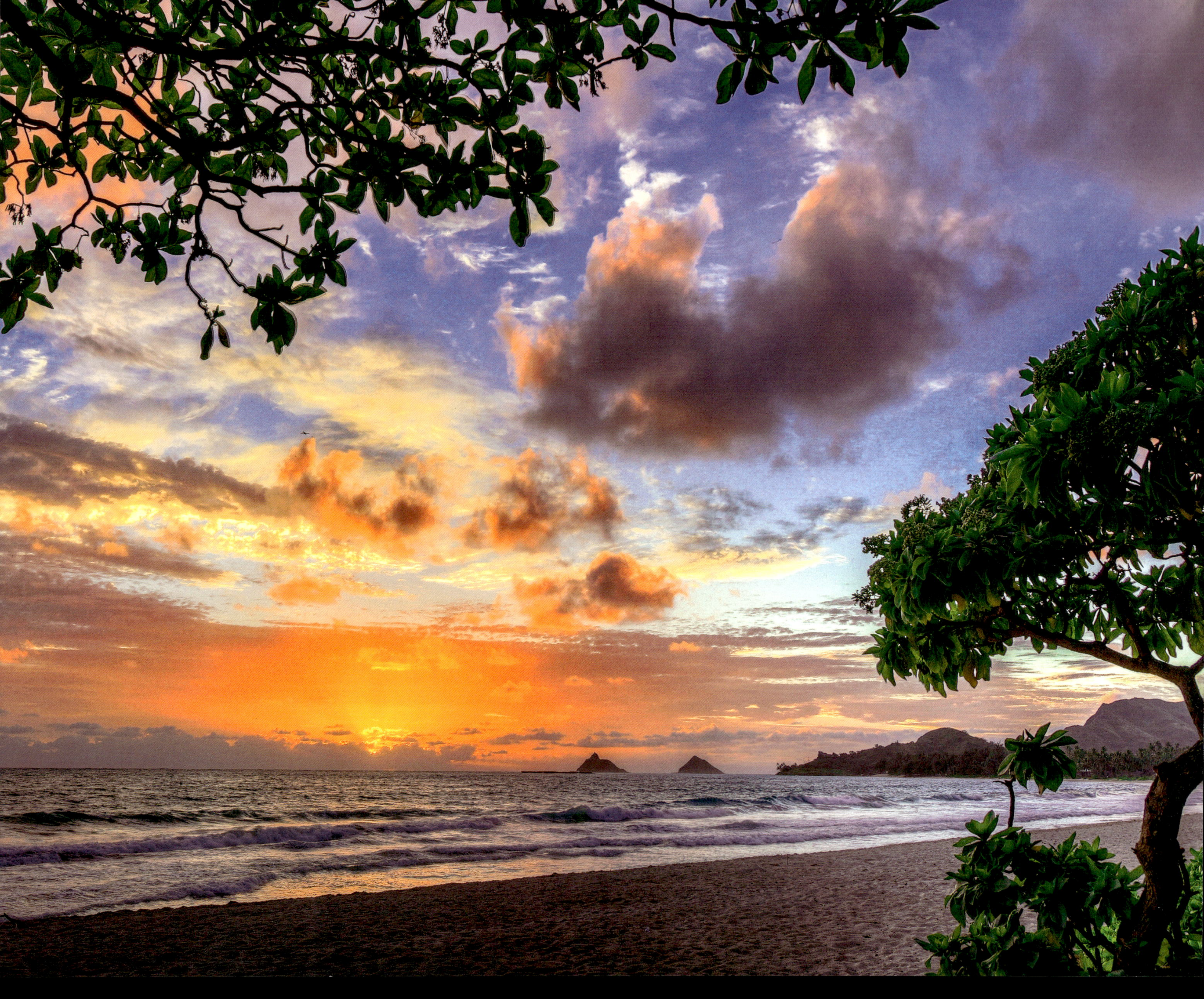

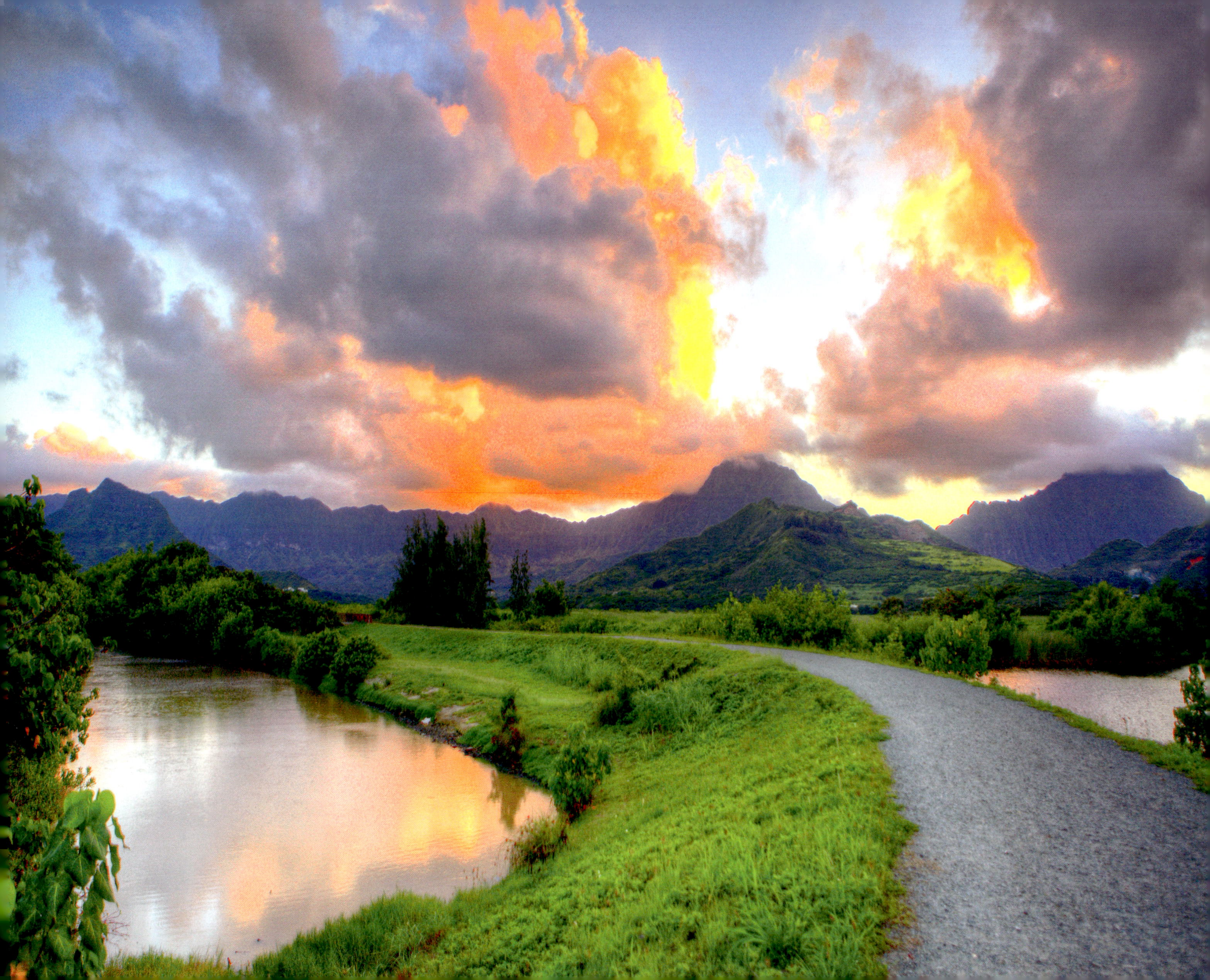

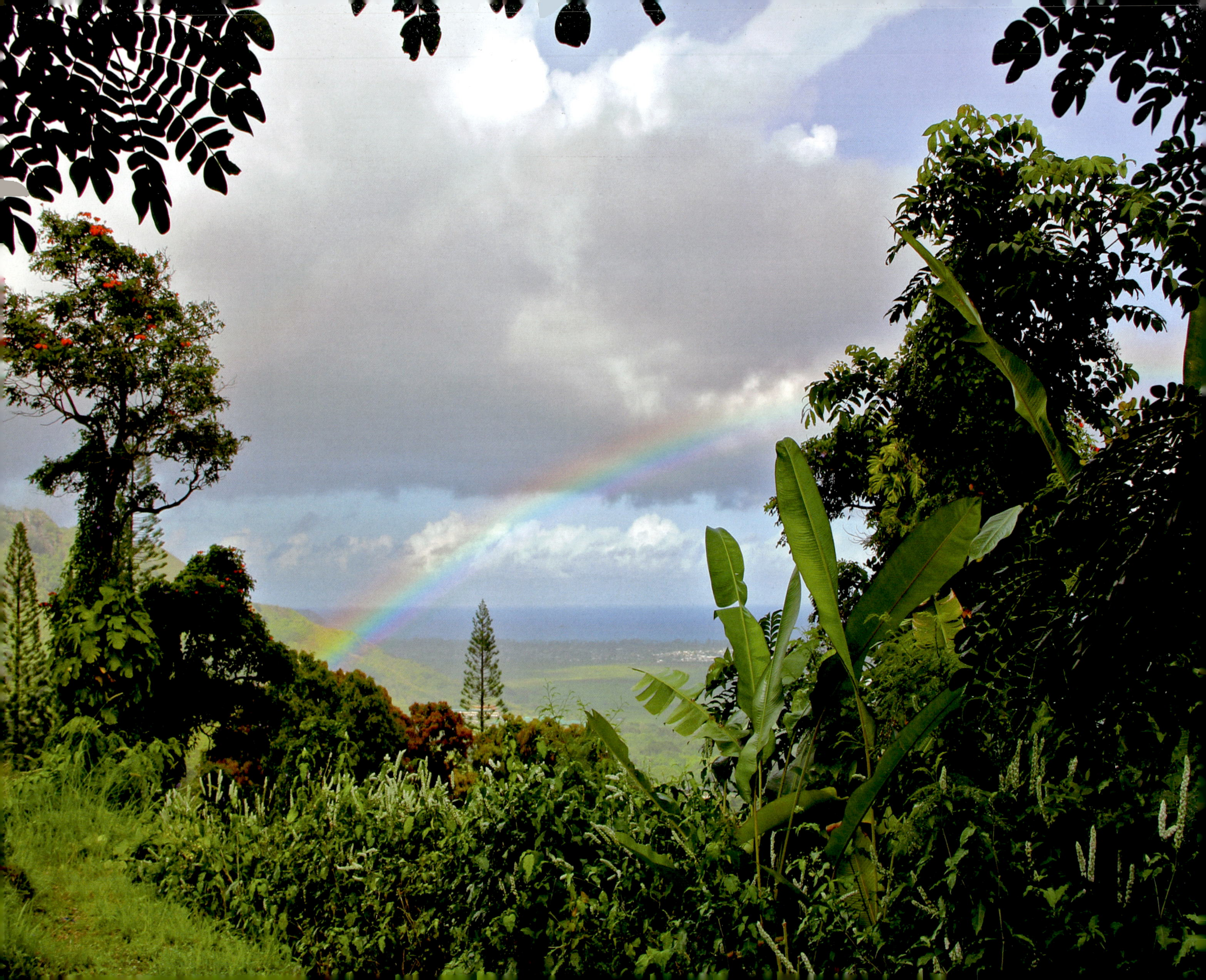

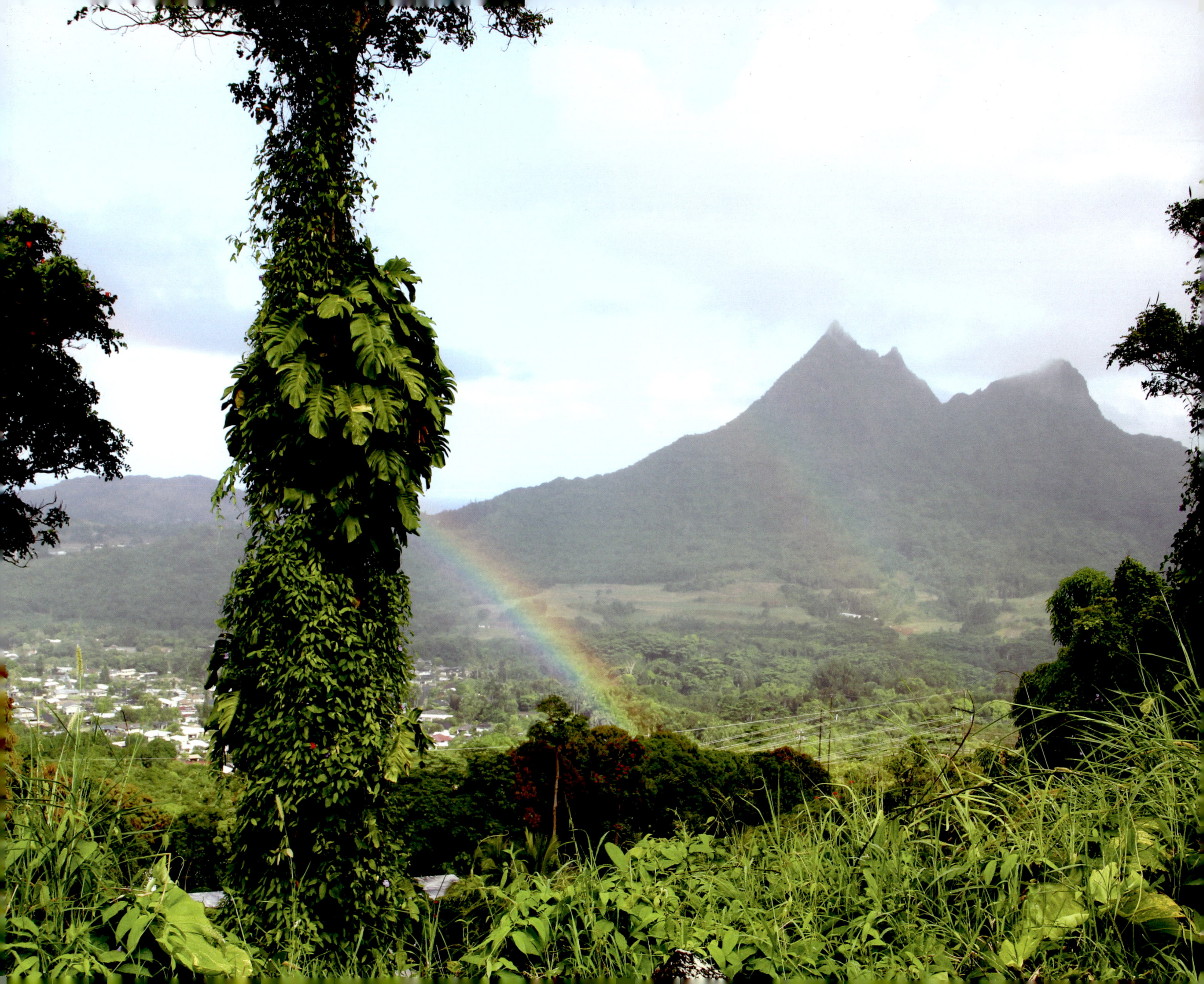

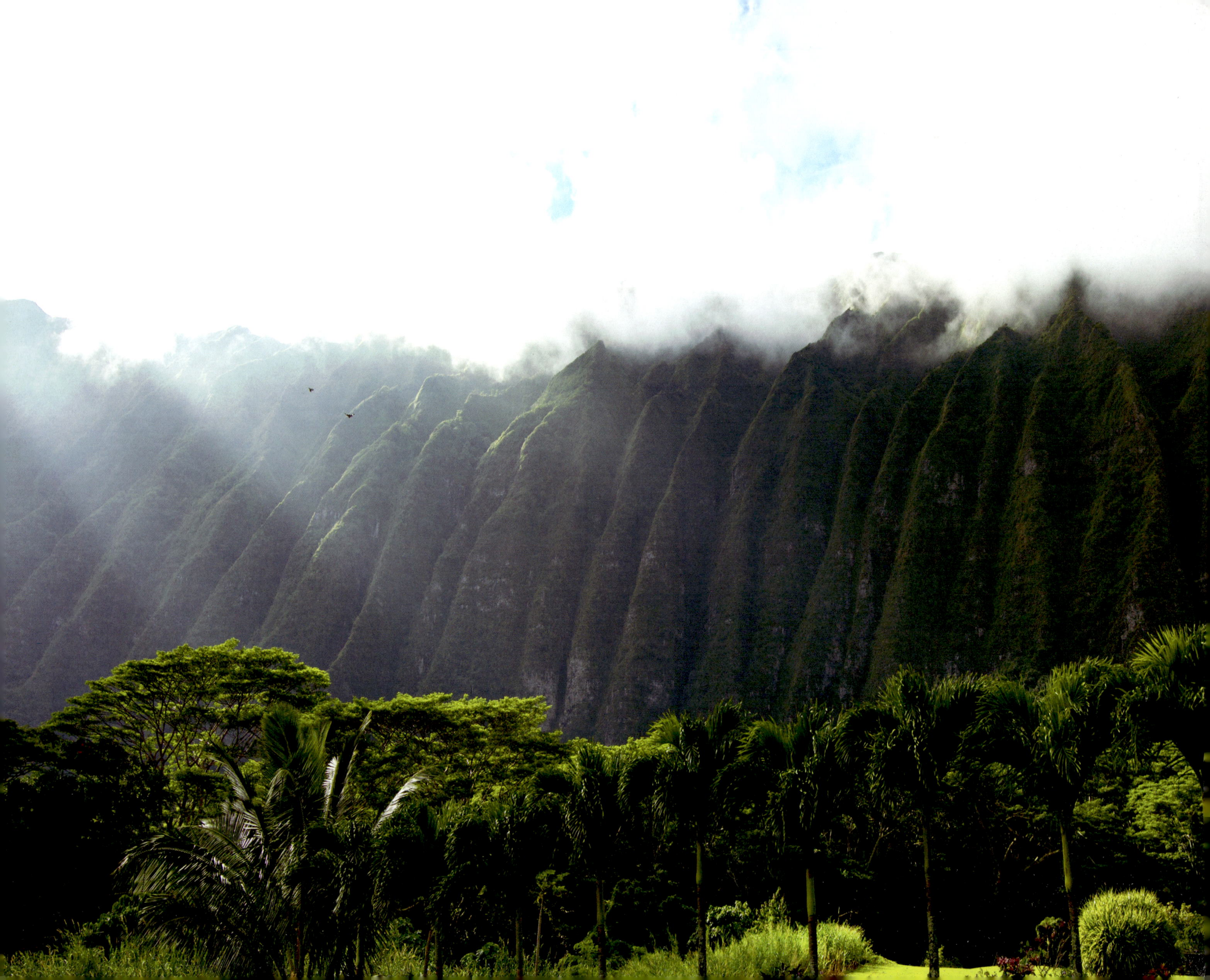

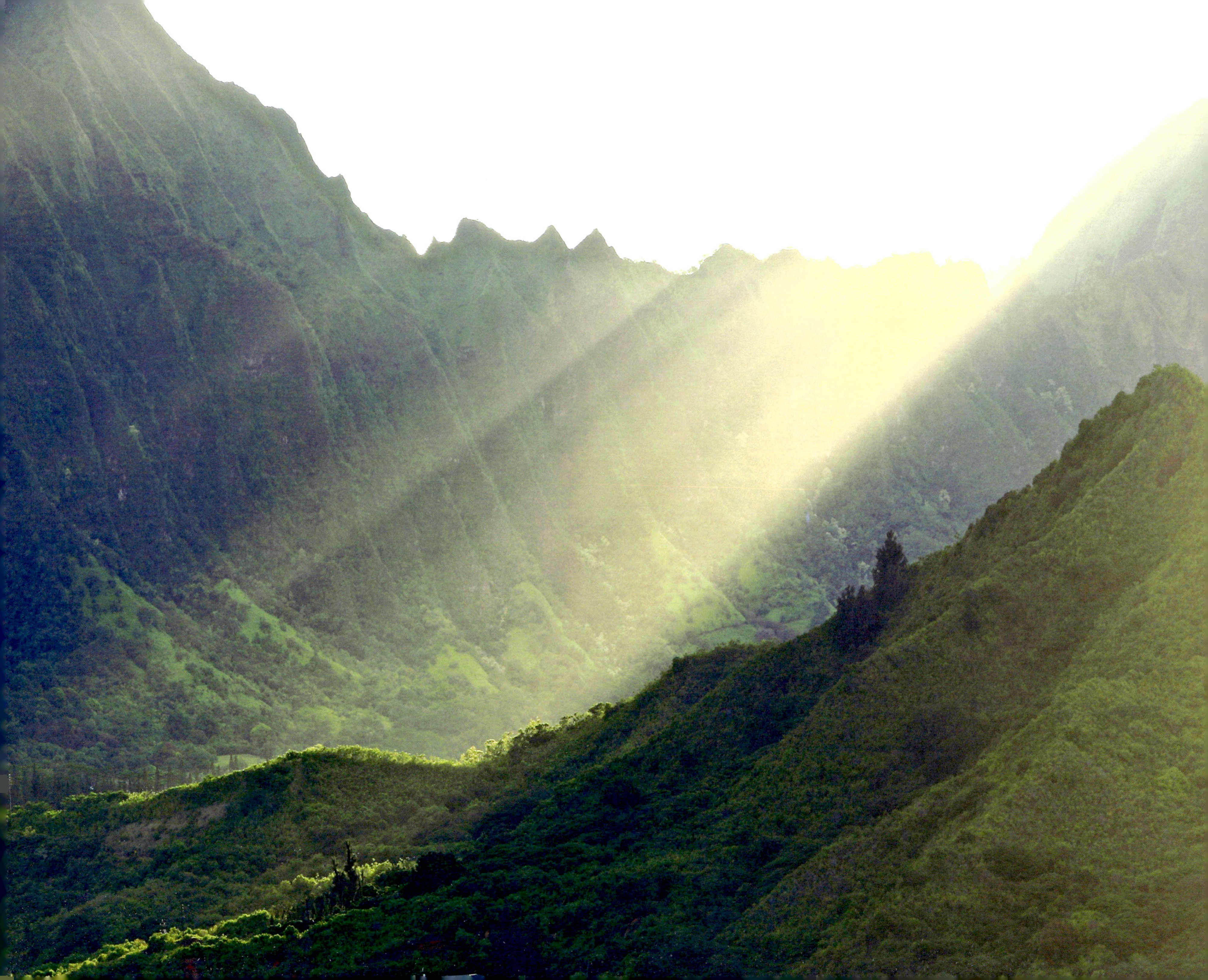

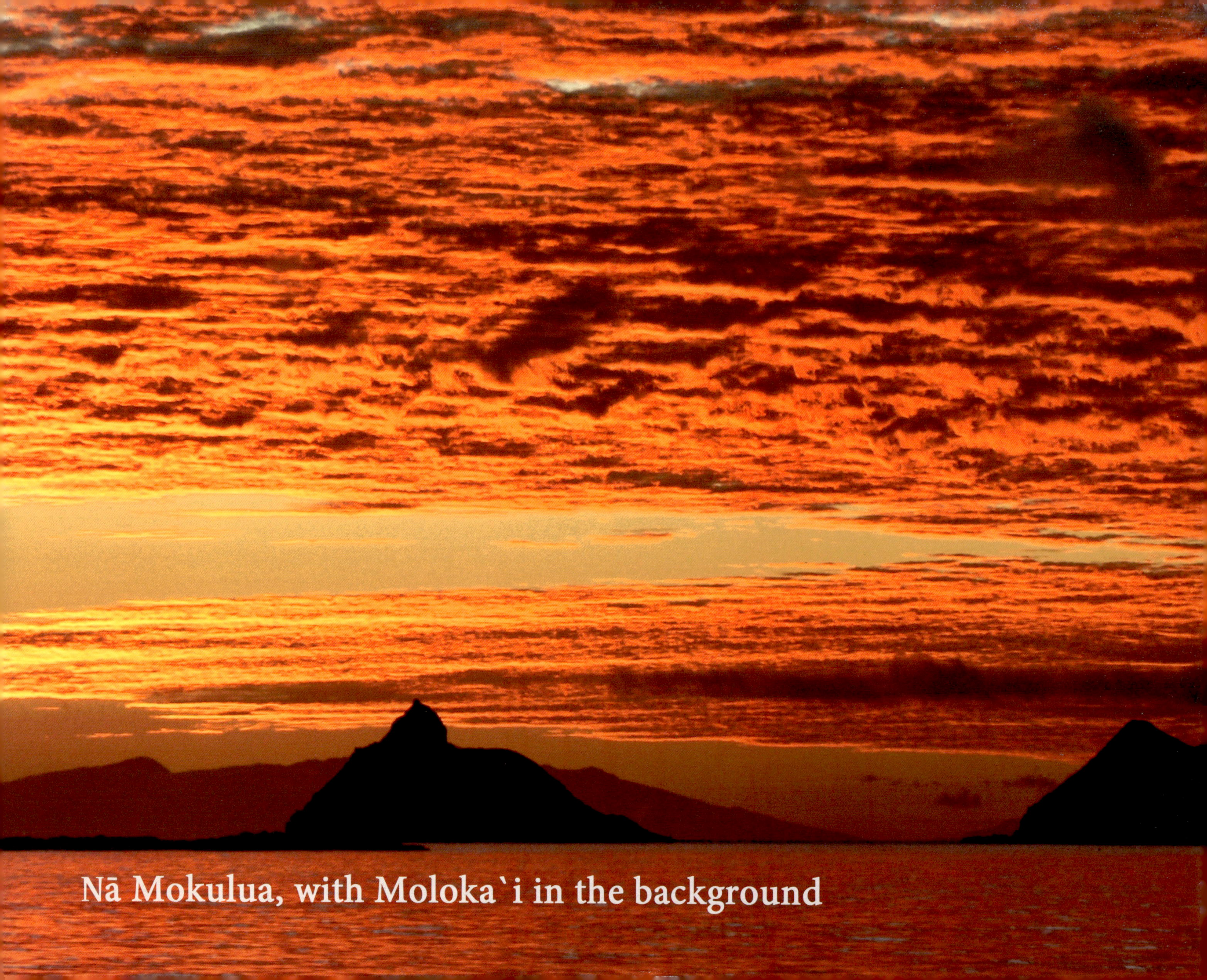

Nā Mokulua, with Moloka`i in the background

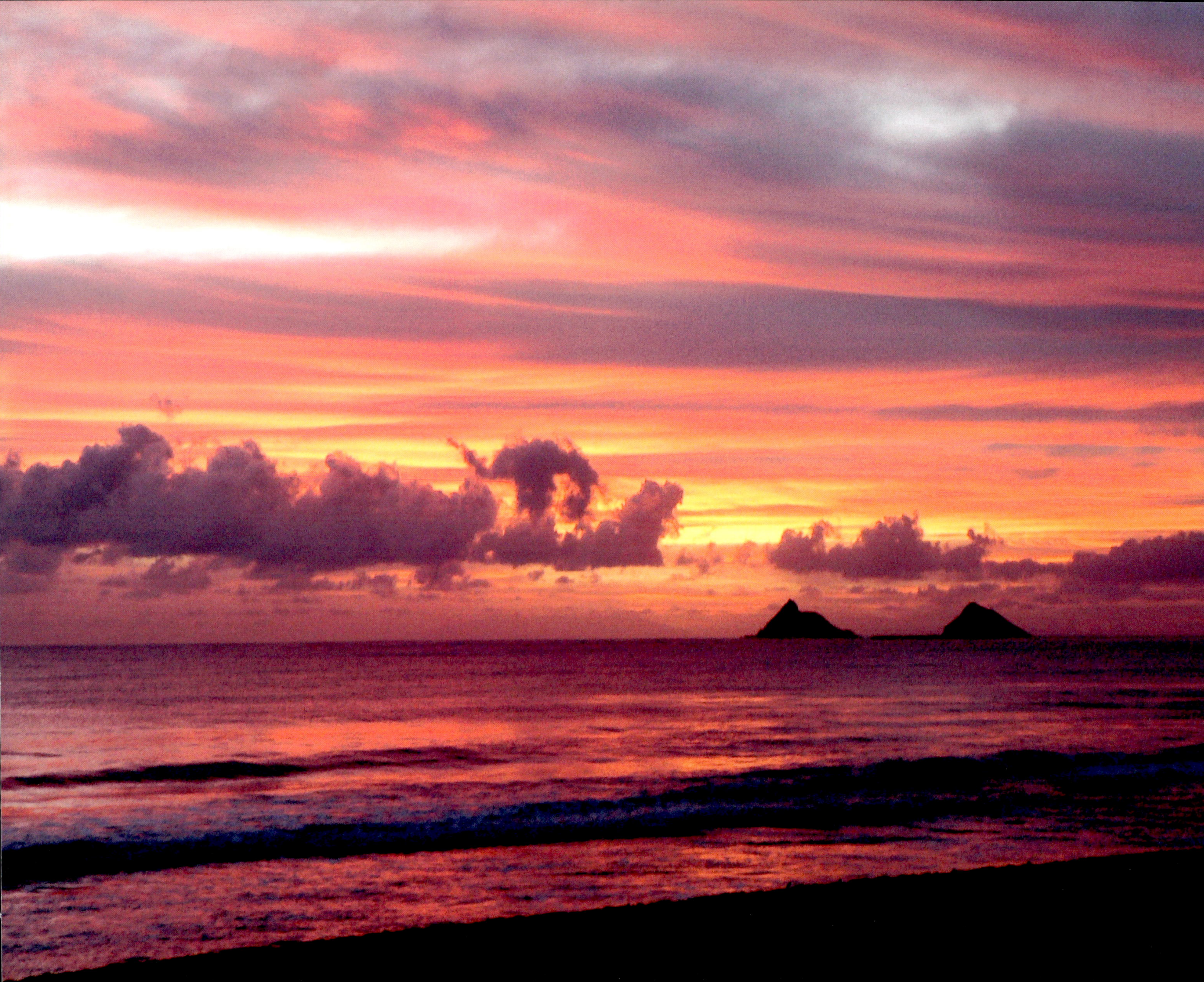

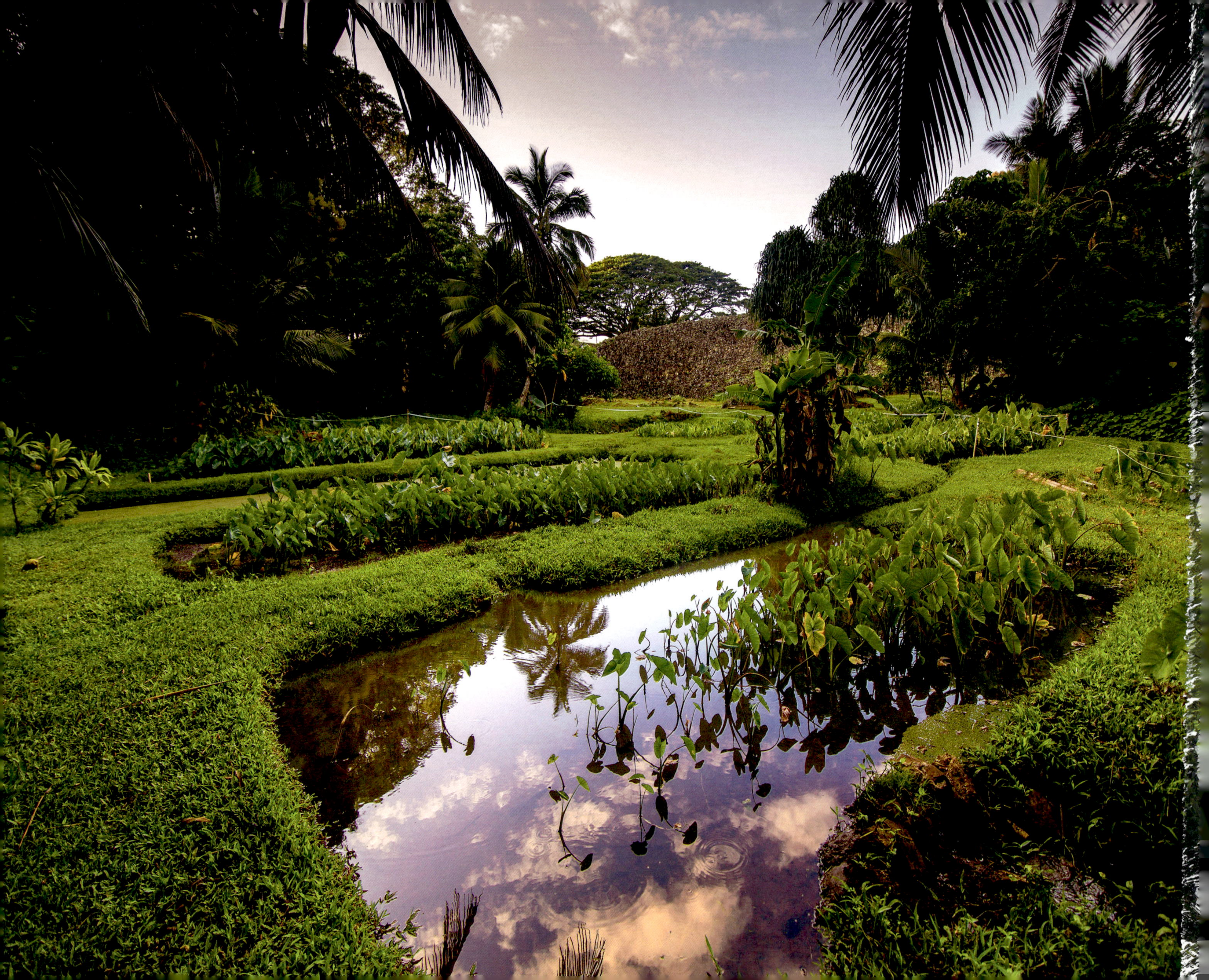